THE LIFE RECOVERY JOURNEY

INSPIRING STORIES

AND BIBLICAL WISDOM

AS YOU WORK THE TWELVE STEPS

AND LET THEM WORK YOU

Stephen Arterburn | David Stoop

TYNDALE
MOMENTUM

An Imprint of
Tyndale House Publishers, Inc.

Visit Tyndale online at www.tyndale.com. Visit Tyndale Momentum at www.tyndalemomentum.com.
Tyndale Momentum and the Tyndale Momentum logo are trademarks of Tyndale House Publishers, Inc.
Tyndale Momentum is an imprint of Tyndale House Publishers, Inc. *Life Recovery* is a registered trademark
of Tyndale House Publishers, Inc. *New Living Translation, NLT*, and the New Living Translation logo are
registered trademarks of Tyndale House Publishers, Inc.

*The Life Recovery Journey: Inspiring Stories and Biblical Wisdom as You Work the Twelve Steps and Let Them
Work You*

Previously published in 2012 as *The Book of Life Recovery* by Tyndale House Publishers, Inc., under
ISBN 978-1-4143-6139-0. First printing as *The Life Recovery Journey* in 2015 by Tyndale House
Publishers, Inc.

Copyright © 2012 by Stephen Arterburn and David Stoop. All rights reserved.

Cover photograph copyright © Darren Falkenberg/Thinkstock. All rights reserved.

Cover design by Stephen Vosloo

Designed by Erik Peterson and Beth Sparkman

Published in association with the literary agency of Alive Literary Agency, 7680 Goddard Street, Suite 200,
Colorado Springs, CO 80920, www.aliveliterary.com.

Unless otherwise indicated, all Scripture quotations are taken from the *Holy Bible*, New Living Translation,
copyright © 1996, 2004, 2007 by Tyndale House Foundation. Used by permission of Tyndale House
Publishers, Inc., Carol Stream, Illinois 60188. All rights reserved.

Scripture quotations marked NIV are taken from the Holy Bible, *New International Version,® NIV.®*
Copyright © 1973, 1978, 1984, 2011 by Biblica, Inc.® Used by permission. All rights reserved worldwide.

Scripture quotations marked NASB are taken from the New American Standard Bible,® copyright ©
1960, 1962, 1963, 1968, 1971, 1972, 1973, 1975, 1977, 1995 by The Lockman Foundation. Used by
permission.

Scripture quotations marked NKJV are taken from the New King James Version.® Copyright © 1982 by
Thomas Nelson, Inc. Used by permission. All rights reserved. *NKJV* is a trademark of Thomas Nelson, Inc.

Scripture quotations marked KJV are taken from the *Holy Bible*, King James Version.

Scripture quotations marked TLB are taken from *The Living Bible*, copyright © 1971 by Tyndale House
Foundation. Used by permission of Tyndale House Publishers, Inc., Carol Stream, Illinois 60188. All rights
reserved.

Scripture quotations marked *The Message* are taken from *The Message* by Eugene H. Peterson, copyright ©
1993, 1994, 1995, 1996, 2000, 2001, 2002. Used by permission of NavPress Publishing Group. All rights
reserved.

The Twelve Steps of Life Recovery are adapted from The Twelve Steps of Alcoholics Anonymous and are
used here with permission of Alcoholics Anonymous World Services, Inc. Permission to adapt the Twelve
Steps does not mean that AAWS has reviewed or approved the contents of this publication, or that AAWS
necessarily agrees with the views expressed herein. AA is a program **of** recovery from alcoholism *only*—use
of the Twelve Steps in connection with programs and activities which are patterned after AA, but which
address other problems, or in any other non-AA context, does not imply otherwise. Additionally, while
AA is a spiritual program, AA is not a religious program. Thus, AA is not affiliated or allied with any sect,
denomination, or specific religious belief.

The stories in *The Book of Life Recovery* are true, first-person accounts. Names, locations, and other
identifying details have been changed to safeguard the privacy and dignity of the individuals involved.

The Library of Congress has catalogued the original edition as follows:

Arterburn, Stephen, date.
    The book of life recovery : inspiring stories and biblical wisdom for your journey through the twelve
steps / Stephen Arterburn, David Stoop.
        p. cm.
    Includes bibliographical references (p.   ).
    ISBN 978-1-4143-6139-0 (sc)
1. Twelve-step programs—Religious aspects—Christianity. I. Stoop, David A. II. Title.
    BV4596.T88A77 2012
    248.8′629—dc23   2012015450

ISBN 978-1-4964-1049-8

Printed in the United States of America

21	0	19	18	17	16	15
7	6	5	4	3	2	1

Table of Contents

The Twelve Steps of Life Recovery

1. We admitted we were powerless over our problems and that our lives had become unmanageable.
2. We came to believe that a Power greater than ourselves could restore us to sanity.
3. We made a decision to turn our wills and our lives over to the care of God.
4. We made a searching and fearless moral inventory of ourselves.
5. We admitted to God, to ourselves, and to another human being the exact nature of our wrongs.
6. We were entirely ready to have God remove all these defects of character.
7. We humbly asked God to remove our shortcomings.
8. We made a list of all persons we had harmed and became willing to make amends to them all.
9. We made direct amends to such people wherever possible, except when to do so would injure them or others.
10. We continued to take personal inventory, and when we were wrong, promptly admitted it.
11. We sought through prayer and meditation to improve our conscious contact with God, praying only for knowledge of his will for us and the power to carry it out.
12. Having had a spiritual awakening as the result of these Steps, we tried to carry this message to others and to practice these principles in all our affairs.

The Twelve Steps used in *The Life Recovery Journey* have been adapted with permission from The Twelve Steps of Alcoholics Anonymous.

Introduction

THIS BOOK IS the basic text for life recovery from a biblical perspective. We believe that when Dr. Bob and Bill W. worked with the Reverend Sam Shoemaker to create the Twelve Steps of Alcoholics Anonymous, they developed their ideas from the text of Scripture. In *The Life Recovery Bible*, we show how each of the Twelve Steps is founded on the principles of the Bible. Now we have added this book as another resource to support your recovery journey.

Inside, you will find an expansion on each of the Twelve Steps to help you better understand what each Step asks of you. The book is structured to allow you to journey through the entire program over the course of a year—one month on each Step. You can begin by reading the personal recovery stories at the beginning of each Step. Then read and reread the Step Insight as many times as necessary to make sure you understand what is involved with that specific Step.

Then you will find four Bible studies for each Step, which will help you interact with passages of Scripture that support the teaching of that Step. You might work through one Bible study each week for the month you are focusing on that particular Step. You will enhance the benefit of these studies if you discuss your responses to the studies in a group with others on the same recovery path.

We have found that the Twelve Steps of Life Recovery outline the principles by which anyone can experience healing and recovery for a variety of issues in life. The obvious application of the Twelve Steps is oriented to the individual alcohol or drug addict. But more and more we find the Steps are just as relevant and helpful to sex addicts, codependents, gambling addicts, workaholics, spendaholics, and any person struggling with a compulsive behavior, emotional problem, or character defect that interferes with their ability to live life as God intended. We believe all these problems will yield themselves to the healing power of these biblically sound principles. We have also found that many people who cannot afford to see counselors can find the help they need in a Twelve Step group.

We trust you will find this resource a powerful tool to assist you as you walk your journey of recovery.

STEP ONE

We admitted we were powerless over our problems
and that our lives had become unmanageable.

*I don't really understand myself, for I want to do what is right, but
I don't do it. Instead, I do what I hate. . . . Oh, what a miserable
person I am! Who will free me from this life that is dominated by
sin and death?*

ROMANS 7:15, 24

Andrea's Story of Recovery: Getting Out of the Insanity

Many years of insanity finally brought me to where I am today. I
could not seem to break the cycle. To my way of thinking, I had to
do it all myself. I had to somehow, someway, pull myself out of the
dark abyss of alcoholism. I tried every which way I could, but I could
not do it. Then, in February 2007, my life started over.

My story is not unique. My childhood, sadly, was not unique. It
was abusive—physically, mentally, emotionally, and sexually. All that
stuff. If you've been there, you know it creates heartache and pain
that don't subside. That's where the drugs came in and took me out
of where I didn't want to be.

I started using drugs when I was twelve years old. The first thing
I ever tried was a hit of acid, and it was on from there because it
made me laugh and feel free, and I knew that's what I wanted. And
so, from twelve years on, my life revolved around drugs in one way
or another. Still, I was known as a good girl. I lived a dual life. At
home I tried to be the peacekeeper, tried not to allow all the craziness

1

to go on—the upending of dinner tables, the random punches, the pulling of knives. That kind of stuff was everyday life in my household. I learned to be the good girl, and that's why, when I was doing drugs, I had to keep my good-girl face on so nobody would know what I was doing. Trying to be two people at once creates a form of insanity in itself.

I have to admit, I really loved to party. Because I had never had a good time when I was young, whenever I went out as a teenager or a young adult, the party was on. My goals and dreams began to revolve around how I could continue to party and still make something of myself—the good girl and the party girl. Instead of going to college, which would have been way too much work, I went to vocational school for a year and became a certified dental technician. At night, I worked in a bar. I thought I had the best of both worlds—I did well at my job, because that's what I had to do, and I was a great partier. Things seemed to be going really well.

My life went on like that for years. I ended up owning my own company and growing in the business world, but I never reached my full potential. Of course, that's all in retrospect. Now I can see where my decisions were hindered by the drugs and the alcohol and the parties.

My unraveling began when I was thirty-one and became a mother for the first time. I had never had a role model and didn't know how to be a mother. Worse yet, I was an alcoholic mother, with an alcoholic husband. He and I had two children together, but by the time the second baby was three months old, we had split up. I became a single mother of two with a business to run, doing speed to keep me going. And, you know, that just doesn't work. After a while, you run down. There just weren't enough hours in the day to do all the things I needed to do, and there wasn't enough speed to keep me going. On top of that, my judgment was impaired and I made one bad decision after another. When my daughters were four and six, I discovered crack cocaine and I lost my soul. Before long, I had also lost my home, my business, and my kids.

For thirteen years, I ran on the insanity that crack brought into my life, along with all the other crazy things that came from the life I had lived. During that time, I also gave birth to a third daughter. But I did not raise any of my girls. (Thank God for the families that loved my children when I couldn't.) And never once did I come to grips with the fact that I was powerless over my problems and that my life had become unmanageable—even though I was going to recovery meetings throughout those thirteen years. I would get sober for a little while—long enough to get the judge off my back and get my kids and a job—but then I would think, *Well, now I can drink.* And pretty soon, after a few drinks, I would decide, *I'll just smoke a little crack.* And, you know, before I knew it, I'd lost my kids again, lost my job, and was right back in the middle of that sick cycle of insanity that we live in as alcoholics and drug addicts.

In 2007, the day finally came when I ran out of chances. My eighty-year-old mother was my last victim. I had already taken everything I could from her, but when I stole her car for the third time—even though I brought it back before the cops could catch me—I ended up in prison with a two-year sentence, of which I had to serve half. My daughters came to court, and they were angry that I wasn't sentenced to more time because I had created so much wreckage and pain during my years of drug addiction. When I went off to prison, I really didn't think I would ever have anybody back in my life after all I had done.

But even after all that, my story is one of recovery. While I was in prison, God spoke to me and I had a spiritual awakening. When the door closed on that prison cell, I thought, *What have I done to myself?* It had never occurred to me I would end up in jail. That was definitely not part of the dream. I was fifty years old and I was really scared. I got on my knees and said, "Okay, God, I surrender to you. If you're here and you hear me, I really need you to speak to me right now."

When my cellmate offered me her Bible, I closed my eyes, opened it up, pointed to the page, and then looked to see what it said. Here's what I read: "The LORD has chastened me severely, but He has not given me over to death. Open to me the gates of righteousness; I will go through them, and I will praise the LORD. . . . I will praise You, for You have answered me, and have become my salvation" (Psalm 118:18-19, 21, NKJV). Today, the Lord is and always will be my salvation. And there is no doubt in my mind that my finger went right to those words so that I would know God was speaking directly to me. The message could not have been clearer to me.

During my year in prison, I worked really hard at getting my act together, and I applied to get into the drug program there. At first, my request was denied, but I kept insisting, "I need this program." The man in charge said, "I really doubt it. But maybe you'll hear from me." The next day, I received permission to enter the drug program. They even let me leave temporarily to appear in court for a hearing on a four-year suspended sentence from an earlier brush with the law. The day I appeared, the judge who had said, "If I ever see you again, you'll do every day of these four years," was not presiding, and the suspended sentence was not revoked. That could only have been the hand of God at work.

When I went back to prison, I worked even harder. I found a sponsor—a woman who was going to be incarcerated for the rest of her life because she had killed two people while driving drunk. When I asked her to sponsor me, she said, "You had better do everything I say, or you will end up right here next to me."

Once I was in the program, I worked the Steps. I had a counselor therapist who assisted me, and I revealed the deep, dark, dirty secrets of what had been done to me and what I had done to others. I also read my Bible every day. At first I didn't know how to read the Bible, so before I opened it, I would pray, "Please, God, give me the understanding of your Word. Let it hit me so I know what I'm reading." Still, in the beginning, the words didn't always make sense. I also started reading *Our Daily Bread*, a devotional booklet produced by RBC Ministries.

While I was in prison, I wrote to my kids every day. I received two letters in return. The first was from my eldest daughter, who wrote, "Dear Andrea, you don't deserve to be called Mother." The second letter was to tell me that my first grandson had been born and what a loser I was to choose crack and end up in prison so I couldn't even be there when my daughter had her first child. Though it hurt to read such harsh words, I said, "That's okay. God is the healer of families." And I just kept writing.

When I walked out of prison, I paroled straight into a drug program, but I left after six months. Four months later, I was back in prison. That just goes to show how you can be in a recovery home for six months and not be doing the deal. I still needed to connect my head with my heart—and I needed to turn to God to lead me every step of the way. I had to learn how to surrender to him. Back in prison, I really hit bottom, but then things began to change for the good, forever, one day at a time.

If you're going to be in a program, you have to do the work. And you have to *decide* that's what you want to do. If you make that choice and continue to walk it out day by day, you will find that you have a life beyond your wildest dreams. That may sound corny, but today my life has turned around so that I don't have to hurt anybody.

My children love me now. I have my own place, along with my youngest daughter, who is sixteen. I hadn't paid rent in twenty years—I'd lived off my mother and anybody else I could—but now I've had a job for three years (thank God for my business experience) and I'm paying my bills. Before I fell off the precipice of life into a deep, dark abyss, I had been promoted a couple of times, and it was the same company that hired me back as a parolee. We hire a lot of parolees and people who are in recovery.

I just want to tell you that recovery is there for the taking. All you have to do is get on your knees and ask God to direct your thinking on a daily basis. I suggest a Bible study resource such as *Our Daily Bread* as a good place to start. Read the daily message. Read the Bible verses that go along with it, and that will begin your journey through the Bible. Ask God to reveal his Word to you, and you will find that it all makes sense somehow. And when you lay your head down at night, say a prayer that you will be better the next day.

STEP ONE INSIGHT

We all know the meaning of the phrase "playing possum." It describes how a certain animal falls over and pretends to be dead when faced with a threatening situation. We humans are apt to do the same thing. When we encounter situations we perceive as dangerous or beyond us in some way, we cop out—we play dead. It's a form of surrender. In the animal kingdom, such a tactic often confuses the predator, and the one playing possum is left untouched. But it doesn't always work that way.

For most of us, playing possum is something we are determined to avoid at all costs. We see it as a sign of weakness, defeat, or humiliation, and there is something inside of us that recoils from such negative ideas. Everything in us wants to say, "No, I can handle it!" Unlike the opossum, we typically are determined to fight on and never surrender.

Recovery from our problems, addictions, and dependencies always begins by playing possum in a *genuine* way—by admitting defeat. When it comes to alcohol, drugs, sex, or food—or whatever the problem is that we can't solve or control—we begin the healing process by coming to terms with the absolute truth that we are *powerless*. Our problem has the upper hand, and we are incapable of breaking free on our own.

Our battle tactics to avoid surrender are common. The first weapon we turn to is our own willpower. "I should be able to handle this on my own," we tell ourselves. "In fact, I *can* handle this all by myself!" We convince ourselves we don't need a program or anyone else to help us. "I can *break* this dependency!" To prove the strength of our willpower, we may succeed in breaking the pattern of our problems or our dependency for a period of time—sometimes for six months or more. "The problem has gone away," we tell ourselves. But then, invariably, because our enemy is stronger than we are, we once again experience defeat and humiliation—left to face the reality of our powerlessness. No matter how hard we try, we always end up in the same place. It's like an endless loop that keeps us chasing after what we can never achieve.

We may also avoid surrendering to the truth of our powerlessness by using the weapon of blame—calling someone or something else the cause of our troubles. We tell ourselves, "I wouldn't have this problem if it weren't for _____." (You can fill in the blank.) The fault always lies outside of us. Blaming is a wonderful way to avoid the reality of our powerlessness. If our problem is someone else's fault, then he or she is the key to fixing everything. We need the other person to get fixed first.

We can spend a lot of time and effort in blaming, and all we get out of it is a continuation of our problem and a growing bitterness within. This bitterness comes not from our powerlessness over our problems, but from our helplessness in changing the other person. There is a world of difference between powerlessness and helplessness.

Denial is probably the most common weapon in our arsenal. Everyone around us sees what is happening to us, but we're blind to it. They tell us we have a problem, and we deny what they are saying. When other people tell us that we are in denial, they may think we're using it as a weapon to keep them off balance in their relationship with us. But the real purpose of our denial is to keep *ourselves* from facing the truth. Denial protects us from the truth. The more we use the weapon of denial, the more everything stays the same.

Another common weapon is isolation. If we tell ourselves that we *almost* have everything under control, we will gradually withdraw from anyone who presses the truth upon us. We often end up destroying friendships and even our family relationships. But when we stand alone, we stand defeated. We are powerless on our own! That's why the first word of Step One is *we*. Nothing changes for very long for the loner. It always takes a *community* to help us recover from our dependencies and our problems.

Our society teaches us the concepts of individualism and self-sufficiency, and thus the suggestion that we can't do it on our own goes against the grain. Further, when we are bound up in our problems, we get the grandiose idea that we don't need anybody—including God. But this prideful attitude will keep us fighting a losing battle with our problems, our addictions, and our dependencies. Honestly, we can never make it for very long on our own.

Maybe you have taken pride in the fact that your work hasn't suffered yet. But that's a hollow achievement. The truth is, our work is usually the last thing to fall apart. We will do everything we can to keep our jobs in spite of our problems. But eventually, as our addiction and our problems grow stronger and our lives become more unmanageable, our work will be affected as well.

The downward spiral will not stop until we finally come to grips with the fact that we are powerless. This is so hard for us to accept. If you're a woman, it may be even harder for you to accept because women have been fighting to regain a sense of power in society for decades. A woman may say to herself, "I need to claim my power as a woman!" But claiming power is not helpful when we are dealing with addictions, dependencies, or perpetual problems. The struggle to retain a sense of control simply keeps us on the treadmill to nowhere. The truth is that once we accept our powerlessness, we stop the erosion of our sense of who we are.

When we finally surrender and accept the reality that we are truly powerless, we begin to develop eyes that gradually open to the truth of our lives. When this happens, our recovery begins—the process of getting our lives and our families back. We begin to see that our lives really have become unmanageable. As we let go of the defensive posture of denial, we see clearly that our relationships have suffered. People have pulled away from us to the point that our only "friend" is our addiction or our problem.

As we see more clearly the consequences of our behaviors, we are left with the pain of how we have hurt those we love. We are filled with an awareness of our guilt and shame—and we may be tempted to go back and bury ourselves in our dependencies so we can avoid the painful truth of what we have done to our lives. But once we begin the steps to recovery, we must stay the course. Remember, this is just the beginning.

When we accept that we are powerless, we discover the paradox of surrender. It's the paradox James identifies when he writes, "Humble yourselves before the Lord, and he will lift you up in honor" (James 4:10). Just as the opossum who seems to "give up" in the face of his attacker survives through an act of surrender, so we find that we are not helpless when we surrender to the reality of our powerlessness.

It's important to look at the difference between being powerless and being helpless. In living with our addictions, dependencies, or problems, we are probably very familiar with the feeling of helplessness. It's a feeling of despair that threatens to overwhelm us. We think there is nothing we can do that will help—all hope is gone. But when we come to the Twelve Steps, we find that we are *not* helpless. There *is* hope. We can begin to work the same Steps that have changed other people's lives. Help is available! But to experience that help, we must change the *feeling of helplessness* into an *attitude of powerlessness*. In other words, we can't do it alone; but help is available!

When we look at Job's experience in the Bible, we see him arguing his innocence before his friends time and time again. "It's not me," he says over and over. He not only argues with his supposed comforters, whose religious advice totally misses the mark, but he also argues with God. It's interesting to note that when God finally responds, in Job 38, he never answers Job's questions. He simply asks question after question of his own, all of which are designed to reveal Job's powerlessness.

Finally Job surrenders. He says, "I am nothing—how could I ever find the answers? I will cover my mouth with my hand. I have said too much already. I have nothing more to say" (Job 40:4-5). In effect, Job says, "I give up. I will shut my mouth and stop trying to defend myself." In the presence of God's absolute power, Job came face-to-face with his own powerlessness, and his arguing with God ended!

That's exactly where Step One is designed to take us. Our arguments and denials are finished, over with, done. Our explanations and defenses have run out completely. We stand before our problems and finally admit that we cannot, by ourselves, defeat this enemy. We put our hands over our mouths and say nothing more.

Think of the life of a child, who is totally dependent on his or her parents for food, shelter, and protection. There is a similar, childlike feeling in being powerless and defenseless before our addictions or problems. Like a child, there is nothing we can do on our own to defend ourselves or to be "in charge." Regardless of how unmanageable a child's life becomes, he or she can do nothing to bring order and sanity to the situation. Likewise, we may think we have power over our circumstances, but like a little child, we are powerless. It takes someone more powerful than the child to handle the child's life circumstances. Jesus speaks directly to this when he says, "The Kingdom of God belongs to those who are like these children. I tell you the truth, anyone who doesn't receive the Kingdom of God like a child will never enter it" (Mark 10:14-15). In our case, we can say that anyone who doesn't begin recovery like a powerless child will never truly experience it.

That's where our recovery begins. Wholeness and healing belong to those who become just like a child, and those who can admit to themselves that they are powerless. If we don't begin our recovery as powerless children, we will never get to the place of wholeness. The demons of our dependencies will continue to battle with us until we learn to "play possum."

Marianne's Story of Recovery: My Father's Helper

To paraphrase Revelation 12:11, "We overcome our enemy by the blood of the Lamb and by the word of our testimony."

I did nothing to deserve being saved by Jesus' blood; that is an unmerited gift. My testimony is a different story. Actually, it's not my story, as someone pointed out to me—it's God's story *about* me. And what an awesome God he is. He transformed my life.

Due to circumstances at home, I became my father's helper at a young age. Taking care of my brother and sister and my alcoholic mother was my responsibility. Every day, I tried hard to keep things running smoothly. As a Catholic school student, I did all I could to hide my home life from the nuns. My parents sent us to church but did not attend themselves.

Despite nights filled with chaos and days filled with anxiety, I earned good grades. When we read the Bible at school, I just thought of it as homework and that none of it applied to me. I found solace in the empty church building, often going there alone to enjoy the peace and quiet, but I had no relationship with God. I felt too ashamed.

Dad was controlling and protective, so it wasn't easy to make friends. He always drove us to school and took us along to run errands. My siblings and I learned helplessness and dependency rather than self-confidence.

In my teen years, I became resentful and rebellious. I began to drink and instantly felt good. I could forget about being responsible for everything and everyone. Alcohol was a way to escape, but it eroded my emotional and spiritual potential.

I started to find ways to stay away from home as much as possible, and I felt as if I was leading a double life. At school, I was angelic to the nuns; at night, I was outside the house, drinking with newfound friends. My father and I fought constantly, and I was always afraid I was going to be found out. I felt ashamed and guilty in front of God and often thought, *I can't imagine what he thinks of me.* And I was right; I couldn't imagine what God thought of me. He loved me!

Before long, I couldn't look at myself in the mirror without feeling pain. I became self-destructive. My distorted thinking led me to make bad decisions. I married, gave birth to two premature babies, and divorced by the time I was twenty-one. Life got harder.

In despair, I begged God to help me. I felt as if I were in a dark hole and the lid was about to close over me. I desperately wanted out. I saw history repeating itself, and I wanted my sons to have a better life.

By God's grace, I became sober in 1974. My mother and I went to Alcoholics Anonymous together. Mother enjoyed twelve years of sobriety before she passed away in 1986. Because of the AA program, much healing took place between us in those years.

Each day, I asked God's help to stay sober. It worked. AA talks about God "as we understood him." I got stuck right there. I didn't have an understanding of God. I felt I knew who God was, but I had no personal relationship with him and didn't have time for one. So I told him, "You keep me sober, and I'll handle the rest from here."

At one point, I tried the charismatic movement in the Catholic Church; but when a priest (who was in the AA program) told me that I didn't need that kind of emotionalism, that it wasn't good for my recovery, I dropped out.

I maintained my sobriety, but happiness and contentment eluded me. I was underdeveloped emotionally and spiritually.

I kept very busy, especially with my two sons. I was trying to prove to God that I was good enough. It was an exhausting way to live, always going and doing, staying in the outer world because I could not stand to be in my inner world. I was unable to practice the presence of God.

I thought my happiness depended on other people's behavior. In order to be happy, I felt I needed to control their behavior, just like I felt when I was a kid. That's why it was very difficult for me to let God take care of me and the ones I loved.

At the AA meetings, two brothers noticed me and decided I would be a good match for their other brother, who was widowed. They asked me to meet him. We dated for a while and decided to get married. His children needed a mother—I knew I could do that—and my boys needed a father. I was determined to make it work. I didn't want to be a failure again.

On the outside, everything looked good. We attended church with the children and kept the appearance of harmony. But there was great turmoil at home. We were outside of a relationship with Christ, and we had married for the wrong reasons. Never once did I ask myself if I loved this man. I knew the answer and I felt ashamed. After six years, we divorced.

Single again, I devoted myself to staying sober, raising my teenage boys, and working. I had a willful personality, very self-reliant and fearful. I tried to do everything right.

At this point, I went to a self-improvement workshop. The people there encouraged me to come face-to-face with myself. Believe me, I was the last person on earth I wanted to meet! This was not a Christian movement, but it had a positive impact on me. I think the shell was beginning to crack. I was searching. There were times when I could see a little light breaking through, but it was overwhelming to me—too bright, too exposing. I'd run back to the darkness.

Psalm 34:18 says, "The LORD is close to the brokenhearted; he rescues those whose spirits are crushed." Because of my negative experiences, I unconsciously avoided true intimacy with God and others. I kept God at a distance. This helped me feel safe, but it left me isolated and alone. *How do I get out of the driver's seat of my own life?* I asked myself. *Maybe if I open the door just a little God will do the rest.*

Around this time I met Jim. We dated and became good friends. We had a lot in common and shared similar backgrounds. I wasn't rushing into anything with this relationship. Five years later, we married and settled into a routine life.

Over the years, I'd gone back to Mass, often bringing my grandchildren with me, but I did not feel spiritually filled. In my sobriety, I became desperate again. Just like when I was a child, my days were filled with anxiety and I couldn't sleep at night because of worry and fear. I wanted to feel God's love, I wanted to love others freely—especially my husband—and I wanted to love myself. I began to pray in earnest for this.

At a meeting, I met an acquaintance I hadn't seen in years. Carol and I became fast friends, and she began to talk to me about Jesus. I watched her, making sure her actions matched her words. Then I asked if I could go to her church. She was happy to take me along.

I loved the warmth of the people at Brookville Baptist Church. I thought Jesus must have made them that way. I wanted to know Jesus.

Romans 10:13 says, "Everyone who calls on the name of the LORD will be saved." Jesus respectfully waited for me to ask him into my life.

I started to attend services and Sunday school at Brookville Baptist in May 2006. In September of that year, in the pastor's office, I asked Jesus to come into my heart and be my Lord and Savior. When I walked out of there, I physically felt as if the pieces were finally fitting together and I was becoming a whole person. I know now I was being filled with the Holy Spirit. I thanked God for his grace toward me. I was so grateful. Membership classes followed, and I was baptized in May 2007.

My eyes were now open to how self-reliant I had become. I knew I still had a lot of work to do—no, *God* had a lot of work to do, and I just had to stay out of the driver's seat. I tended to stay very busy— a human *doing* instead of a human *being*. And though I have since found out that I can change what I'm doing, I realize that I can't change who I am. Only God can do that. I ask for lots of help and get strength and encouragement from his Word. Many kings and prophets in the Bible felt inadequate and afraid, so I know I'm in good company.

God invites me to talk to him. He promises to pay attention. He says he will always be interested and compassionate. The Bible tells me Jesus was forgotten, devalued, and distressed and that he asked for God's mercy. Jesus understands shame. He knows my affliction. When shame comes up, I can imagine Jesus welcoming me with open arms, the same arms he opened for me on the cross. He holds me and tells me I'm okay. He tells me that I am made perfect in his sight.

Second Corinthians 5:17 says, "Anyone who belongs to Christ has become a new person. The old life is gone; a new life has begun!"

I've been shown God's mercy. I've been shown a way out of my distress. I can be helpful to others who suffer the same affliction because I understand.

I have experienced many miracles, both big and small. I recently read that slow miracles are just as effective as fast miracles. Prayers have been answered. Jim started going to church with me and was deeply touched. He accepted Christ as his Savior a couple of years ago. We have a prayer life together, we read the Bible together, and we praise and serve God every day. It's a great blessing to see the Holy Spirit working in our lives. Jim even plays harmonica on the worship team! I am cochairing the women's Bible study this year and also discipling a fourteen-year-old girl in the youth group.

I have adopted Psalm 143:5 as my life verse: "I remember the days of long ago; I meditate on all your works and consider what your hands have done" (NIV).

When I look back, it feels as if that life happened to a different person altogether. I am amazed at the life I have today. With the Holy Spirit, I have the capacity and enthusiasm to help others in a healthy way, not a codependent way. Pastor Dennis said that God has been very good to me and Jim. This is so true.

As a short person (I'm four feet eleven), I can relate to Zacchaeus. Being a small man, he climbed a tree, hoping to get a glimpse of Jesus. When Jesus spoke to him, Zacchaeus must have felt ten feet tall. He climbed down from the tree and came forward. Jesus has the same effect on me.

I've now learned how to come forward each day. I feel loved, accepted, and part of God's wonderful family. Thank you, Lord. You are the perfect Father.

STEP ONE BIBLE STUDIES

For each Step, there are four Bible studies. You can work on them on your own—perhaps doing one study per week as you focus on each Step for a month. Better yet, do the studies with your recovery group by having members complete each study at home and then discussing what you've learned. Either way, you will be learning the biblical basis for each of the Twelve Steps, expanding your understanding of what is needed for recovery and what God wants to do for you as you work through the Steps.

Study #1: The Progression of an Addiction

This study is based on Proverbs 23:29-35 (page 812 in *The Life Recovery Bible*). Read the passage several times before working on the study.

1. IT ALL SEEMED SO MANAGEABLE AT FIRST

Things keep getting progressively worse—that's one way to define an addiction. And that's part of its deception—we start out thinking it's not a problem. By the time it becomes a problem, everyone but us can see it. We blindly continue to operate on the premise that "I can handle it." But what started out as manageable eventually manages us. We say to ourselves, "I can handle using this drug," or, "It's not a problem if I watch a little pornography," or, "I can manage my eating," or, "My spending is not out of control." In other words, "I'm not an addict!" It's too easy to ignore the progressive nature of behavioral problems that can become addictions. Addictions can and will take over and run our lives. They progress as Proverbs describes for us:

> *Who has anguish? Who has sorrow?*
> *Who is always fighting? Who is always complaining?*
> *Who has unnecessary bruises? Who has bloodshot eyes?*
> *It is the one who spends long hours in the taverns,*
> *trying out new drinks.*
> *Don't gaze at the wine, seeing how red it is,*
> *how it sparkles in the cup, how smoothly it goes down.*

PROVERBS 23:29-31

Here the passage is talking about alcohol, but you can easily substitute drugs, food, pornography, gambling, spending, or whatever your dependency might be. For example, it might read like this: *"Who spends long hours in front of the computer, surfing new porn sites? Don't gaze at those images, seeing how sensual they are, or how well those body images are put together. Don't dwell on how turned-on you have become."*

Now it's your turn to try it. Rewrite these verses based on your own problem, in a way that describes your dependency:

Think back to the beginning—before you were addicted or dependent. What attracted you to your problem behavior?

How did you get started?

How did you minimize any thought of risk at that time?

2. AT SOME POINT, WHAT ONCE WAS ATTRACTIVE WILL TURN ON YOU

For in the end it bites like a poisonous snake;
it stings like a viper.
PROVERBS 23:32

Here the writer of Proverbs jumps ahead. Eventually, what was once so attractive, and appeared to be so manageable, becomes dangerous.

Instead of the pleasure we thought we would experience, the alcohol leads to what the writer describes as a dangerous threat to our lives. Apply this verse from Proverbs to your own situation.

Over time, how did what seemed manageable turn against you? When did you begin to recognize the danger?

How did it all change in your experience?

What were some of the "dangers" you encountered? Who was involved?

3. THE CONSEQUENCES

Who has anguish? Who has sorrow?
   Who is always fighting? Who is always complaining?
   Who has unnecessary bruises? Who has bloodshot eyes? . . .
You will see hallucinations,
   and you will say crazy things.
You will stagger like a sailor tossed at sea,
   clinging to a swaying mast.
And you will say, "They hit me, but I didn't feel it.
   I didn't even know it when they beat me up."

PROVERBS 23:29, 33-35

Now the writer describes the progression of alcoholism. The person being described is where the alcoholic typically ends up—with bloodshot eyes, experiencing blackouts and crazy thinking, fighting, staggering and not feeling pain when beaten—all experiences common to the later stages of alcoholism. But the same principle applies to any addiction. What happens when your spouse discovers the pornography, or when your weight balloons to obesity, or when you lose everything due to your gambling? Write out your version of these verses and put your personal experience into what you write.

What would be a parallel to "hallucinations" for your dependency?

Describe some of your "crazy talk."

How have you tried to dull the pain?

4. THE FINAL STAGE: POWERLESSNESS

*When will I wake up
  so I can look for another drink?*
PROVERBS 23:35

What was initially attractive has taken control of our lives. We have become obsessed with the next drink, the next website, the next binge, or the next hit. All of our thinking seems to be controlled by a substance or an experience of something that we "must have"!

Describe times when you have been obsessed with pursuing your addiction or dependency.

When you realized that most of your thoughts were about that "next time," describe the feeling of powerlessness you experienced.

How close to "the bottom" did you come?

Jesus says, "The truth will set you free" (John 8:32). Look back over what you have written. How truthful have you been with yourself as you studied this passage? Is there anything you want to add or change?

Even when we are in the clutches of our addictions and dependencies, we lie to ourselves and think we are in control. But we aren't in control, and that's why the concept of powerlessness is so important in Step One of your recovery. When we read Proverbs 23, we see the futility of the drunkard's life, and we see how powerless he or she really is. Now we need to see this in *ourselves* and believe that admitting our powerlessness is the key to breaking the power of our addictions.

Study #2: Running Away—The Alternative We've All Attempted

This study is based on Genesis 16, the story of Hagar, Sarah's servant (page 23 in *The Life Recovery Bible*). Read the chapter several times before working on the study. (Note: In the biblical text, Sarah is called Sarai and Abraham is called Abram. Their names were later changed by God.)

1. SLAVERY

God promised Abraham countless heirs. He compared the number to the grains of sand on a seashore and to the stars in the sky—both beyond calculation. But to have that many descendants, Abraham knew he had to start with at least one. And he and his wife, Sarah, were advanced in age and had no children. I imagine that one night they were sitting and talking about this problem, when Sarah came up with a way to "help God" keep his promise. They would have the promised child through Sarah's servant—a practice that was quite common at the time.

> *Now Sarai, Abram's wife, had not been able to bear children for him. But she had an Egyptian servant named Hagar. So Sarai said to Abram. "The LORD has prevented me from having children. Go and sleep with my servant. Perhaps I can have children through her." And Abram agreed with Sarai's proposal. So Sarai, Abram's wife, took Hagar the Egyptian servant and gave her to Abram as a wife.*
>
> GENESIS 16:1-3

But what sounded like a good idea at the beginning turned into a nightmare for Sarah once Hagar became pregnant. The conflicts between them escalated, and Sarah came to regret her decision. Hagar was now in a power position, or so she thought, and she made life miserable for Sarah. But Sarah was still in charge, and the conflict grew to the point that Hagar's life became unmanageable and she ran away.

In this picture we have of Hagar, we see the frustration and anger of a slave who was being treated harshly. When we are lost in our addictions and dependencies, we are in much the same predicament as Hagar—we're slaves—and any addiction will eventually turn on us and beat us into oblivion. We really are powerless and faced with a life without choices, but our denial keeps us stuck. We believe the lie that we are not powerless, that our lives are not unmanageable. So we keep running away from the truth, and nothing changes in our lives.

In what ways is living with our dependencies like Hagar's life?

What choices does it appear Hagar had about sleeping with Abraham?

Who had the power in this passage, and who was powerless?

2. FAMILY CHAOS PREVAILS

So Abram had sexual relations with Hagar, and she became pregnant. But when Hagar knew she was pregnant, she began to treat her mistress, Sarai, with contempt. Then Sarai said to Abram, "This is all your fault! I put my servant into your arms, but now that she's pregnant she treats me with contempt. . . ."

Abram replied, "Look, she is your servant, so deal with her as you see fit." Then Sarai treated Hagar so harshly that she finally ran away.

GENESIS 16:4–6

Notice how everyone seems to be at everyone else's throat in this passage. Hagar treats Sarah with contempt, so Sarah takes it out on Abraham. Abraham opts out of the problem, and Sarah deals harshly with Hagar until Hagar runs away.

What effect has your addiction or dependency had on your family relations?

Describe some of the times when your anger spilled out on everyone else.

When have you felt like "running away"?

There are various ways to run away. How did you run away? Or why didn't you?

3. THE LESSONS LEARNED BY RUNNING AWAY

Hagar didn't have a plan when she ran away; she just wanted to get away from Sarah. Staying would only have reinforced the reality of her powerlessness. At first, being pregnant with her master's baby must have given her a sense of power, and even the act of running away must have felt empowering at first. But once she left the familiar surroundings of home, she was faced with the reality of her powerlessness, for she had no place to run.

> *The angel of the LORD found Hagar beside a spring of water in the wilderness, along the road to Shur. The angel said to her, "Hagar, Sarai's servant, where have you come from, and where are you going?"*
>
> *"I'm running away from my mistress, Sarai," she replied.*
>
> *The angel of the LORD said to her, "Return to your mistress, and submit to her authority." Then he added, "I will give you more descendants than you can count."*
>
> GENESIS 16:7–10

When you've thought of running away from your problems, how did that idea empower you? How long did the feeling of empowerment last?

Notice that Hagar only answered the first question the angel asked. She didn't tell him where she was going, for she obviously didn't have a plan. If she did, she wasn't about to share it. What plans have you had in the past for running away from your addiction?

What is the first lesson that Hagar learns from the angel?

Submit is another way of saying "surrender." How do you think Hagar experienced the words "submit to her authority"? Describe your own response to that phrase.

When the angel left Hagar, Scripture says that Hagar used another name to refer to the Lord who had spoken to her. She said, "You are the God who sees me." She also said, "Have I truly seen the One who sees me?" (Genesis 16:13). What an incredible insight Hagar had about her experience with the angel. She had a new experience of God. As she surrendered and accepted Sarah's authority, she became aware of God's interest in her. This is the paradox of powerlessness, of surrendering: We meet God in a new way, and we're no longer helpless, as we'll see in the next two steps. The all-powerful God actually sees us and is intimately interested in us. That's a life-changing realization.

Based on Hagar's experience in this passage, what new insights do you have about God?

As you admit your powerlessness, can you also open yourself to "the God who sees you"?

Regardless of where you are in the process of surrendering and accepting your powerlessness, the God of the universe cares enough about you that he sees you. And as he looks at you, there is no judgment, nor is there condemnation; there is only the desire to walk with you on your journey of recovery. Be assured that you are loved, just as the Egyptian slave Hagar was loved and blessed by God.

Study #3: The Man Who Had Everything, and Lost It All

This study is based on Judges 13-16, the story of Samson (beginning on page 320 in *The Life Recovery Bible*). The book of Judges gives more space to the life of Samson than to any of the other judges. Read the full story several times before working on the study.

1. A GREAT BEGINNING

Not many people have had an angel announce their birth, but that is what happened with Samson. He had a great beginning. His parents had tried unsuccessfully for years to have a child, and they were old at the time of his birth. They may even have been old enough to have given up on the idea of having children. But suddenly an angel appeared to Manoah's wife (whose name is not given in the text) and made the announcement that she would become pregnant. She must have laughed to herself, but she believed the announcement enough that she went and told her husband. At first, Manoah didn't believe her, so the angel had to return and make a second announcement to the father-to-be. Here's how it started:

The angel of the LORD appeared to Manoah's wife and said,
"Even though you have been unable to have children, you will
soon become pregnant and give birth to a son. So be careful; you
must not drink wine or any other alcoholic drink nor eat any
forbidden food. You will become pregnant and give birth to a
son, and his hair must never be cut. For he will be dedicated
to God as a Nazirite from birth. He will begin to rescue Israel
from the Philistines."

JUDGES 13:3-5

What is the meaning of being a Nazirite? Look at Numbers 6:2-3
for help.

What do you think was the purpose of someone taking
a Nazirite vow?

A person would take a Nazirite vow in order to develop a deeper
relationship with God. He or she would typically do it for a period
of time—similar to how some people today give up something for
Lent. But Samson was *born* a Nazirite, set apart from birth for a special purpose. He was to be a judge and lead Israel in its fight against
the Philistines. In the story of Samson, it seems he never really took
his vows seriously. He was to be a leader, but he never led. Still, in
spite of himself, he accomplished some of God's purposes. He created
havoc in the towns of the Philistines and killed many of the enemy.
But he never acted intentionally. To him, it was just a lark or something done in anger when he was provoked. His story is certainly not
one of success, but God was nonetheless at work.

Are there any examples in your life where God has worked in spite of yourself? Describe what happened.

2. FAMILY ISSUES

Perhaps it was because Samson's parents were older when he was born. Or maybe it was because they were so happy to have a son that they simply gave him everything he wanted. He obviously knew nothing about delayed gratification—he was totally spoiled. His parents really didn't know how to parent him.

Samson was to have nothing positive to do with the Philistines—he was to rescue Israel from them, not become part of their culture. His parents tried to steer him on the right path, but he didn't listen. When he met an attractive Philistine woman, he wanted to marry her! And his determination to do what he wanted set him on a path that would lead to his destruction.

One day when Samson was in Timnah, one of the Philistine women caught his eye. When he returned home, he told his father and mother, "A young Philistine woman in Timnah caught my eye. I want to marry her. Get her for me."

His father and mother objected. "Isn't there even one woman in our tribe or among all the Israelites you could marry?" they asked. "Why must you go to the pagan Philistines to find a wife?"

But Samson told his father, "Get her for me! She looks good to me."

JUDGES 14:1-3

Usually, when we start down the path of addiction, there are plenty of warnings. What were some of the warnings given to you?

How did you respond to the warnings? Why?

Obviously, Samson wanted what he wanted, and his parents gave in. They probably had a pattern of giving in to Samson, for he was so "special." They were his enablers. Who have been your enablers?

3. BROKEN VOWS

As a Nazirite, Samson was to be set apart to serve God. Instead, he served himself and broke his vows many times. For example, he was forbidden to touch anything that was dead—as a Nazirite, he wasn't even to be in the presence of something dead—but the prohibition meant nothing to him.

> *When he returned to Timnah for the wedding, he turned off the path to look at the carcass of the lion. And he found that a swarm of bees had made some honey in the carcass. He scooped some of the honey into his hands and ate it along the way.*
> JUDGES 14:8-9

> *One day Samson went to the Philistine town of Gaza and spent the night with a prostitute.*
> JUDGES 16:1

Describe some of the vows you have made to yourself about your problem or dependency that you haven't been able to keep.

If you were retelling the story of Samson, how would you get him to understand his powerlessness?

4. SAMSON'S DOWNFALL

Samson's wife came to him in tears and said, "You don't love me; you hate me! You have given my people a riddle, but you haven't told me the answer." . . . So she cried whenever she was with him and kept it up for the rest of the celebration.

JUDGES 14:16-17

Then Delilah pouted, "How can you tell me, 'I love you,' when you don't share your secrets with me? You've made fun of me three times now, and you still haven't told me what makes you so strong!" She tormented him with her nagging day after day until he was sick to death of it.

JUDGES 16:15-16

We can say that Samson's downfall was caused by his addiction to sex. He wanted to marry a forbidden woman—a Philistine. That marriage didn't last very long. Later, he slept with a prostitute and got caught in a web of intrigue with Delilah. He couldn't stand up to Delilah's nagging pressure, and he couldn't stop toying with her as she tried to discover the secret of his strength.

What do you think he should have done?

We've already seen that running away doesn't work. What did you learn from Hagar that applies to Samson? How would he "surrender"?

Unfortunately, Samson, through his own addiction to sex and to women, became powerless—literally. He lost his eyesight and his great physical strength, becoming a prisoner of Israel's enemy, the Philistines. Notice what he did next:

> *Then Samson prayed to the LORD, "Sovereign LORD, remember*
> *me again. O God, please strengthen me just one more time.*
> *With one blow let me pay back the Philistines for the loss of my*
> *two eyes."*
> *Then Samson put his hands on the two center pillars that*
> *held up the temple. Pushing against them with both hands,*
> *he prayed, "Let me die with the Philistines." And the temple*
> *crashed down on the Philistine rulers and all the people.*
> JUDGES 16:28-30

Here is an example of what we mean about powerlessness. By himself, Samson had always been powerless. He believed he was the source of his own power. He believed his own lies. Now, however, he couldn't lie to himself anymore, and he turned to the One who was the real source of power: Almighty God.

Describe some of the ways you have lied to yourself.

Who alone has the power to break your addictions, dependencies, and compulsions?

Why do you think Samson was in denial for so long?

Is there any other source of power that is strong enough to break the lies of denial and heal the broken places in your life?

Samson accomplished God's purpose in spite of himself, but it took tragedy for him to do it. He was called to be a leader, but he never led. He could be called the first sex addict in the Bible—not a great way to be recognized. But in the end, when he faced the reality of his powerlessness, he succeeded. We can only guess what he could have accomplished if he had lived out his Nazirite vow. If only he had done what was right, he could have been one of the greatest examples of a godly man.

Study #4: A Psalm Dedicated to Powerlessness

This study is based on Psalm 116 (page 762 in *The Life Recovery Bible*). Read the complete psalm several times before working on the study.

1. FACING THE REALITY OF OUR POWERLESSNESS

When we finally come to the end of ourselves, it feels almost like a death. Sometimes, just before we hit bottom, it may even feel like we are dying. We become completely overwhelmed with depression and the consequences of our self-destructive behaviors, and we may even contemplate suicide. But something stops us, and we finally come to the end of ourselves. We accept our powerlessness, and we find there is someone waiting to help us at the bottom. We may be powerless, but we are not helpless or hopeless. We can turn to the One who can help. The psalmist describes what he did when he faced the end, his death.

> *Death wrapped its ropes around me;*
> *the terrors of the grave overtook me.*
> *I saw only trouble and sorrow. . . .*
> *I was facing death, and he saved me. . . .*
> *He has saved me from death,*
> *my eyes from tears,*
> *my feet from stumbling. . . .*
> *"I am deeply troubled, LORD."*
> *In my anxiety I cried out to you,*
> *"These people are all liars!"*
>
> PSALM 116:3, 6, 8, 10-11

When have you felt this hopeless?

In what ways have you experienced the bondage of your addiction as a death?

2. TAKING THE FIRST STEP

Let's look at the rest of the psalm and rearrange the order to see the psalmist's progression as he moves forward after hitting bottom. It begins with an awareness of the kindness and mercy of God.

How kind the LORD is! How good he is!
  So merciful, this God of ours!

PSALM 116:5

How do you view God? How does it compare with how the psalmist views God?

We have to begin by seeing that God is *good*, *kind*, and *merciful*. What does God's mercy mean to you?

The next step is to call upon the Lord:

Then I called on the name of the LORD:
  "Please, LORD, save me!"

PSALM 116:4

When the psalmist cried out to God, he gained a new experience of God's character:

I love the LORD because he hears my voice
  and my prayer for mercy.
Because he bends down to listen,
  I will pray as long as I have breath! . . .
The LORD protects those of childlike faith. . . .
The LORD cares deeply.

PSALM 116:1-2, 6, 15

Which of these statements do you have trouble accepting?

Do you feel as if God is listening?

Now look at the psalmist's response to being heard in his cry for help:

> *And so I walk in the LORD's presence*
>   *as I live here on earth! . . .*
> *What can I offer the LORD*
>   *for all he has done for me? . . .*
> *O LORD, I am your servant. . . .*
>   *born into your household;*
>   *you have freed me from my chains.*
> PSALM 116:9, 12, 16

What does it mean to you to "walk in the LORD's presence"?

The psalmist feels great gratitude and relief that his chains have been broken. Even as you begin to understand the reality of this first step, the chains of your addiction and dependency are being broken. Describe what it will feel like to have your chains broken.

> *I will keep my promises to the LORD*
>   *in the presence of all his people. . . .*
> *I will fulfill my vows to the LORD*
>   *in the presence of all his people—*
> *in the house of the LORD*
>   *in the heart of Jerusalem.*
> PSALM 116:14, 18-19

The psalmist concludes by reminding us that we can't go forward while living an isolated life. True recovery takes place "in the presence of all his people." What makes it difficult to be a part of the "we" in this first step?

Why is the psalmist so insistent that recovery is experienced in the context of "we, the people"?

Who are some of the people who are part of your "we," who will be included in your growth and recovery?

As you've fought your addiction or dependency, you've probably broken many vows. Vows don't work with problems, addictions, and dependencies. But the psalmist seems to suggest that there is one vow we must keep, and that is to stay connected in the process with people who care. Can you make that vow?

STEP TWO

We came to believe that a Power greater than
ourselves could restore us to sanity.

*After this time had passed, I, Nebuchadnezzar, looked up to
heaven. My sanity returned, and I praised and worshiped the
Most High and honored the one who lives forever.*

DANIEL 4:34

George's Story of Recovery: Love Is an Action

I am an Alaskan Native from a village of about one hundred and
twenty people on the Alaska Peninsula. As in most Alaskan villages,
I grew up in the Russian Orthodox church, which for me meant a
static faith, based on repetition, with no change involved. Later in
my life, I was transformed by God and discovered that our Lord is
both dynamic and gracious. I started writing a daily journal, which
became a way for me to let go of the sins of my past and move forward in Christ.

I first accepted Christ while I was in high school. Some friends
of my parents had invited me to Ivan Bay to stay for a while and go
hunting and fishing. I didn't know much about Jesus then, but as I
was watching a program with the family on the Trinity Broadcasting
Network, I found myself convicted of my sinful life. I was so upset,
I went into another room and cried and cried. My friend's wife came
into the room and asked if she could pray for me. I agreed. I accepted
Christ that day, and my life seemed to change. I felt loved and cared
for with every step I made. Up until I went back home, that is. That

is when I learned how important it is to have Christian fellowship. Without other Christians to support and encourage us, we are vulnerable to the enemy's attacks. When I got home, my life seemed to go back to normal. When I thought of praying, I felt discouraged because of the evil that was around me.

About a year after my first experience with Christ, I fell back into the ways of the world and started experimenting with alcohol. I loved how it made me feel—almost as if I had no problems. This was far from the truth, and somehow I knew it. I continued this way for years and became a slave to alcohol. Today, I am thirty-eight years old, and I drank regularly for at least ten years before I became sick of it.

I still vividly remember the day I came to rely on alcohol for solace, when I was working as an EMT.

I received a call about two o'clock one morning saying I needed to go to a patient's house. When I arrived, I was shocked to see a fellow EMT doing CPR on a woman who was nonresponsive. I was upset because the EMT had the woman on the bed. I carefully transferred the patient to the floor and continued CPR with the assistance of the patient's husband. He and I worked on her for an hour and a half, during which time I was in radio contact with a doctor, who kept telling me it was time to let the woman go. I looked at the husband and said, "We aren't done yet."

Finally, out of sheer exhaustion, I told the husband it was time to stop. Those were the hardest words I have ever had to say to any man. I looked at him, with tears in his eyes, as I got up and walked out of the house. For the next several minutes, I sat on the porch and cried. I blamed God, asking him, "Why did you allow her to leave?" I was so angry, I went home and tore up my Bible.

From that moment on, I had to deal with the loss. It took me about six months to get over it. That's not to say the memories aren't still there, even today. I blamed myself for losing her and couldn't bring myself to face her family. I buried my heartache in the bottle and was content to do so for a long time. After all, it was my solace.

Whenever I turned on the TV and saw TBN, I got angry and said things like, "Yeah right, whatever!"

When I had earned enough money to buy a ticket to Anchorage, I flew over to visit friends I had made during other trips. Every friend I had was homeless, so I camped out with them wherever they were staying. We drank to drown our sorrows and worries.

I remember one day when I was sitting at a park and the Lord spoke to me. All he said was John 3:16. Over and over again in my mind I heard the same thing: "For God so loved the world . . ." Every time, however, my heart grew harder and harder. I drank for four months straight and was starting to feel the effects of my drinking. I would wake up at four or five in the morning and have to drink a beer so I wouldn't shake. My body came to rely on alcohol. After a couple weeks of this, I finally brought myself to get help.

I went to the hospital and they got me into a detox center, where I stayed for five days. The first two or three days were pure torture. Every time I closed my eyes, I saw the most grotesque faces I had ever seen—the kind you would see in the most horrible horror movies. They never said anything; they just stared at me. It was almost as if they were looking into my soul.

It was terrifying to go to sleep, but it was difficult to stay awake because of the drugs they gave me. I had no choice but to shut my eyes. I told myself it was the price I had to pay for my choice to drink. When I got out of the detox center, I went back to the homeless camp, but I didn't drink for a couple of days. Then the sorrow and self-pity came back and the bottle called to me.

Another attempt at sobriety came when I was in the Pacific Northwest. I prayed one evening, telling God that if he wanted me to quit drinking, he'd have to bring someone to me to say so. My friend and I were walking around a lake and talking about our drinking habits. Out of the corner of my eye, I saw a man and a woman sitting at a table. It looked as if they were praying. Then the man stood up and approached my friend and me. He said, "I have been led to talk to you about your life." He asked me if I needed prayer. I said yes. After I spilled out my story, the man said, "The Lord wants you to go home." The next day, I got on a plane back to Anchorage. It was an eye-opening experience and part of the journey that led me back to God.

During my life, I have learned a lot about God—how faithful he is to us and how he loves us. I learned that love is not just a word. To me, love is an *action*. Otherwise, God could have sent Jesus just to visit us, talk about love, and go back to paradise. Instead, he sent his Son to die for us, to make the ultimate sacrifice so that we would not die in our sin. I asked myself once if I loved my family. Sadly, I could not say yes to that question. If I loved my family, my life would reflect that love. Again, John 3:16 pops into my head: "For God loved the world so much that he gave his one and only Son, so that everyone who believes in him will not perish but have eternal life." Powerful, powerful words. *God loves us.* How do we know this? He tells us in his Word, and he proved it through his sacrifice. Love is an *action* word.

I ask myself where I would be today if God had not helped me to overcome my addictions and to love—to truly love. Thanks be to our Lord in heaven for his grace and mercy.

STEP TWO INSIGHT

We've taken the first step. We've surrendered. We have admitted complete defeat. We agree that we cannot overcome our problem behaviors. We are powerless! So now what do we do? Step Two begins to move us outside of ourselves to the place where we genuinely believe that we need Someone who is actually powerful enough to defeat our problem—a power we know we do not have. It's one thing to admit we are powerless, but it's something else again to actually believe there is a Power that can restore us to sanity.

The first two Steps not only confront us with our powerlessness, they also confront us with the reality of the insanity we have been living with in our lives. For far too long, we have tried and tried, harder and harder, to solve our problems on our own, never recognizing the insanity of doing the same thing and expecting a different result. Step One breaks the cycle of insanity as we admit that we are powerless over our problems, and that our lives have become unmanageable. Step Two introduces us to a way to live that will actually lead us forward in our recovery and to our healing.

As you read this Step, you may already be forming an opposing argument. Maybe you want to say that you've turned to God in the past and nothing ever happened. God was apparently busy with someone else's problems, and he either forgot about you or didn't have time for your problems. So why will this time be any different?

First, think back to how you "tried" to get God's help in the past. Often when our lives feel totally out of control, we turn to God and we tell him what we need from him right now. Our "God help me" quickly moves into "this is what I need you to do right now!" After all, at the point we desperately needed help in a specific way, we thought we knew best what was needed.

Now ask yourself: Who's in control in that scenario? Obviously *we* still are! We are *telling* God what we need from him. Typically, God is not interested in our solutions because *his* way of dealing with our problems and addictions is quite different from our way of dealing with them. So when we make our demands, is it any surprise that he seems to be busy somewhere else? People may tell us we have no faith, or not enough faith. We wonder what's wrong with us, why God doesn't do what we ask, or what we tell him. We've "claimed the promises," memorized the appropriate verses, and for a time, we've tried harder and harder to get God to act. And we've ended up frustrated and in despair.

Maybe at one time you trusted God for the solution to your problems, but now as you come to this Step, you're at a place where you have simply given up on God. You're tired of the Bible verses, the prayers, the well-meaning suggestions of other believers. Maybe you are so jaded by religion that when you see this Step, and several others, suggesting that the answer begins with God, you respond,

"I'm finished with God." Maybe you're ready to quit before you even begin, because you've had enough of religious talk.

Some people will admit to being powerless—for a while—but they soon take back the reins of their lives. Because they have always operated on the premise that they don't need anyone else's help, they are satisfied to be self-sufficient. One man we counseled was so sure he didn't need anyone's help that he consciously decided that the "greater Power" was merely an untapped part of himself. He was still determined to take care of the problem on his own. When we talked about this and he saw that admitting powerlessness meant he had to go *outside* of himself, he decided that his greater power would be one of the magnificent trees growing near the site of his AA meetings. He was convinced he would find help there because the tree was "mightier" than he was. Finally, he became aware that whatever he turned to for help had to be *able* to help, not just inspire. And who is more powerful and able to help than God?

Remember, we are now coming to God with a recognition and acknowledgment that we are powerless! We have given up. We have surrendered our will. And so we don't *tell* him what to do; instead, we wait for him, moment by moment, to lead the way. Because we have surrendered, he is now responsible for what happens next.

The apostle Paul understood the struggle of trying to solve our own problems. He writes, "The trouble is with me, for I am all too human, a slave to sin. I don't really understand myself, for I want to do what is right, but I don't do it. Instead, I do what I hate" (Romans 7:14-15). He ends up in despair, saying, "Oh, what a miserable person I am! Who will free me from this life that is dominated by sin and death?" (Romans 7:24). He might have said "this life that is dominated by my problems or my addictions." But notice how he answers his own question: "Thank God! The answer is in Jesus Christ our Lord" (Romans 7:25). Paul came to the one person who was more powerful than he was. And when he turned to Jesus, he found love, grace, and forgiveness. He later adds, "There is no condemnation for those who belong to Christ Jesus!" (Romans 8:1). When he surrendered his struggle with sinful behavioral patterns, Paul recognized that a Power greater than himself could restore him to sanity without condemning him in the process.

What about people who are stuck because they say they don't believe in God? They claim to be either agnostic or atheistic. If they don't believe there is a God, how can they admit that a Power greater than themselves will actually help them win the battle against their problems and dependencies? The idea of God or anything like God shuts them down, and there's no point in going any further. They say, "If you bring God into the discussion, I'm out." They want nothing to do with the recovery process if God is involved.

So where does that leave them? Obviously, no single person—not even a sponsor—is more powerful than we are, so the answer is not going to be a person. But what about a *group* of people? What about the power of ten people who are committed to walk with us on our journey out of insanity? Can we start there in our understanding of the "greater Power" and deal with the "God issue" in Step Three? We can, but why delay the process?

The early developers of the Twelve Steps knew that no human power, either singular or collective, could help them. They clearly recognized their need for God, and that idea, for them, was not debatable. Our "higher power" is not a lightbulb or a tree or even a recovery group. God is the only one who can and will deliver us from our insanity—*if* we will seek him.

"But I've been disappointed with God."

"I'm tired of all the religious jargon."

"I don't want any of this God stuff."

All of these responses share the same problem: They discourage us from turning to God for help in the proper way. If we say we're disappointed with God because he didn't help us the way we wanted in the past, we're really no different from the person who says God doesn't exist. Both are resisting help. Both are operating with a closed mind and haven't yet admitted complete defeat. Both would rather dictate the terms of surrender. Being open to the ongoing healing process requires complete surrender and a placing of trust in that greater Power.

Think of it this way. We've been fighting our problems our own way, even though we are part of a larger army. We're like rebellious soldiers, second-guessing the general, and even disobeying orders. When we finally get caught, we come to a place where we are forced to admit complete defeat in doing things our own way. We must end our rebellion and submit (surrender our will) to our general. In doing so, we admit that our general is, and has always been, more powerful than we are. We may have resented our general, not respected him, resisted his leadership, and only pretended allegiance to him. But once we have given up our rebellion, we cannot negotiate the terms of our surrender or tell the general what he is supposed to do. We may have tried that in the past, but now we must realize and accept the fact that *he* is in charge. He determines what our next steps will be. We don't correct him; we don't argue with him; we don't resist him. It's like when General Robert E. Lee surrendered at the end of the Civil War: He gave up his authority and submitted to the Northern general. He had no control over what would come next— he could only surrender.

Look at how this differs from what we tried when we thought we were in charge of our recovery. We tried telling God what we needed from him, and nothing changed. Or we kept trying harder on our own, hoping that somehow our best efforts would change things. We thought we could do it our way, and we thought we could do it on our own. Now, however, if we have truly surrendered and admitted complete defeat, we simply say to this Power that is greater than ourselves, "Your will be done." We let go and we let God do what is needed. He is the General to whom we have surrendered.

What does it mean to surrender? Webster's defines surrender in this way: "To yield to the power, control, or possession of another. . . ; to give up completely . . . ; to give (oneself) up into the power of another . . . ; to give (oneself) over to something (as an influence).[1]

When we surrender to God, we allow God's Holy Spirit to

empower us. But first we must humble ourselves. "Humble yourselves before the Lord, and he will lift you up in honor" (James 4:10).

Jesus said, "Anyone who chooses to do the will of God will find
out whether my teaching comes from God or whether I speak on my
own" (John 7:17, NIV). This is an important point, one that under-
girds this Step. In essence, Jesus is saying, "Test my teaching to see if
it is true." Applied to your recovery, we could say, "Test this Step—by
doing what it says—and you will find out if God is for real or not."

So, what do we have to do? We must believe that God is the only
power that is greater than ourselves and can restore us to sanity.

This Step is often called the "Hope Step" because when we admit
we are powerless, we may also feel that everything is hopeless. But
that's not true. And when we realize that we are powerless but not
helpless, we find there is hope. We can change! We can move from
insanity to sanity!

But hope is always a corollary to faith. Notice what the writer
of the book of Hebrews says: "Faith is the confidence that what we
hope for will actually happen; it gives us assurance about things we
cannot see" (Hebrews 11:1). That's why this Step could also be called
the "Faith Step."

This time you could be saying, "Look, I don't have any faith.
I'm not sure that doing this Step is going to make any difference."
Again, the writer of Hebrews helps us: "Anyone who wants to come
to [God] must believe that God exists and that he rewards those who
sincerely seek him" (Hebrews 11:6). We begin by simply *choosing* to
believe God exists, and then we begin to seek him. And we seek him
in order to get to know him. How is this different from before? This
time, we're starting from a place of surrender. We aren't telling God
what to do; we simply desire to *know* him, and we're willing to *wait*
for him to help us in his own way and to guide us one moment at
a time.

We need to be willing to *believe*—to put our trust in God—
because that becomes the foundation for all that is to follow. Once
we are willing to surrender—to admit that we can't do it on our own,

that we need the help of a Power greater than our own—we are one step further in the process of our recovery. We may say, "God, I'm angry with you for the past," or, "God, I'm not even sure you are there," or, "God, I'm just plain tired of trying to do it all alone and I'm willing to be open to your reality." In whatever way we are able to express our faith in God's existence and power—from the tiniest particle of faith to faith as big and strong as you can imagine—we put ourselves in the position to receive his help. It all begins with the *willingness* to believe that God has the power to restore us to sanity.

Our willingness to believe becomes the foundation for doing "first things first." What comes first? God does. Jesus said, "Seek the Kingdom of God above all else, and live righteously, and he will give you everything you need" (Matthew 6:33). We don't get ahead of ourselves. We start by doing what comes first, and the priority at this point is to *seek God*. We want to know him. We seek him first because when we do, he is going to give us everything we need. That doesn't mean he's the great Santa Claus in the sky who gives us all kinds of goodies. No, he gives us what we need. And getting what we need begins with our knowing God and learning to trust him with our entire lives on a daily basis. Then we will begin to see his healing power at work in our lives.

How long will it take to restore sanity to our lives? Be patient. In our insanity, we become desperate and want everything *now*. But when we become serious about seeking to know God, we will also be content with the fact that our recovery process will take a lifetime—a lifetime of continuing to grow in our relationship with God. And as we continue through the Steps, our relationship with God will become stronger and stronger, and we will see more and more the reality of his power in our lives.

Cliff's Story of Recovery: Recovery Is a Process

I'm a Christian, and I'm an addict. I've got some issues with drugs, alcohol, sex, and relationships.

I'm just going to be extremely real and honest here. There's no point in being pretentious; it's really not about me, anyway. I grew up angry. My dad died when I was two, and that really ticked me off. I now see it as necessary. I don't understand it, but my sponsor recently pointed out that it was necessary, and there are a lot of things in my life that are that way, you know? I've had a sense of worthlessness pretty much my whole life.

I started looking at dirty pictures at a very young age. I remember finding *Playboy*s and whatnot in some fields near my house. I started getting loaded and having sex at thirteen. I think I did acid for the first time when I was fifteen. The first time I got drunk was to impress some girls. I went over to a slumber party at a girl's house when I was thirteen and stole a little bit of booze out of all the different bottles in her parents' liquor cabinet and filled up a big glass. That's all I remember about that night.

That's how my life as a user started out. I've had run-ins with booze, meth, and freebase—that's what we called it back in the day. It was the booze that really destroyed me. I also learned how to manipulate girls and I got really strung out on porn. I've never been married, but I've got two daughters. One is twenty-five, and the other is thirteen. I have little contact with either of them. I pray for restoration of those relationships all the time. I've devastated every relationship I've ever been in.

Okay, about my strength. Christ has redeemed me, and that started when I embraced the principles of the Twelve Step program. I can clearly see now that the Twelve Steps are directly based on the Bible's instruction on how to live life and honor God. It's basically about repenting—admitting your wrongs and turning around and going in the other direction. It's a lifelong process, and I'm still on the path—it's ongoing.

My hope is in God.

I proclaim that Jesus Christ is the only begotten Son of God. He died for my sins and rose on the third day and is with the Father and is one with the Father. I'm in the midst of a process called sanctification. I'm reckoning the old man dead. I'm trusting God, and I know that all my hope resides in God's grace.

What is insanity? You know, I hear things in the program—that insanity is doing the same thing over and over and expecting different results. Sure, that's one definition. Here's another: living recklessly through high-risk sex and deadly situations. I could give you plenty of examples of that kind of insanity. Living in rebellion and defying God is insane. *Okay?* That's what insanity is.

So what is *sanity?* Surrendering to Step One. You know, that's the beginning of becoming sane—when you admit that you're powerless, that in your own strength you're hopeless. That was my beginning: admitting I was hopeless.

Submitting to and accepting God's love and his grace and obeying his laws has not been easy. Recovery is a *process*—you know that, right? I mean, I'm a wreck right now. If I had written my story a couple of weeks ago, it would be very different than it is right now. I really did not want to share my story. But this isn't about me. This is about Jesus Christ, and it's about my trying to reach out to a newcomer. Life is not rosy, but I'm learning how to live it on God's terms. I'm learning to surrender my will.

Here is a little bit of insight about sex addiction. In the United States, 50 percent of men and 30 percent of women look at pornography weekly, and that's in general society. Those are hard numbers. I think these numbers apply to churchgoers, as well, and they would probably be even higher for people in recovery, who often exchange their addictive behavior to relationships, sex, and porn. That sums up the first couple years of recovery for me. I stopped smoking heroin and started chasing skirts. I'd meet women in recovery and you know—yeah. I'm on my ninth Step, and I've got some serious amends to make in that regard. I've got a really tough sponsor, too. I recommend you get a really tough sponsor. That's working for me. I can't overemphasize the value of getting a good, tough sponsor.

My relationship addiction, my sex addiction, has cost me a lot. God has put some amazing people in my life, and I destroyed one of them. I acted out of my selfishness and my pride. My sin nature got the better of me yet again. My sponsor tells me that committing sin is like committing suicide. I agree. The wages you get for sin is death. But even though I'll never be without sin, as long as I'm truly trying to walk the right path, God is there to pick me up if I stumble. I wish I had the words to tell you what God's grace means. Recovery is truly a process. And I'm a long way from where I want to be.

Stephanie's Story of Recovery: Watching My Dad Die

I grew up going to a Christian school. In first grade, I asked God to be my personal Lord and Savior. But Christianity is hard enough to understand when you're an adult, let alone in first grade. As I got older, I began to understand more about the Christian faith and walking out my relationship with God in my daily life.

When I was in fourth grade, my aunt collapsed from two brain aneurysms. The doctors told my family that she wasn't going to make it. God showed me what prayer and having hope were all about, and my aunt didn't die from the aneurysms. However, a few weeks later, she was diagnosed with malignant melanoma cancer, and she passed away shortly after that. God gave me strength through that difficult experience, and I learned to have more faith in him.

When I was in fifth grade, I decided to rededicate my life to Christ. And am I happy I did! As I look back on the things I've gone through, I can't imagine going through life without Jesus. Little did I know what was to come in the next couple of years.

One night when I was in seventh grade, I rode home with my mom from a gymnastics class and we stopped to pick up my dad at a bar, where he was having drinks and playing pool with some friends. He told my mom he wasn't ready to come home yet, so my mom said, "That's fine. Call us when you're ready—but remember there's school in the morning and I have to work."

About twenty minutes later, my dad called to say he had been thrown out of the bar and he thought his knee was broken. Of course, we rushed across town to pick him up and to see what was wrong, but we couldn't even move him. Finally, an ambulance came and took him to the hospital.

That was one hard, late night—just one of many to come. My dad's knee had been shattered, and he had to undergo surgery. He was in the hospital for a few weeks, and even after he got out and was recovering at home, he continued to have checkups. Before we knew it, his knee had become the least of his problems.

During one of his follow-up appointments, the doctor told my dad that his liver was failing and that he was going to die if he didn't stop drinking. My dad was pretty stubborn, and I remember him saying, "Well, I'm not going to stop." And I remember thinking, *What? How could he say that?* I didn't understand. I remember talking with him on numerous occasions, telling him that if he loved me and loved my mom, he would stop drinking. I didn't understand why the alcohol meant more to him than we did.

As time went on, my dad wasn't working because his knee was shattered and he couldn't walk. So he had more and more time to sit around at home and drink. Things got worse.

Then, after a while, his knee started getting better. I said, "Oh, thank God. Finally." I knew God had his hand in this, and I think everybody at my school was praying for my dad.

As my dad continued to improve, he realized that his drinking was really hurting my mom and me—and himself as well. So he gave it up for, I think, about six months, and he even got back to work, and back walking. I remember being so proud of him and so thankful to God for this apparent miracle, because the doctors hadn't known if my dad would ever walk again.

A couple weeks after my dad went back to work, my mom and I traveled to New Mexico to visit my grandparents, whose health was failing. Because my dad had been out of work for so long, he stayed behind to work.

One night, he got lonely I guess. I don't know. I didn't really understand it, but he started drinking again and ended up falling down the stairs and re-shattering his knee.

When we got back home and went to the hospital, we found out that not only was my dad's liver failing, but so were his kidneys. Around that same time, my great-grandma died, and it felt as if my mom and I just couldn't get a break. I started questioning and wondering, "God, are you there?" But then I realized, *What am I thinking? How am I questioning God? He knows way more than I do. His plan is perfect.* So I didn't understand what was going on, but I realized that it's okay not to always be at a spiritual high, and that it's okay to question. That's how we learn. That's how we grow stronger. That's how we grow deeper in our relationship with Jesus Christ.

By the time my eighth-grade year came along, my dad had gotten more and more sick. It felt as if, for the past two years, the hospital had become our second home. It felt like we were always there. And when my dad wasn't in the hospital, I think both my mom and I lived with the fear that we would come home one day and he wouldn't be alive. If we called him and he didn't answer right away, we imagined him lying somewhere, dead. We just never knew for sure. It was a really hard time.

Before I knew it, it was time for my eighth-grade graduation and going off to high school. We didn't know if my dad would be able to attend the ceremony because the doctors kept telling us, "Oh, he's not going to make it." But we continued to pray and have faith and hope, and we knew God could work miracles. I had already seen him do so many amazing things in my life.

My dad was able to make it to my eighth-grade graduation, but something in my heart told me that it would probably be the last graduation of mine he would be able to attend. We made it through most of the summer, but one day my dad got really sick and we had to call for an ambulance again. In the hospital, they put him on a respirator, but both his liver and his kidneys were failing and his blood wouldn't clot. Then he contracted a staph infection, called MRSA, which in itself could have killed him. It felt like the end for my mom and me. It was almost like he was already dead because he couldn't talk or respond to us. But then they transferred him to UCLA, which was the best hospital for someone whose liver is failing. And while he was there, he started to get better. "Thank you, God," was all I could say. It was just amazing.

Over the next several days, he continued to improve, and they scheduled him for a liver transplant. But then, all of a sudden, everything went haywire again. His vital signs plunged and he got pneumonia, so they had to postpone the transplant. If they had gone ahead with the surgery, he might have bled to death.

That night, my mom and I went home and slept for a couple of hours. At one o'clock in the morning, we got a call saying they didn't know how much longer my dad was going to make it. Once again, we rushed to the hospital. I remember the whole time we were driving there just praying, "God, you know what is going to happen. Whatever is in your will I know is the better plan for me."

When we arrived, I didn't want to believe that my dad was going to pass away, but as I sat there and looked at him, I knew that he probably was. We had only a couple of minutes with him before he flatlined. On August 26, he went to his eternal rest with God. Three weeks later, I started high school.

The transition from junior high to high school is such a big step, and I couldn't believe that God was putting this on me. I couldn't believe I would have to start this new chapter of my life without my dad there to share all the memories with me. I just didn't understand.

Starting high school distracted me from my dad's death. Not that I forgot about it, but I moved on. A couple of months later, it hit me harder than anything, and I started grieving. I still didn't understand—and I don't know if I'll ever understand—why God took my dad so young. And when I was so young. But I know that God had a plan for my dad's life and I've had to learn to trust him with that. I started thinking about who I am. I'm not a cheerleader. I'm not the daughter of an alcoholic. That's not what makes me who I am. That's not what my identity in Christ is all about. I am a child of God, and I'm made in his image. And I was put here on earth to do his work.

So even though my dad is not here anymore, God is here and he's my Father, and I have amazing faith. My dad had his faults, like we all do, but he was an amazing father, and I have memories that will last a lifetime. My dad's early death made me realize that I should not get caught up in the stupid things of life—like drugs and alcohol or any of the other temptations we encounter in high school. I'm determined to live every day to the fullest and to remember who I am in Christ.

All that I've experienced—including my dad's alcoholism—has helped me to be who I am today. I am so thankful and happy that God stayed with me through everything, and I hope he continues to use me as I go on in life.

STEP TWO BIBLE STUDIES

Study #1: Coming to Believe

This study is based on Romans 1:16-23 (page 1431 in *The Life Recovery Bible*). Read these verses several times before working on the study. Before that, you might also want to read the entire chapter.

1. HURDLES TO BELIEF

Step Two calls on us "to believe that a Power greater than ourselves" actually exists and is there wanting to "restore us to sanity." That sounds like something everyone in recovery could easily accept, but if it were that easy, we wouldn't have to define it as a formal step in the process. Especially if you have been disappointed by God in the past, at times you may have found that it just isn't that easy to believe. In Romans 1:16-23, the apostle Paul affirms his belief in the Good News, but then he quickly begins to tell us why believing is so difficult. We disbelieve because of what Paul calls our "wickedness," or what we might call our dependent behaviors. In essence, Paul tells us that when we are trapped in self-defeating behaviors, our minds become clouded and confused and we deny the truth about God and about our own lives. Notice what he says:

> *But God shows his anger from heaven against all sinful, wicked people who suppress the truth by their wickedness. They know the truth about God because he has made it obvious to them. For ever since the world was created, people have seen the earth and sky. Through everything God made, they can clearly see his invisible qualities—his eternal power and divine nature. So they have no excuse for not knowing God.*
>
> ROMANS 1:18-20

If we modify some of the harsh-sounding words—changing *wickedness* to "addictive behaviors" and *sinful, wicked people* to "struggling, powerless people"—how does this passage describe your struggle with believing that God has the power to restore you to sanity?

In what ways have you "known" that God is the only Power that can help you?

Do you remember times in the midst of your struggle when you looked at a sunset, or a range of mountains, or a beautiful sky, and were aware for a moment of the reality of God? Describe that experience. How did you "push it aside" and go back to your "unbelief"?

Paul says we "have no excuse for not knowing God." What excuses have you used in the past for not knowing God's power? Circle any excuses you still hold on to.

2. THE COST OF DENIAL

Paul describes what happens to us when we are in denial. He says that at one point we knew something true about God, but now we deny the reality of who God is. Instead, we have created our own version of God, while at the same time rejecting the truth about him. It's something that is all too common.

> *Yes, they knew God, but they wouldn't worship him as God or even give him thanks. And they began to think up foolish ideas of what God was like. As a result, their minds became dark and confused. Claiming to be wise, they instead became utter fools. And instead of worshiping the glorious, ever-living God, they worshiped idols made to look like mere people and birds and animals and reptiles.*
>
> ROMANS 1:21-23

In what ways have you "redefined" God, as compared to how the Bible portrays God's character?

If in the past you have created your own understanding of God, how has that led to your disappointment with God?

What kinds of vows or behaviors did you think you had to change before going to God?

Do you still harbor any "foolish ideas" about what God is like?
Describe them.

Our recovery begins when we "come to believe." Describe any new
insights you have discovered about God.

3. THE GOOD NEWS

We've changed the order in which we're studying these verses to make
the point that Jesus Christ is "the power of God at work, saving
everyone who believes" (Romans 1:16). That's why Paul calls it the
Good News. If Jesus Christ is the one who has the power to bring us
back to sanity, that is indeed good news!

> *For I am not ashamed of this Good News about Christ. It is the*
> *power of God at work, saving everyone who believes—the Jew*
> *first and also the Gentile. This Good News tells us how God*
> *makes us right in his sight. This is accomplished from start to*
> *finish by faith. As the Scriptures say, "It is through faith that*
> *a righteous person has life."*
> ROMANS 1:16-17

How is this good news for you? Be specific as you describe what you
mean.

The Bible's definition for faith is "the confidence that what we hope for will actually happen" (Hebrews 11:1). How would you describe your faith right now? What is your confidence level?

Jesus talks about having faith the size of a mustard seed, which at that time was the smallest seed known. In Mark 2:1-12, Jesus heals a paralytic man because the stricken man's friends had faith (verse 5). It says nothing about the man's own faith. So it seems clear that it isn't the size of our faith that matters; what matters is the object of that faith—Jesus—and that we exercise even the tiniest bit of faith we have. Begin where you are, and as God works, watch your faith increase.

Study #2: The Grandiosity of Self-Sufficiency

This study is based on Daniel 4:19-33 (page 1081 in *The Life Recovery Bible*). Read the passage several times before working on the study. You may also want to read the entire chapter to understand the context.

1. GRANDIOSE THINKING

Before we admitted we were powerless, we operated on a false foundation of grandiose thinking. "I'm different," we told ourselves. "My situation is unique. No one really understands. I can and must handle life on my own—no help needed!" If anyone had a basis for thinking this way, it was King Nebuchadnezzar. He had it made. He was so successful that he lived in his palace "in comfort and prosperity" (Daniel 4:4). It doesn't get much better than that. Nebuchadnezzar felt so good about his life that he sent a message of peace and prosperity to everyone in the known world—"to the people of every race and nation and language throughout the world" (Daniel 4:1). That's power! And Nebuchadnezzar had that kind of power. He also had a belief in God, for he said, "I want you all to know about the miraculous signs and wonders the Most High God has performed for me" (Daniel 4:2).

But there is a danger in grandiose thinking. It may begin with an acknowledgment that God is the source of all power, but eventually it runs the risk of coming to the place where we think *we* are godlike and we take credit for everything. When Nebuchadnezzar reached that point, he forgot God. Daniel tried to warn the king, but grandiose thinking doesn't make us good listeners.

> *This is what the dream means, Your Majesty, and what the Most High has declared will happen to my lord the king. You will be driven from human society, and you will live in the fields with the wild animals. You will eat grass like a cow, and you will be drenched with the dew of heaven. Seven periods of time will pass while you live this way, until you learn that the Most High rules over the kingdoms of the world and gives them to anyone he chooses. . . . King Nebuchadnezzar, please accept my advice. Stop sinning and do what is right. Break from your wicked past and be merciful to the poor. Perhaps then you will continue to prosper.*
>
> DANIEL 4:24-25, 27

In the midst of his comfortable life, Nebuchadnezzar had an unusual dream. When he awakened, neither he nor anyone else could interpret the dream. It took Daniel to tell the king the dream's meaning. You could call this dream a wake-up call!

What have been some of the wake-up calls relating to your problem?

Assuming there were wake-up calls that didn't wake you up, how did you move past the wake-up calls to continue in your problem?

When the dream failed to "wake up" Nebuchadnezzar, Daniel gave him a more specific warning. Who tried to warn you of the dangers connected with your problem?

When we are totally absorbed with ourselves and with our problems, wake-up calls and direct warnings are often to no avail. We don't pay attention to them. Not only did Nebuchadnezzar ignore the signs and the warnings, but his grandiose thinking now burst into full bloom. *He* was all that mattered. Likewise, our problems and dependencies eventually not only control us; they take over our lives, our relationships, and our thinking. Our world revolves around *us*. Notice what happened to the king:

> *Twelve months later he was taking a walk on the flat roof of the royal palace in Babylon. As he looked out across the city, he said, "Look at this great city of Babylon! By my own mighty power, I have built this beautiful city as my royal residence to display my majestic splendor."*
>
> DANIEL 4:29-30

How has your grandiose thinking been displayed?

2. THE FALL TO INSANITY

While Nebuchadnezzar was saying these things to himself, God intruded into his life to remind him who had the real power:

> *While these words were still in his mouth, a voice called down*
> *from heaven, "O King Nebuchadnezzar, this message is for you!*
> *You are no longer ruler of this kingdom. You will be driven from*
> *human society. You will live in the fields with the wild animals,*
> *and you will eat grass like a cow. Seven periods of time will*
> *pass while you live this way, until you learn that the Most High*
> *rules over the kingdoms of the world and gives them to anyone*
> *he chooses."*
>
> *That same hour the judgment was fulfilled, and*
> *Nebuchadnezzar was driven from human society. He ate grass*
> *like a cow, and he was drenched with the dew of heaven. He*
> *lived this way until his hair was as long as eagles' feathers and*
> *his nails were like birds' claws.*
>
> DANIEL 4:31-33

Even though Nebuchadnezzar had been forewarned, his fall into insanity was sudden. With our problems and addictions, we typically have the opposite experience; our fall into insanity takes time. We're like the frog in the pot of water on the stove. As the water heats, there is no sense of what's ahead. When we finally realize what we have done, it's too late—we're trapped.

What were some of the warnings you ignored about your problem?

The picture of Nebuchadnezzar is of someone who is truly insane. What has your insanity looked like to you? To others who cared about you?

3. THE RETURN TO SANITY

Just as it does for us, Nebuchadnezzar's return to sanity started when he "came to believe." His recovery began with the tiniest seed of faith—he merely "looked up to heaven." His sanity returned when he acknowledged God.

> *After this time had passed, I, Nebuchadnezzar, looked up to*
> *heaven. My sanity returned, and I praised and worshiped the*
> *Most High and honored the one who lives forever.*
> DANIEL 4:34

When his sanity returned, Nebuchadnezzar's faith grew to where he was able to express his beliefs. He said:

> *Now I, Nebuchadnezzar, praise and glorify and honor the*
> *King of heaven. All his acts are just and true, and he is able to*
> *humble the proud.*
> DANIEL 4:37

Describe your first small step in "coming to believe."

How has God responded so far to your step of faith?

What has been different for you since your step of faith?

Nebuchadnezzar lived in his insanity for some time. His coming to believe didn't happen instantly. His faith grew progressively, but there was also a decisive moment when he turned and looked up to heaven. Recovery is a lifelong process because it is really just another word for "growth," but it begins with the barest expression of faith. Be patient—God is at work!

Study #3: Examples of Faith

This study is based on Hebrews 11:1-10 and 12:1-2 (pages 1590 and 1592, respectively, in *The Life Recovery Bible*). Read the passage several times before working on the study.

1. OUR HOPE IS FOUND IN OUR FAITH

In fighting our addictions or our problems, we have often been filled with hope, only to have our hopes dashed time and time again. With this Step, we have come to believe that hope alone—without faith in someone more powerful than we are—is simply empty and meaningless. Hope in ourselves is simply more of our powerless self-sufficiency. We cannot make our hopes a reality by ourselves; otherwise we wouldn't be where we are, and we wouldn't be studying this Step. Genuine hope is built on the foundation of our own powerlessness by placing our faith in God's almighty power. Because we can't literally see God's almighty power, we must exercise faith when we choose to believe in that power.

> *Faith is the confidence that what we hope for will actually happen; it gives us assurance about things we cannot see. Through their faith, the people in days of old earned a good reputation. By faith we understand that the entire universe was formed at God's command, that what we now see did not come from anything that can be seen.*
>
> HEBREWS 11:1-3

As you begin to work through the Twelve Steps, what are some things you hope to see change in your life?

What would *sanity* look and feel like for you?

On what, or on whom, is your faith based?

As an example of "small faith" in action, a man asked Jesus to heal his son, then added the words "if you can." "What do you mean, 'If I can'?" Jesus asked. "Anything is possible if a person believes" (Mark 9:23). The man cried out, "I do believe, but help me overcome my unbelief!" (verse 24). What part of believing is easy for you? What part do you still struggle with? Are you able to say what the man said?

2. EXAMPLES OF FAITH

Hebrews 11 gives us four examples of faith. Look at each one and try to identify the key to each person's faith, or the difficulty each one faced by believing.

> *It was by faith that Abel brought a more acceptable offering to God than Cain did. Abel's offering gave evidence that he was a righteous man, and God showed his approval of his gifts. Although Abel is long dead, he still speaks to us by his example of faith.*
>
> HEBREWS 11:4

How did Abel know what to offer?

It was by faith that Enoch was taken up to heaven without dying—"he disappeared, because God took him." For before he was taken up, he was known as a person who pleased God. And it is impossible to please God without faith. Anyone who wants to come to him must believe that God exists and that he rewards those who sincerely seek him.

HEBREWS 11:5-6

Look at Genesis 5:23-24 and describe how you think Enoch showed faith.

It was by faith that Noah built a large boat to save his family from the flood. He obeyed God, who warned him about things that had never happened before. By his faith Noah condemned the rest of the world, and he received the righteousness that comes by faith.

HEBREWS 11:7

Noah faced a total unknown, yet he exercised faith. How did he show his faith?

It was by faith that Abraham obeyed when God called him to leave home and go to another land that God would give him as his inheritance. He went without knowing where he was going.

HEBREWS 11:8

How did Abraham show faith? What did he do?

3. WHAT IS OUR GOAL?

In Hebrews 12, the writer sets a goal for us.

> *Therefore, since we are surrounded by such a huge crowd of*
> *witnesses to the life of faith, let us strip off every weight that*
> *slows us down, especially the sin that so easily trips us up. And*
> *let us run with endurance the race God has set before us. We do*
> *this by keeping our eyes on Jesus, the champion who initiates*
> *and perfects our faith.*
>
> HEBREWS 12:1-2

The "crowd of witnesses" refers to the examples of faith mentioned in chapter 11. It can also extend to include everyone who is standing with us in our recovery. What for you is the "sin that so easily trips" you up? How can you protect yourself?

The text talks about our running with endurance. What resources are you gathering to help you do this?

Finally, the writer tells us where our focus must be as we run with endurance. What are we to keep our eyes on?

The last part of this passage gives us great hope regarding our faith. It is Jesus who initiates our ability to believe in the Power that is greater than we are. Like Nebuchadnezzar, all we need to do is turn our focus to Jesus, who not only initiates our ability to believe but is also the one who completes our faith. He is like a gardener. He plants the seed of faith and then he waters and fertilizes it, completing what he initiated. What a deal! All we need to do is become the willing, fertile ground.

Study #4: The Patient Source of Our Power

This study is based on Luke 15:11-32 (page 1318 in *The Life Recovery Bible)*, which is the familiar story of the Prodigal Son. Read these verses several times before working on the study.

1. RIOTOUS LIVING

This is one of the more popular stories told by Jesus. It is typically called "The Story of the Prodigal Son," but it could just as easily be called "The Story of the Welcoming Father." It seems the point of the story, from Jesus' perspective, was more about the character of the father than the riotous living of the younger son. Rembrandt painted a magnificent portrait of the reunion between father and son in this story.[2] He clearly understood that the father in the story is a symbolic representation of God the Father. If you look closely at the painting, you will notice that the father's hands are different from each other. One hand is very masculine, and the other hand is very feminine. In fact, the artist used a man as a model for the masculine hand and a woman as a model for the feminine hand. Rembrandt wanted us to understand that God as father also possesses all the warm, tender characteristics of a mother. With that in mind, let's look at the parable.

> A man had two sons. The younger son told his father, "I want my share of your estate now before you die." So his father agreed to divide his wealth between his sons.
>
> A few days later this younger son packed all his belongings and moved to a distant land, and there he wasted all his money in wild living. About the time his money ran out, a great famine swept over the land, and he began to starve. He persuaded a local farmer to hire him, and the man sent him into his fields to feed the pigs. The young man became so hungry

that even the pods he was feeding the pigs looked good to him.
But no one gave him anything.
LUKE 15:11-16

We already see this was an unusual father, because no father in that culture would have done what he did by giving his sons their inheritance while he was still alive. But the father did it. At this point, one might say the father was a codependent enabler—that is, someone who enables a person to continue in his or her problem. Enablers don't mean to make things worse; they just try too hard to be helpful.

Who have been the enablers—the codependents—in your struggle with your problem?

The son's wild living may be a parallel to your own life up to this point. If you were the son in this story, what would the text say about the way you have lived?

As we see in the life of the younger son, things seldom get better by themselves. Before long, he ran out of money and was left doing the most horrible job a young Jewish boy could have: feeding pigs. Eventually, things got so bad that he looked longingly at the food he was giving to the pigs.

Describe how your life came to the same point of hopelessness the son experienced.

2. A TIME FOR HUMILITY

As a Jewish boy feeding pigs, the Prodigal Son understood what humility was all about, as well as *humiliation*! He was living a life of insanity.

> *When he finally came to his senses, he said to himself, "At home even the hired servants have food enough to spare, and here I am dying of hunger! I will go home to my father and say, 'Father, I have sinned against both heaven and you, and I am no longer worthy of being called your son. Please take me on as a hired servant.'"*
>
> LUKE 15:17-19

One translation of these verses says, "When he came to himself . . ." (Luke 15:17, KJV). It was as if he had a meeting with himself and said, "Enough of this!" Suddenly, he saw reality as it truly was for him. And it wasn't even close to being tolerable.

Have you had a similar experience of coming to your senses? What happened?

A big part of the young man's "coming to himself" occurred when he finally came to a place of humility. Things became so bad for him that he was even willing to become a hired servant for his father. It was one thing to hire himself out to feed someone else's pigs—that could be hidden from anyone who mattered to him. But to ask his father to treat him as a servant instead of a son—that would be humbling!

In what ways have you been humbled?

3. SURPRISED BY GRACE

Now the story takes an incredible turn. When the desperate young man returned home, he had no idea how love and grace would come together to greet him.

> *So he returned home to his father. And while he was still a long way off, his father saw him coming. Filled with love and compassion, he ran to his son, embraced him, and kissed him. His son said to him, "Father, I have sinned against both heaven and you, and I am no longer worthy of being called your son." But his father said to the servants, "Quick! Bring the finest robe in the house and put it on him. Get a ring for his finger and sandals for his feet. And kill the calf we have been fattening. We must celebrate with a feast, for this son of mine was dead and has now returned to life. He was lost, but now he is found." So the party began.*
>
> LUKE 15:20-24

Notice the surprises:

1. His father had been watching for him.

2. He doesn't even get to finish his appeal to be a servant.

3. Instead of judgment, he received grace—the best robe, the important ring, sandals, and a party.

What are some of the positive things that have surprised you as you have begun your recovery?

In the story Jesus tells, the father represents God, our Father. As you have begun your search for God as a "Power that is greater than you," have there been any surprises? Describe them.

At this point, are you able to see God as one who is loving and accepting, as the father is in the parable, or do you see him as someone who is critical and judging? What would it take for you to see God acting as the father in Jesus' story?

In the rest of the story, the father's older son is the one who is critical and not accepting of the younger brother. The French writer André Gide wrote a short story based on the parable of the Prodigal Son, in which he imagines the returning prodigal in conversation with a younger brother, who is not part of the biblical narrative. In Gide's story, the prodigal tell his brother, "Perhaps you should go off to a far country and live riotously; then you might understand and experience the love of our father."[3] When we are finally able to admit to ourselves that our lives are unmanageable and that we need someone more powerful than ourselves to return us to sanity, we have already been to the far country. Much of our future depends on how we experience God when we want to return to sanity. We need to find that he is like the father in the story: He loves us extravagantly and he accepts us right where we are when we come to him. If you have trouble with this, then reread the story several times and put yourself in the young man's place. Imagine you are the Prodigal Son and that the father in the story is God himself welcoming you back.

STEP THREE

We made a decision to turn our wills and
our lives over to the care of God.

Dear brothers and sisters, I plead with you to give your bodies to
God because of all he has done for you. Let them be a living and
holy sacrifice—the kind he will find acceptable.

ROMANS 12:1

Michael's Story of Recovery: Free Indeed

Even though I was raised in a decent, middle-class family, I was hurt
deeply as a child. Consequently, I grew up with a low self-image and
a negative outlook on life.

When my best friend introduced me to drugs, I thought they
would solve all my problems. I soon escaped the realities of life by
plunging into the hippie culture: hash, LSD, cocaine, speed, pot,
rock concerts, protests, and the peace/love movement. I flunked out
of college and blew an opportunity to play bassoon in the US Army
Band. Depression drove me to an attempted suicide and a visit to a
Christian psychiatrist, who told me that Jesus was the answer to all
my problems. I rejected his advice and turned instead to a secular psychiatrist, who prescribed mood elevators. Later, I moved to Hawaii.

There, I was a lone hippie, still bound and desperate. My supplier,
a man we called Satan, controlled my life. Of greater torment than
the drugs, though, were the terrifying thoughts of suicide—voices
urging me to drive off bridges or jump off volcanic peaks and high
buildings.

To silence the voices, I again turned to psychiatrists and psychiatric drugs. One day, my crazy roommate tied sheets together and hanged himself outside our window. I was living in a nightmare and I wasn't getting better. When I found out that the doctors planned to commit me to the state mental hospital, I got desperate enough to see another Christian psychiatrist. As this man shared Scriptures and ministered to me, I was lifted out of my depression. Shortly thereafter, he released me and I flew to California to join my younger brother, Richard, who had found Jesus and was eager to share his faith. I turned to him a couple of times, but each time I was so filled with conviction that I had to leave.

I got on a plane headed east, back to where my mess had started seven years before. My mind flew back as well, recalling all that I had gone through. I thought, *Man, if something drastic doesn't change my life soon, I'll wind up right where I started.* I began thinking about all the people who had shared Jesus with me: the doctors, my brothers, and my grandmother, who was a real prayer warrior. Looking out the window at God's magnificent creation, I couldn't help but believe in him. Still, I felt so empty inside.

Nothing I tried had satisfied me; the things of this world only led me to despair. I looked again and commented to my neighbor how wonderful the clouds were laid out in the heavens.

As I spoke, an amazing sense of peace swept over me, drawing me and gently filling me with comfort. I recalled a verse:

> *If you confess with your mouth that Jesus is Lord and believe in your heart that God raised him from the dead, you will be saved.*
> ROMANS 10:9

When I began to doubt, another verse came to mind:

> *Jesus told him, "I am the way, the truth, and the life. No one can come to the Father except through me."*
> JOHN 14:6

To find God, I knew I had to go through Jesus. My conviction of sin was so real that I knew I needed his forgiveness. So I prayed, "Lord Jesus, please take away my sins and come into my heart this day." It was amazing. All of a sudden, I felt guiltless and forgiven for all my past.

Later, I prayed for Jesus to take away my dependency on drugs. That was nine years ago, and I haven't used drugs or depression medication since. Praise God! "If the Son sets you free, you will be free indeed" (John 8:36, NIV).

STEP THREE INSIGHT

Now comes the time for action. Steps One and Two have laid the groundwork for our recovery, but Step Three calls us to *act*. We must make a decision! We have admitted defeat, and we have surrendered to the only one who is powerful enough to defeat our addictions, our problems, and our dependencies. But without our taking an action step, nothing will ever change.

Like soldiers in a war, we can surrender. But soldiers will only lay down their weapons reluctantly when they surrender to their enemy. In their minds, they have only been defeated *temporarily*, on the inside they will continue to resist giving in to the enemy. They are like the rebellious child in the classroom who refuses to sit in his seat. The teacher tells him to sit, but to no avail. Finally, the teacher orders him to sit down. With great hesitancy, he faces the fact that he is being forced to sit, and slowly he obeys the teacher. But he says to the teacher, "You may be able to make me sit down on the outside, but on the inside, I am still standing!"

It's one thing to admit that our lives are out of control, and that we need someone more powerful than we are to restore us to sanity. But all too often, on the inside, we're still thinking there are some parts of our recovery we need to do on our own. After all, we still think we know best what will work for us. On the outside, we have surrendered, but on the inside, we're still holding parts of ourselves in reserve—parts that remain under our control and haven't really been surrendered.

When we're "still standing on the inside," we need to go back and review the first two Steps and ask ourselves some searching questions: *Is my life really unmanageable? Do I really understand that I am* powerless *in the face of my problems and dependencies?* If so, then we must let go of *every* attempt to hold on to control in *every* area of our lives. Out of that reality, we must find someone powerful enough to restore us to sanity. It goes beyond simply "admitting defeat." It involves *believing* and *accepting* that an outside source of power *can* and *will* change our lives. And it involves truly *surrendering* to that power, on the inside as well as on the outside.

How much must we believe? Unless we can answer this pivotal question, our decision to surrender our will to God may appear too big of a jump. Dr. Bob, one of the founders of Alcoholics Anonymous, described himself as an agnostic. While he was drinking, he and his companions discussed God and the teachings of religion, but in their skepticism, they always ended up dismissing it all. After all, they reasoned, if they were still active in their addictions, it must mean that God hadn't really done anything for them. Nevertheless, Bob said, there was always a question mark at the end of the discussions. When, in the darkness of the middle of the night, a new question emerged in their minds—"Who, then, made all this?"—they began to reconsider. Bob said that as soon as the questioning stopped and they accepted their powerlessness and moved on to admitting that a greater power had to exist, God started to work in their lives. The decision to turn their wills and their lives over to God began by simply ceasing to question God. Dr. Bob found that God does not make it hard for those who seek him to find him! It can be as small a beginning as letting go of the questions about God's existence.

The simple truth is that making the decision to turn our wills and our lives over to God begins with our willingness to do so. Until then, it's as if we face an insurmountable wall that blocks our path to recovery. Like the Great Wall of China, it stretches as far as we can see in either direction, and its height is clearly insurmountable. What are we to do? Let's imagine that as we examine the bricks in the wall, we notice some writing on one of the bricks. Moving closer, we see the word *willingness*. What does it mean? We don't know exactly, but we accept the fact that in some way we must be willing to do something. As an act of faith we press on the brick, and to our surprise a doorway opens in the wall, allowing us to move to the other side.

So far, that describes the first two Steps. We believed and the doorway opened. But now we are faced with a decision. Do we take our willingness to the next level? Do we *walk* through the doorway, or do we just *look* through the doorway? Maybe we lean in and tentatively look around on the other side of the wall. Maybe we start by sticking our heads through the opening. Each of these *actions* expresses our willingness to begin the next phase of the journey. Some are more tentative than others, but they are all actions. We are *doing something*.

At the risk of pushing the analogy too far, imagine there is a voice on the other side that says, "It's safe. Come on over." That voice is the voice of the others who, through their own willingness, have walked through the door and are farther along on the path of recovering sanity in their lives.

During the seventeenth century in France, François Fénelon was the spiritual director to the court of Louis XIV. In a modern translation, some of Fénelon's letters were compiled into a book titled *Let Go*. In one of his letters he writes, "All that lies in your power is the *direction* of your will. Give that up to God without reservation. The important question is not how much you enjoy religion, but whether you desire whatever God wills."[4]

This letter was titled by the publisher, "The true source of peace is in the surrender of the will." Fénelon understood the meaning of Step Three. When we surrender our will, it must include everything—nothing can be held back!

If our willingness opens the pathway to our recovery, why are so many still unwilling to turn their wills and their lives over to God? Let's look at several obstacles we may need to overcome.

The first potential obstacle has to do with how we understand God. AA adds the words "as we understood him" to this Step, and that may be our problem. Our *understanding* of God may be negative, based on our past frustrations with him. How often have we prayed for God's help and as far as we could see nothing happened? How often has someone thrown God at us, or told us, "Just trust God," but nothing changed? We've developed an image of God based on his seeming failure to help us in the past. But we must not define God by our experiences, especially when we're in our problems and dependencies; often, we simply want to be rescued from the consequences of our behaviors.

If this has been your experience, then before you can turn your will and your life over to God, you need to refresh your understanding of who God really is and what he is really like.

How are we to understand God? First, we need to see that he can be trusted. As we look at God's character, keep in mind that our relationship with him is now based on our recognition of our own powerlessness and our search for the one who is most powerful. In this Step, we give that higher power a name. He is God.

To begin our redefinition of this greater power—that is, to seek to *understand* God—we must first see him as our *Creator*. Because he's our Creator, by definition he knows everything there is to know about us. Here's what King David says about our Creator God in the Psalms:

> *You made all the delicate, inner parts of my body*
> *   and knit me together in my mother's womb.*
> *Thank you for making me so wonderfully complex!*
> *   Your workmanship is marvelous—how well I know it.*
> *You watched me as I was being formed in utter seclusion,*
> *   as I was woven together in the dark of the womb. . . .*
> *How precious are your thoughts about me, O God.*
> *   They cannot be numbered!*

PSALM 139:13-15, 17

God knows us at the deepest levels, and his thoughts about us are precious. He made us, so he knows all about us—both the good and the bad.

Next, we need to understand that God desires to be our *refuge*, our place of safety. Perhaps your first thought is that if God knows so much about you, then he must also know all about your failures; and because you have failed so often, he will judge you and reject you. But again, King David writes that this God to whom we have surrendered our wills and our lives desires to be our refuge. He is the safe place we can come to at any time.

> *O God, listen to my cry!*
> *Hear my prayer!*
> *From the ends of the earth,*
> *I cry to you for help*
> *when my heart is overwhelmed.*
> *Lead me to the towering rock of safety,*
> *for you are my safe refuge,*
> *a fortress where my enemies cannot reach me.*
> *Let me live forever in your sanctuary,*
> *safe beneath the shelter of your wings!*
>
> PSALM 61:1-4

Over and over throughout the Psalms, David affirms that God is his safe place. In another psalm, he writes:

> *Those who live in the shelter of the Most High*
> *will find rest in the shadow of the Almighty.*
> *This I declare about the LORD:*
> *He alone is my refuge, my place of safety;*
> *he is my God, and I trust him.*
>
> PSALM 91:1-4

If, when we come to this safe place, we are going to be judged and rejected, it obviously isn't a safe place. But David, with all of his problems, found that turning to God gave him a place of safety.

Next, we need to understand that God is a God who loves. In fact, the Bible makes it very clear that God's very nature is love. When we live in the shame of our problems and dependencies, our perception of God may center on his judgment. But that's because of our guilt and shame. God has deferred until the end of time his role as judge. So when we come to him now, he doesn't judge us—he accepts us and receives us. To understand God as he is, we must see him as one who unconditionally loves us.

> *Anyone who does not love does not know God, for God is love.*
> *God showed how much he loved us by sending his one and only*
> *Son into the world so that we might have eternal life through*
> *him. This is real love—not that we loved God, but that he loved*
> *us and sent his Son as a sacrifice to take away our sins.*
> 1 JOHN 4:8-10

Not only is God a loving God, he is a good God. He is the epitome of goodness.

> *"For I know the plans I have for you," says the LORD. "They*
> *are plans for good and not for disaster, to give you a future and*
> *a hope. In those days when you pray, I will listen. If you look*
> *for me wholeheartedly, you will find me. I will be found by*
> *you," says the LORD. "I will end your captivity and restore your*
> *fortunes."*
> JEREMIAH 29:11-14

God is our good and loving Creator and refuge, who wants the best for each of us, regardless of our past.

Lastly, we must understand that we can depend on God. When we surrender our wills and our lives to him, we can trust him to be faithful. As Moses told the people of Israel as they were about to enter the Promised Land, "Do not be afraid or discouraged, for the LORD . . . will be with you; he will neither fail you nor abandon you" (Deuteronomy 31:8).

Another obstacle that may stand in the way of our accessing the "willingness" brick is the fear that God will become just another dependency in our lives. We tell ourselves, "I've got to be me—and to be me, I have to have some control. If I give control of everything to God, I will cease to be me." But depending on God will actually make us *more free*.

Let's look at a different kind of "dependency" to help us understand. Let's say we're dependent on our car. We need it to get around. There are too many places that public transportation won't take us, so we must have a car. But now it feels as if we're too dependent on our car, so we must give it up, because we want to be self-sufficient. Then what happens? We suddenly realize that we have limited ourselves in what we can do and where we can go. Our life has become *more* limited. The truth is, our dependency on our car makes us more independent!

In the same way, our complete dependence on God will help us discover who we really are. Surrendering our wills and our lives to our loving God, far from causing us to cease to be ourselves, actually will help us find our real selves. This is one of the "healthy dependencies" that will help us in our recovery and in our lives in general. Other healthy dependencies may include our recovery group, the people in the group, and our sponsor. As we depend on them to guide us on the path of recovery, we learn what true independence really is.

In our fear of being dependent on God and seeing it as a negative thing, we meet another obstacle: our desire for self-sufficiency. Our motives about this may be good, but the results will always get worse and worse. How easily we forget that our self-sufficiency is what led our lives to become more and more unmanageable. We thought all we needed was a slight adjustment to make our lives work better; in our self-sufficiency, we tried to do and be everything ourselves. The result was that our lives became increasingly insane, and despite our best efforts, we couldn't get back on course. God designed us to be dependent on *him*. We need to quit playing God and decide that God is our Father and we are his children.

Some may look at this Step as a conversion experience, and for many it is. But it also goes deeper than conversion, for it means that *daily* we will bring our will into conformity with God's will for us. When we do this, we begin to live out the reality of the Serenity Prayer: "God, grant me the serenity to accept the things I cannot change, courage to change the things I can, and wisdom to know the difference." And as we will see, this Step becomes the foundation for our success in each of the following Steps.

STEP THREE BIBLE STUDIES

Study #1: The End of Shame

This study is based on Isaiah 54:4-8 (page 908 in *The Life Recovery Bible*). Read the passage several times before working on the study.

1. THE PROMISE

One big obstacle to our decision to turn our wills and our lives over to God is that we are too ashamed of our pasts. Shame is different from guilt. When we feel guilty, we either think or know we have done something wrong. Shame goes beyond our actions to a sense of who we are as people—that is, our sense of self. Shame operates at the core of our personhood. We think we are "rotten to the core." It's not just that our behaviors are wrong or bad, but *we* are bad. This deep-down sense that there is no goodness in us *feels* beyond redemption, and we don't see how God could be interested in us.

For many people, this is an all-too-common experience. We're told that we are to see ourselves differently, but in our guilt and shame we hold back. We try to hide our real selves, showing only a false bravado that pretends everything is okay. Or we may try the opposite strategy. Still holding on to a sense of self-sufficiency, we may believe that before we can come to God, we have to clean up our lives on our own; we have to in some way appear *worthy*.

Whatever is holding you back, Isaiah issues a great invitation, beginning with the words, "Fear not"! Notice what he says next:

> *Fear not; you will no longer live in shame.*
> *Don't be afraid; there is not more disgrace for you.*
> *You will no longer remember the shame of your youth*
> *and the sorrows of widowhood.*
>
> ISAIAH 54:4

Shame, disgrace, and sorrows—all part of a life of problems, addictions, and dependencies. The "sorrows of widowhood" could be likened to the broken relationships we often experience in our families.

What are some of the things you have done that fit into these categories?

What have you typically done to hide your shame or disgrace?

Does it feel impossible not to remember, as Isaiah suggests? How has remembering kept you trapped in your problem?

2. THE ONE WHO PROMISES

How does God propose to help us break the cycle of our shame? For one thing, he makes promises to us. Why does that matter? Remember, shame leads us to believe we are worthless. Why then, if we are worthless, would the "God of all the earth" (Isaiah 54:5) even take an interest in us? Yet he does. From that starting point, the rest of this passage answers the question of how we break free from the cycle of shame. (See the devotional, "Redeeming the Past," on page 909 in *The Life Recovery Bible*, for more insight on this passage.) Notice what Isaiah says first:

> *"Your Creator will be your husband;*
> *the* LORD *of Heaven's Armies is his name!*
> *He is your Redeemer, the Holy One of Israel,*
> *the God of all the earth.*
> *For the* LORD *has called you back from your grief—*
> *as though you were a young wife abandoned by her husband,"*
> *says your God.*
>
> ISAIAH 54:5-6

Start with the last phrase in this section—"as though you were a young wife abandoned by your husband" (or a young husband abandoned by your wife). How does this help to explain the meaning of "your Creator will be your husband" (or wife)?

What characteristics of God's nature and character do you find in these verses?

1.

2.

3.

4.

How can your personalize these characteristics in terms of God's relationship with you? What does it mean to you that God is your Redeemer?

3. THE TIME OF ABANDONMENT AND ANGER—AS OPPOSED TO NOW

Isaiah is honest in this passage. He does not deny that, in the past, we experienced God's abandonment, and that his anger was directed toward us. We know that our lives didn't measure up and that nothing ever changed despite how hard we tried through our own efforts. But now that is all in the past. We have now turned our wills and our lives over to God, and he is now in charge of our change. Twice Isaiah tells us what we are going to experience as a result.

> *"For a brief moment I abandoned you,*
> *but with great compassion I will take you back.*
> *In a burst of anger I turned my face away for a little while.*
> *But with everlasting love I will have compassion on you,"*
> *says the LORD, your Redeemer.*
>
> ISAIAH 54:7-8

Describe times when you felt abandoned by God.

Have there been times when you have felt God's anger? Explain.

According to Isaiah, those experiences are now in the past. What do we experience today?

How have you experienced God's everlasting love and compassion?

Write God a note, responding to his promise of love and compassion.

The theme of God's unfailing love and great compassion is woven throughout several biblical passages that we will study. We need to have that message reinforced often. How this image of God differs from the one we often struggle against—that of a harsh, judgmental God. The apostle John concurs with Isaiah that God's nature is *love* (see 1 John 4:8).

Study #2: The Unknown God

This study is based on Acts 17:22-31 (page 1409 in *The Life Recovery Bible*). Read the passage several times before working on the study.

1. GOD THE CREATOR

St. Augustine, the bishop of Hippo at the turn of the fifth century, said of God, "Thou hast made us for thyself and restless is our heart until it comes to rest in thee."[5] Augustine could well have been thinking of the Athenians described in Acts 17 when he made that statement. When the apostle Paul visited Athens, he was deeply troubled by all the idols he saw throughout the city. Given the opportunity to address the council of Athens, he commented on a shrine he had seen that was dedicated "to an unknown god." To Paul, it was apparent that the Athenians had a hunger to know God. They had idols to every god they could imagine; but in Paul's mind, this only meant they had no idea who God really was. The idol to the "unknown god" proved it. They wanted to be certain they hadn't overlooked any gods, so they created an all-purpose idol. Paul used it to tell them about the God of the Bible.

Paul, standing before the council, addressed them as follows: "Men of Athens, I notice that you are very religious in every

*way, for as I was walking along I saw your many shrines. And
one of your altars had this inscription on it: 'To an Unknown
God.' This God, whom you worship without knowing, is the one
I'm telling you about.*

*"He is the God who made the world and everything in it.
Since he is Lord of heaven and earth, he doesn't live in man-
made temples, and human hands can't serve his needs—for he
has no needs. He himself gives life and breath to everything, and
he satisfies every need. From one man he created all the nations
throughout the whole earth. He decided beforehand when they
should rise and fall, and he determined their boundaries."*

ACTS 17:22-26

In our recovery, when we make a decision to turn to God and surrender to him our wills and our lives, we may need to rediscover
who God really is and how he acts. We may need to revise how we
understand God and how we understand his relationship with us.

List the things that Paul tells the Athenians about the nature and
behavior of God.

Which of these characteristics is the most important to you? Why?

Which characteristic of God is the hardest for you to experience?
Why do you think it is so hard for you?

2. WE ARE TO SEEK HIM

When we try to understand God through our own reasoning or our own experiences, we continually miss the mark. It's as if God plays "hide and seek" with us. But when we surrender our lives and our wills to him, we find that he doesn't make it hard for us to find him. He really is not far away, and he has promised that when we seek him, we will find him.

> *Anyone who comes to [God] must believe that he exists and that he rewards those who earnestly seek him.*
> HEBREWS 11:6, NIV

> *[God's] purpose was for the nations to seek after God and perhaps feel their way toward him and find him—though he is not far from any one of us.*
> ACTS 17:27

As you surrender your will and your life to God, how does that fit into God's purpose for you?

Notice how Paul says that God is not far from any of us. How does that make it easier to find God?

How does your willingness play into your understanding of God as he truly is?

3. AN INTIMATE CONNECTION

Part of the reason we can find God when we look for him is that he is right here—he is close to us. Notice how Paul explained it to the citizens of Athens:

> *In him we live and move and exist. As some of your own poets have said, "We are his offspring." And since this is true, we shouldn't think of God as an idol designed by craftsmen from gold or silver or stone.*
> ACTS 17:28-29

If we *live* and *move* and *exist* in God, where is he in your life?

Where has he been in the past?

Paul's main argument seems to be that we cannot create our own gods, our own idols. What were some of the idols in your life before recovery?

Are there any that still "call out to you"?

When we surrender completely to God, there is no room in our lives for any idols. The key here is the word *completely*. Take some time now to examine the completeness of your surrender, and clean out any remaining idols. Write out how you will do this.

Study #3: God's Total Provision for Us

This study is based on 2 Peter 1:2-9 (page 1622 in *The Life Recovery Bible*). Read the passage several times before working on the study.

1. GROWING IN GRACE

In our first study for this Step, we learned from Isaiah that God loves us with an everlasting love filled with great compassion. When we consider that we don't *deserve* to be loved that way, we begin to understand the concept of *grace*. Grace is unearned and undeserved favor. When we were actively struggling with our problems and dependencies, we spent all kinds of effort trying to clean up our act, only to discover that nothing we did lasted for very long. That's why Step Three calls us to shift our thinking and surrender our wills and our lives to God. A major part of that shift is to begin to understand and receive grace. When we show our willingness to surrender our lives and receive unmerited favor, God moves into our lives in a new way.

One of the first gifts he gives us is an understanding of his grace. The apostle Peter personally knew the reality of grace. After Jesus was arrested, and before he was crucified, Peter denied three times that he even knew him. When Peter realized what he had done, he was convinced that all was lost. He had blown it completely! But after Jesus' resurrection, when the disciples were gathered together, Jesus specifically sought out Peter to restore their relationship. Peter experienced God's grace in an incredible way. And he never forgot what it felt like! Here's how he begins his second letter, written years later:

> *May God give you more and more grace and peace as you grow in your knowledge of God and Jesus our Lord.*
>
> 2 PETER 1:2

God keeps giving us more and more grace. How have you experienced God's grace so far?

If we understand grace as an experience of undeserved compassion, it
is a small step on our way to finding peace. François Fénelon said that
we experience peace when we completely surrender to God. God's
peace is an expression of his grace.

Where in your recovery journey do you still need to experience God's
grace and peace?

2. THE FRUIT OF STEP THREE: GOD'S PROVISION FOR US

Grace is only the beginning of what God will do for us when we turn
our lives and our wills over to him. Peter moves forward from his
opening salutation of grace and peace to show us what else God will
do for us when we simply choose to believe in him.

> *By his divine power, God has given us everything we need for
> living a godly life. We have received all of this by coming to
> know him, the one who called us to himself by means of his
> marvelous glory and excellence. And because of his glory and
> excellence, he has given us great and precious promises. These
> are the promises that enable you to share his divine nature and
> escape the world's corruption caused by human desires.*
>
> 2 PETER 1:3-4

Before we surrendered our wills and our lives to God, we typically
asked him for help in dealing with our *consequences*. All too often,

he didn't seem to be listening. But when we choose to believe and do things God's way, everything else changes.

> What do you think Peter meant when he said, "God has given us everything we need"? In what way is this different from our *asking*? How is God's provision for us an expression of his grace?

> Can you think of some of God's promises to us? Write them down. If you have trouble remembering, look up the following passages in *The Life Recovery Bible*: Matthew 6:14; Matthew 7:11; John 3:16-17; John 5:24-25; John 14:18; Philippians 1:6; Philippians 4:6-7; Philippians 4:13. These are just starting points.

> How can you personalize Peter's promise that we will "escape the world's corruption caused by human desires"? Write it out in your own words.

3. THE "END GAME"

Thus far, we've read what God is willing to do for us. Now Peter tells us what the result will be if we faithfully stay on the path of recovery. It is a process that takes time. It doesn't happen all at once. It begins with our willingness—just respond!

> *In view of all this, make every effort to respond to God's promises. Supplement your faith with a generous provision of moral excellence, and moral excellence with knowledge, and knowledge with self-control, and self-control with patient endurance, and patient endurance with godliness, and godliness*

with brotherly affection, and brotherly affection with love for
everyone.
2 PETER 1:5-7

There is a progression, a growth pattern, in what Peter describes here. It's almost as if he is outlining the recovery process and telling us what lies ahead in our growth. Look at each of the steps Peter describes and write out your definition of each one:

Moral Excellence

Knowledge (of what?)

Self-control

Patient Endurance

Godliness

Brotherly Affection

Love for Everyone

Now rewrite the Scripture passage, using your own definitions.

4. A WARNING

Peter's warning is introduced with a promise.

The more you grow like this, the more productive and useful
you will be in your knowledge of our Lord Jesus Christ. But
those who fail to develop in this way are shortsighted or blind,
forgetting that they have been cleansed from their old sins.
2 PETER 1:8-9

We are not expected to have arrived. After all, we are only on Step
Three. But even in the warning we can see the promise. What
does Peter promise to those who stay the course—who continue in
recovery?

What happens to those who fail to stay the course?

How would you define *shortsighted*? Would a definition of *blind*
be "in denial"? Write Peter's warning in your own words, and keep
it before you as you continue to grow. Remember, a relapse isn't a
failure unless we stay there.

Recovery is simply one way that we can talk about our personal
growth. It is growth in the right direction. It is growth in our understanding and knowledge of God. It is growth in our experience of
God's activity in our lives. That's why we can call it *life recovery*—our
lives are now characterized by growth in the right direction. That's
the path to serenity and character.

Study #4: The Easy Yoke

This study is based on Matthew 11:25-30 (page 1214 in *The Life Recovery Bible*). Read the passage several times before working on the study. You might also consider reading all of Matthew 11 to get the context of the passage.

1. THE CHRIST OF RECOVERY

After a visit from some disciples of John the Baptist, who were questioning Jesus' identity, Jesus begins talking to the crowds surrounding him about the evidence they've seen that he is the long-awaited Messiah. As he talks about the witness of John and the evidence of his own miracles, Jesus becomes increasingly frustrated by the people's lack of faith and belief. As he told the disciples of John, "Go back to John and tell him what you have heard and seen—the blind see, the lame walk, the lepers are cured, the deaf hear, the dead are raised to life, and the Good News is being preached to the poor" (Matthew 11:4-5). It's as if he is asking, "What more do you need?" After Jesus expresses his frustration, he prays the prayer that begins our study passage.

> *O Father, Lord of heaven and earth, thank you for hiding these things from those who think themselves wise and clever, and for revealing them to the childlike. Yes, Father, it pleased you to do it this way!*
>
> *My Father has entrusted everything to me. No one truly knows the Son except the Father, and no one truly knows the Father except the Son and those to whom the Son chooses to reveal him.*

MATTHEW 11:25-27

There was one powerful thing Jesus did in his frustration—he prayed! And as he prayed, he regained his perspective. If Jesus needed to pray when he was frustrated by the events of his daily life, how much more do we need to do the same thing?

What do you typically do when you get frustrated?

What perspective did Jesus gain by praying?

What do you think he meant by the term *childlike*?

If you were to be childlike in your faith, how would that change how you view situations?

What small step can you take to be more childlike in your walk with Jesus?

2. THE INVITATION

When Jesus finished his short prayer, he began to speak to the people again—especially to those who were burdened with problems, addictions, and dependencies. To them—and to us—he made an offer and a promise.

Come to me, all of you who are weary and carry heavy burdens,
and I will give you rest.

MATTHEW 11:28

Let's connect our progress through the Twelve Steps to this place in our study. How did we get here? We admitted that we were powerless over our problems and that our lives had become unmanageable. That sounds like a heavy burden! We needed someone powerful enough to end our insanity. It's wearying to even think about that again. Obviously, the invitation is given to us who are on the path of recovery. We are invited to come into a relationship with God through Jesus Christ. In so doing, we will find rest.

Restate Jesus' invitation above to reflect your own weariness and your previous heavy burden.

3. THE EASY YOKE

A yoke is used to link together two animals, typically oxen, so that they can pull a load together. A yoke is associated with heavy work, such as plowing a field or pulling a wagon. When we were yoked, or tied, to our addictions and dependencies, we knew we were trying to pull a heavy burden. Being yoked to any form of slavery is a burden that brings no rest, only weariness. Jesus invites us to put off the yoke of our heavy burdens and to be yoked together with him.

Take my yoke upon you. Let me teach you, because I am humble
and gentle at heart, and you will find rest for your souls. For my
yoke is easy to bear, and the burden I give you is light.

MATTHEW 11:29-30

As we read Jesus' invitation, he tells us something about himself. He says he is humble and gentle at heart. Is this news for you? How do you include this in your understanding of Jesus?

There is a paradox in what Jesus is saying. Yokes are naturally burdensome, but Jesus says his yoke is different. If you think of your own yoke as heavy and Jesus' yoke as light and easy to bear, what do you think makes the difference?

If I only have two oxen, and one is stronger than the other, there is a way to yoke the two together so that the stronger one bears the heavier load. Jesus is our higher power, and he is infinitely stronger than we will ever be. When we yoke ourselves to him, he carries the heavy burden. What a tremendous picture of God's grace and provision! When we are willing, when we decide to turn our wills and our lives over to God, we are responding to Jesus' invitation to be yoked together with him.

STEP FOUR

We made a searching and fearless
moral inventory of ourselves.

Let us test and examine our ways. Let us turn back to the LORD.
LAMENTATIONS 3:40

Rick's Story of Recovery: The Second-Scariest Step

My name is Rick. I am an alcoholic. I am a porn addict. I am a recent
member of the unemployed and a Step Four survivor. What I hope
to accomplish is to prove to you that yes, there is life after Step Four.
I have been attending a life recovery group for about six years, and
I am on the leadership team there. The following is my experience
during Step Four.

First of all, this was, and is, the second-scariest Step for me. The
absolute scariest Step is Step Nine, which is when we go and make
amends to all the people we have harmed. I'm not looking forward
to that one. But even with Step Four, my fear made me try to put
this Step off for as long as possible.

When I met with my previous sponsor and I knew I was supposed to start working on Step Four—the "searching and fearless
moral inventory" of myself—I came up with as many delay tactics
as I could. Whenever he brought up the subject of Step Four, I tried
to steer the conversation as far away as possible. We met with two
other guys, and whenever my sponsor said, "Well, Rick, I want you
to start on Step Four," I would say, "Okay, Chris. Okay. By the way,
how is that issue with your father going?" Sure enough, I'd get him

talking about something else, and by the time the meeting was over, I hadn't heard another word about Step Four.

Once or twice, I even went out for a few drinks, just so I could start back at Step One and postpone my appointment with Step Four. So this was a big deal for me.

With my new sponsor, my delay tactics were not going to work. When I tried to change the subject, or when I relapsed with my drinking, he would always say, "Well, that's too bad, Rick. But I still want you to start on Step Four." So I finally had no choice. I had to do the work.

Now, there are many ways you can approach this Step. The way I did it was the method recommended in the AA *Big Book*. The first thing you do is write the names of all the people, places, or things in your life that you resent or feel angry toward. It sounds like an easy task, but it took me forever to get started. The first couple of times I worked on my list, I came up with only a few names. Just two or three. Well, I knew that wasn't everything.

The reason it was so hard was that as I wrote down the names, I went back in my mind and relived whatever the person had done to me that caused me to feel the anger or resentment. I had to relive the shame and embarrassment I felt when my high school English teacher called me a fag in front of the entire class because I had said I was going to be in a play. Or the humiliation I felt when two big guys spat on my back during class multiple times but I was too afraid to turn around and confront them. I can still feel that on my back to this day. Or the time when a young woman I had a crush on said to a group of people we were sitting with, "Rick, you look like someone from another planet."

I did not want to relive these negative experiences, but I finally figured out, with God's help, that if I wanted to heal from all the crud in my life, I had to put everything out there to be healed. Once I got started, the floodgates opened and all the shameful and hurtful things came out. My list grew.

Next you're supposed to write down what it was in you that was injured. What part of you was damaged by those experiences? This part was a breeze for me. Even though I felt a lot of anger and sadness while I was writing everything down, I was able to complete my list with God's and my sponsor's help.

If you read further in the AA *Big Book*, it says this: "Putting out of our minds the wrongs others had done, we resolutely looked for our own mistakes." That was hard. You mean I have to write down something *I* did wrong in those situations? This part I really, really resented. I mean, these people hurt me. These people did these things to me. I did nothing wrong. Why do I have to look at this? I hated this part of Step Four and it was a struggle for me, but I did it—grousing and moaning the whole time, by the way, but that's a different story.

When I finally finished—it felt like it took forever—I had a list of my own character flaws that I wanted to be healed. This is not what Step Four is about, but I still would like to share with you my character defects because I think you might find it helpful.

The part of me that was most affected by the events of my past was my *self-esteem*. This was no surprise to me because I still have an issue with self-loathing. To this day, all the things those people said about me echo in my head.

The second part of my character that I had to come to grips with was *fear*. This also did not surprise me because I am very careful about not doing things outside of my comfort level.

Coupled with my sense of fear are *feelings of abandonment*. When I realized this, it made perfect sense to me because I tend to get a little clingy in my relationships. I test people a lot before I allow them in. I don't ask women out because I'm afraid they will say no and I will feel abandoned.

As I continued to search myself, I became aware of my own *pride*. At first I did not understand this because I had always thought of myself as a humble, quiet man—which leads directly to the next item on my list, which is *arrogance*. I didn't want to face that one, but it wasn't even the worst thing on my list. The one character trait about which I felt the most disgust, and the one I hated the most, was *intolerance*. I hate that word. I hate people who are intolerant of other people, and yet I'm no different. It still bothers me, but at least now I can see it in myself.

The last three items on my list were *jealousy*, *dishonesty*, and *lust*. Yes, I am jealous of people who have something or someone I wish I had. And I will lie to protect myself or to make people like me. And yes, I constantly deal with lust. I lust after women. I lust after things. I lust after power.

Those are my major character defects. When you get through Step Four, you may discover that yours are similar to mine, or they may be totally different. The one thing I can promise you, though, is that you will be surprised by your list—that is, if you are brutally honest in your inventory.

Remember earlier when I said there is life after Step Four? Well, there really is. The nice thing about the Steps, and the reason why I personally believe they are from God, is that they help us deal with the darkness in our lives—they help us bring all the crud out into the light where it can be healed so we don't have to deal with it anymore. I'm still working my way through the Steps, but now I have hope, and I hope you do too.

STEP FOUR INSIGHT

The purpose of the first three Steps in our recovery has been to bring us out of a state of denial into a relationship with God, who will restore us to sanity. If you have faithfully worked these three Steps, you are already on a path of growth into a life characterized by serenity and humility. Now that you have faced your powerlessness and your brokenness, and have surrendered to God, Step Four will force you to put what you've learned into concrete action. Now the real work of recovery begins.

Sadly, all too often, people either delay starting this Step, or simply stop working on their recovery at this point. Some are too proud to continue, thinking they've got the basics down and that's all they need. What is there to do beyond surrendering? Others stop because they are too fearful to take a deep look at themselves. The task seems large or too intimidating. Either way, they stop, and when they do, their journey of growth to healthy living stops as well. Perhaps, also, it's the wording of this Step. When we use words like *searching*, *fearless*, and *moral*, it sounds like a lot of work that will require us to look inside ourselves more deeply than we are comfortable doing.

There's another reason why some people stop at Step Four. When we're forced to take an inside look, we realize we have made it a practice to blame others for our problems. We have a list of people to blame for our addictions or dependencies or for every problem we can't fix. For years, we have been saying, "If only he would . . . ," or, "If only she wouldn't . . ." (You can probably finish these sentences yourself.) We would love to make a searching, fearless, moral inventory of everyone else—that sounds much more doable than making an inventory of ourselves. The thought that we are in some way responsible for our troubles is not only scary, it just seems so wrong. *"It's not my fault—it's everyone else's fault!"* To begin to take responsibility for our own lives feels like it's too much. We can't change the way we think, so our recovery just dries up and stops.

Maybe some people stop at Step Four because they don't know where to begin. So let's start with a question: What's an inventory? Webster's defines it this way: "an itemized list of current assets; . . . a list of goods on hand; . . . a list of traits, preferences, attitudes, interests, or abilities used to evaluate personal characteristics or skills."[6] In a business, when people take inventory, they count everything in stock at that moment and make a list of everything they've found.

When we come to Step Four, it's time to take stock of our lives up to this point and make a searching and fearless list of every place we've fallen short. We use the word *shortcomings*; we could also use the words *sins* and *failures*. If this Step required us to make a list of our successes, we would be feeding our pride and our sense of self-sufficiency, which would be counterproductive to our recovery. Instead, we look at the negative attitudes, thoughts, and behaviors we have practiced in our lives.

The next question is obvious: How do we know what to include in our inventories?

Early in the history of Twelve Step programs, people in recovery began their inventories by looking at how they measured up to the "four absolutes": *honesty, purity, unselfishness,* and *love*. These are positive absolutes, but they are absolutes that everyone fails to meet. So our inventories will include our failures to be honest, our failures to be sexually and morally pure, our failures to be unselfish, and our failures to love.

Dr. Bob, one of the developers of the original Twelve Steps, said that these four absolutes are the yardstick to measure our conduct and take our inventory, and that they are what block us in our relationship with God and with others. Let's look at each one so that we understand why they are absolutes.

Honesty

We begin with *honesty*. In John 8:31-59, Jesus is embroiled in a heated discussion with people about who he is. At one point, he says to them, "You are the children of your father the devil, and you love to do the evil things he does. He was a murderer from the beginning. He has always hated the truth, because there is no truth in him. When he lies, it is consistent with his character; for he is a liar and the father of lies" (John 8:44).

In Luke 16:10, Jesus tells his disciples, "If you are faithful in little things, you will be faithful in large ones. But if you are dishonest in little things, you won't be honest with greater responsibilities." When we were trying to fix our problems on our own, one of the characteristics of our "out of control" lives was a shading of the truth or just plain dishonesty. Addicts are liars, for how else can they maintain their addictions? Anyone with a dependency has to lie to maintain that lifestyle—and their lies are often *about* themselves and *to* themselves. When we are overwhelmed by our problems, we lie not only to others, but also to ourselves.

Get a notebook to use for your inventory, and write "Honesty" at the top of a page. Think back over your life and write down every lie and every dishonest thing you have done that you can remember. Remember, this is a *fearless* list! What have you done that was dishonest? To whom have you lied most often? How do you lie to yourself? Write it all down. Include names if that helps. For now, you will guard your list, keeping it private, so you can be totally honest in what you write. You don't have to remember everything—just get started. Don't shortcut the process. Write down everything you can remember.

Purity

Next we'll look at *purity*. In Mark 7:15, Jesus says, "It's not what goes into your body that defiles you; you are defiled by what comes from your heart." His disciples didn't understand, so Jesus explained his words to them. "Can't you see that the food you put into your body cannot defile you? Food doesn't go into your heart, but only passes through the stomach and then goes into the sewer" (Mark 7:18-19). He was explaining that the Jewish food laws were no longer in force—the issue now was a *heart* issue. In the Sermon on the Mount, Jesus says, "God blesses those whose hearts are pure, for they will see God" (Matthew 5:8). Later in that same sermon, he makes a radical statement about purity: "If your eye—even your good eye—causes you to lust, gouge it out and throw it away. It is better for you to lose one part of your body than for your whole body to be thrown into hell. And if your hand—even your stronger hand—causes you to sin, cut it off and throw it away. It is better for you to lose one part of your body than for your whole body to be thrown into hell" (Matthew 5:29-30).

These are harsh words from Jesus, but they illustrate how purity in thought and actions, including sexual purity, is to be a part of our lives when we have turned our wills and ourselves over to God. Remember, we are not *solving* our problems at this point; we are simply *facing* them by putting them on paper. You may have ruminated over your sins, shortcomings, or failures, but have you ever made them concrete by listing them on a page? That's what we are doing now. So start another page and write "Purity" at the top. Be sure to include your thought life as part of your inventory.

Unselfishness

The third absolute is *unselfishness*. Jesus told the disciples, "Among you it will be different. Whoever wants to be a leader among you must be your servant, and whoever wants to be first among you must be the slave of everyone else. For even the Son of Man came not to be served but to serve others and to give his life as a ransom for many" (Mark 10:43-45). Jesus' example is one of unselfishness.

In Luke 22:27, he asks, "Who is more important, the one who sits at the table or the one who serves? The one who sits at the table, of course. But not here! For I am among you as one who serves." The way of life that characterizes our surrender to Jesus, and will characterize our recovery, is one of unselfish service to others.

In Luke 9:23, Jesus makes an even more direct statement about unselfish living when he says, "If any of you wants to be my follower, you must turn from your selfish ways." If we are going to walk the road of recovery, we must learn to turn from our selfish ways. To do this, we need to face the facts by taking an honest, searching inventory. Start another page, and at the top of it write "Unselfish." In what ways have you acted selfishly, and how has that affected the people in your life? One of the most common selfish behaviors is to try to control other people, so add that to your list as well. How have you tried to control other people in your life?

Love

The fourth absolute is *love*. There is a lot of misinformation in our culture today about love. To many, it is just a feeling. If I feel loving, great; if not, too bad. But to look at love as an absolute, we must go beyond feelings and emotions. We must define love by our behaviors. John 13 begins with the story of Jesus and the disciples preparing for their Passover meal in the upper room. John tells us that Jesus "loved his disciples during his ministry on earth, and now he loved them to the very end" (John 13:1). When the disciples arrived at the home where they would eat the Passover meal, there was no servant there to wash their feet as they came in from the dusty road. Because they hadn't yet grasped the concept of serving one another in love, they all sat there with dirty feet. When Jesus came in, he demonstrated his love for them by becoming their servant and washing their feet. Jesus *showed* his love by his actions.

First Corinthians 13, often called the "love chapter," doesn't mention a single emotion. Instead, it's all about *behavior*. The apostle Paul writes, "Love is patient and kind. Love is not jealous or boastful or proud or rude. It does not demand its own way. It is not irritable, and it keeps no record of being wronged. It does not rejoice about injustice but rejoices whenever the truth wins out. Love never gives up, never loses faith, is always hopeful, and endures through every circumstance" (1 Corinthians 13:4-7). When you start your inventory page with "Love" at the top, you will be looking for ways in which you have *not* acted in love; you'll be identifying your behaviors that do not fit the criteria of these verses.

Honesty, purity, unselfishness, and love: These are the four absolutes in a life of recovery—in a life well lived. But our *fearless* inventory must continue by examining negative behaviors head-on.

Resentment

Perhaps the primary negative area in our lives is the place where we hold on to *resentments* and *grudges*. James tells us, "Don't grumble about each other, brothers and sisters, or you will be judged" (James 5:9). Jesus gave a similar warning when he said, "If you are even angry with someone, you are subject to judgment! If you call someone an idiot, you are in danger of being brought before the court.

And if you curse someone, you are in danger of the fires of hell" (Matthew 5:22).

Why do we cling to bitterness and hold on to grudges? In Proverbs we read, "Each heart knows its own bitterness, and no one else can fully share its joy" (Proverbs 14:10). Isn't it interesting that bitterness and joy are put together in this passage? But then, we already knew this, for we will often say of someone holding on to bitterness that he or she is having a "pity party." But resentments and bitterness are dangerous. As the writer of Hebrews warns us, "Watch out that no poisonous root of bitterness grows up to trouble you, corrupting many" (Hebrews 12:15). Not only does bitterness spell trouble for us, it affects others as well. The solution is to root it out of our lives.

In your inventory, begin a page with "Resentments" at the top. Write the names of people you resent and what they did that led to your resentment.

Fear

Another major negative quality is *fear*. In fact, fear is probably at the root of many of the other things you will list on your inventory. David writes in Psalm 27:1, "The LORD is my light and my salvation—so why should I be afraid?" When we have turned our wills and our lives over to God, we are ready to hit fear head-on. The more God is active in our lives, the less we will fear. As you work on your inventory, you might add the word *fear* in parentheses next to things you have already listed where fear is a factor. You may also want to make a separate page for fears that are more specific.

Others We Have Harmed

Another important category to list is people we have harmed along the way. Write the names of people toward whom you have acted in selfish, controlling, and unloving ways. Add the names of people with whom you have been dishonest. What about people you have hurt by your lack of purity in your thoughts and in your life?

If your lists begin to feel overwhelming, remember that we aren't going to do anything with our inventories at this point; that's reserved for later Steps. And when we come to that point, we will have an opportunity to choose what we're going to do with all this information. Right now, however, at Step Four, our task is to make a list of as many people we can think of who have been negatively affected by our problems, addictions, or dependencies. By writing down what we have done to harm other people, we begin the process of recovery in those relationships.

Facing the Truth

The purpose of "taking inventory" of our lives is to help us face the truth about ourselves. Truth is the opposite of denial. By putting the truth in writing, we demonstrate that we are ready to break free from the patterns and behaviors of denial.

We also know that facing the truth will be painful because we must also face the reality of what we have lost in our lives. It's never easy to look at our deceits, abuses, shame, and disappointments. But even though this is a time of discomfort, we know that the steps of recovery will lead us to humility and to a life full of happiness. It may not feel that way as we work on our inventories, but those who have made the journey before us will testify to that truth.

When Jesus came to earth, he brought with him "grace and truth" (John 1:14, NIV). Here's how the New Living Translation puts it: "So the Word [Jesus] became human and made his home among us. He was full of unfailing love and faithfulness." Step Four is a process of facing our truth, with God's help. When we face the truth, we also experience God's grace—his "unfailing love and faithfulness." The more we experience the truth, the more we will experience God's grace, and the more we will experience an attitude of humility, have a teachable heart, and feel accepted for who we are.

Perhaps at this point you're wondering, "How long do I work on this step?" or "Do I do it more than once?" The truth is, there is great value in "taking inventory" regularly throughout our lives. It is something we will do now, but only to a point before we move on to Step Five. When we come to Step Ten, we will continue "to take personal inventory." From that point forward, taking inventory of our lives and our behaviors will become an ongoing process. Each time we do an inventory, we may go deeper or we may hit areas we were previously unaware of. Remember, *recovery is a process of growth*, and *growth is a lifelong journey*.

As you walk this journey day by day, remember that by inventorying our sins and our shortcomings, we are identifying the things that block us from God, who loves us, believes in us, and accepts us as we are. So don't shortcut the process; do a fearless inventory of yourself. Begin with the areas that are the most troublesome for you and the most obvious. Then follow wherever that path leads. The more fearless and honest you are, the more you will benefit. This is *your* inventory and you're doing it for yourself!

STEP FOUR BIBLE STUDIES

Study #1: A Preface to Recovery

This study is based on Nehemiah 9:1-6 (page 612 in *The Life Recovery Bible*). You might consider reading Nehemiah 8-9 several times before working on the study.

1. A SERIOUS CELEBRATION

The events in this chapter were of monumental importance to the people of Israel. Through blood, sweat, and tears—and many fears—they had restored the walls of their once-great city, Jerusalem. There was great opposition to the rebuilding of the walls, in part because people don't like change, even when it's for the better. As a result, they had endured opposition that had forced them to literally guard each other's backs. Now Nehemiah had called for a great celebration to mark the dedication of the walls. In recovery language, they had done all the Steps, and now they were celebrating this huge milestone in their recovery process.

One could easily read the short book of Nehemiah as a parallel to the work of recovery. Just as the people worked to rebuild the walls that would provide safety for the city of Jerusalem, we are working to rebuild our internal boundaries to be able to enjoy sanity in our lives. Both tasks began in a state of despair—the task seemed impossible. But the wall builders had two "sponsors" who kept them focused on the task at hand: men named Nehemiah and Ezra. As they persevered and worked together, the impossible became not only possible, but a reality. Let's begin by looking at the successful outcome—and the celebration.

On October 31 the people assembled again, and this time they fasted and dressed in burlap and sprinkled dust on their heads.
NEHEMIAH 9:1

At first, it doesn't look like there will be a celebration. Notice how they dressed. Obviously, there was a very serious tone to what was about to happen. As you celebrate the progression of your sobriety and your return to sanity, there is seriousness to that celebration as well.

How would you describe the seriousness of your work in recovery to this point?

Some people, those who don't understand the serious nature of breaking free from our problems and dependencies, see Step Four as "inventory lite." But those who are on the path of recovery know that the fourth Step is fraught with difficulties. No one likes to work on an inventory of his or her sinfulness. The people of Israel marked the seriousness of their work by how they dressed. How can you mark the seriousness of your recovery on this Step?

2. SEPARATION TIME

Our success in navigating Step Four may involve separating ourselves from some of the friends of our past. As crazy as it may sound, other people feel threatened when we make changes in ourselves, even if those changes are for the good. Here's how Nehemiah says it:

> *Those of Israelite descent separated themselves from all foreigners*
> *as they confessed their own sins and the sins of their ancestors.*
> *They remained standing in place for three hours while the*
> *Book of the Law of the LORD their God was read aloud to*
> *them. Then for three more hours they confessed their sins and*
> *worshiped the LORD their God.*
>
> NEHEMIAH 9:2-3

The Israelites covered all the bases in their inventory of sin—their own sins and the sins of their ancestors, the sins they had committed and the sins that were committed against them. At this stage of our recovery, it is important that we focus on what we ourselves have done. If you are recovering from an addiction, including drugs or alcohol, you must focus your inventory on "the sins *I* have done." Because so much of your addicted life has been spent blaming others for your problems, now is the time for you to take responsibility and look only at yourself.

Describe what it is like to shift from blaming others to taking responsibility.

If you are struggling with a dependency, such as eating, caretaking, codependency, shopping, or the like, you will need to take the opposite approach that an addict does. Instead of blaming others for your dependencies, you have taken all the blame on yourself. Rather than looking at "the sins *I* have done," you need to look at "the sins that have been done to me." Dependent behaviors usually develop because of gaps in how we've been treated by the significant people in our lives.

Describe what it is like to shift from taking all the blame to actually blaming the right source.

In Matthew 6:12, Jesus prays, "Forgive us our sins, as we have forgiven those who sin against us." Take some time now and begin your inventory. Depending on what issues you are working on, begin the list of "My Sins" or "Sins Done to Me."

3. CONFESSION AS A PART OF WORSHIP

Nehemiah set up the celebration as an act of worship. For the people of Israel, worship always included confession. Confession brings a person into alignment with reality. In this situation, Nehemiah calls for a corporate confession because he wants the people to be in alignment with each other as well as aligned with the truth.

The Levites—Jeshua, Bani, Kadmiel, Shebaniah, Bunni, Sherebiah, Bani, and Kenani—stood on the stairway of the Levites and cried out to the LORD their God with loud voices.

Then the leaders of the Levites—Jeshua, Kadmiel, Bani, Hashabneiah, Sherebiah, Hodiah, Shebaniah, and Pethahiah—called out to the people: "Stand up and praise the LORD your God, for he lives from everlasting to everlasting!" Then they prayed:

"May your glorious name be praised! May it be exalted above all blessing and praise!

"You alone are the LORD. You made the skies and the
heavens and all the stars. You made the earth and the seas and
everything in them. You preserve them all, and the angels of
heaven worship you."
NEHEMIAH 9:4-6

The Levites named were the priests who were in charge of corporate
worship. For them, confession—making an inventory—was done
in the realization of the one to whom they were confessing. At this
point, you are doing your inventory only in the context of yourself
and God. Perhaps you have known God for years, but haven't served
him. Perhaps your awareness of God began when you got serious
about Step Three. Either way, write out a description of your understanding of God as you fearlessly begin your inventory.

Thank God for listening to your confession in love and compassion,
not in a spirit of judgment.

Study #2: Making Our List

This study is based on Romans 12:1-3 and 13:8-10 (pages 1447 and
1449 respectively in *The Life Recovery Bible*). Read these passages
several times before working on the study.

1. RENEWING THE MIND

We are not alone in this recovery journey. When we turn our wills
and our lives over to God, he becomes the one who leads us forward. In Romans 12:1-2, the apostle Paul encourages us and reveals
a secret that, until recently, we didn't fully understand. Paul tells us
that God wants to transform us, and he will do it by *renewing* our
minds. What does that mean? Recent studies of the human brain tell
us that the way we choose to think shapes our brains throughout our
lives; our brains will shape our lives until the end, as well. In other

words, "Change the way you think, and you will change your brain, which will change your life!" "For as he thinks in his heart, so is he" (Proverbs 23:7, NKJV). Paul expands on this idea in 2 Corinthians 10:3-5:

> *We are human, but we don't wage war as humans do. We use God's mighty weapons, not worldly weapons, to knock down the strongholds of human reasoning and to destroy false arguments. . . . We capture their rebellious thoughts and teach them to obey Christ.*

God designed us in such a way that our thoughts affect our daily lives. The battle is in our minds—in our thoughts. Every day, we face a battle between what the world, or human culture, tells us and what God wants for us.

> *Dear brothers and sisters, I plead with you to give your bodies to God because of all he has done for you. Let them be a living and holy sacrifice—the kind he will find acceptable. This is truly the way to worship him. Don't copy the behavior and customs of this world, but let God transform you into a new person by changing the way you think. Then you will learn to know God's will for you, which is good and pleasing and perfect.*
> ROMANS 12:1-2

Paul assumes we have turned our wills and our lives over to God, and now he tells us how we can truly worship God. It has to do with the way we think—either the way of the world or God's way.

What are some of the behaviors and customs of the world that we should not copy in our recovery?

Our recovery, according to 2 Corinthians 10:3-5, includes knocking down "strongholds of human reasoning." Write down some of your thought patterns that, with God's help, you need to change.

Practice changing your destructive thoughts into God's thoughts. Describe some of the differences you experience emotionally as a result.

2. TIME FOR EVALUATING

Our searching and fearless moral inventory is basically an evaluation of ourselves. When we do this self-evaluation, Paul warns us to be honest with ourselves. It is easy to compare ourselves with someone who is worse off than we are. To keep us honest, Paul says we are to measure ourselves by God's standard.

> *Because of the privilege and authority God has given me, I give each of you this warning: Don't think you are better than you really are. Be honest in your evaluation of yourselves, measuring yourselves by the faith God has given us.*
> ROMANS 12:3

Paul could just as easily have said, "Don't think you are *worse* than you really are." What he wants is an *honest* evaluation of ourselves. He wants us to fearlessly deal with our relationships in a morally sound way.

Do you have a tendency to think more or less highly of yourself?

How will you find the balance, so that your inventory is fearless, searching, and honest?

3. NEED HELP REMEMBERING?

In Romans 13:8-14, Paul gives us clear guidelines about what to include in our inventories. His standard is that we act in love. We are to love ourselves, and then use that as a measure for how we love others. He gives some specifics, all clearly based on the underlying principle of *love*.

> *Owe nothing to anyone—except for your obligation to love one another. If you love your neighbor, you will fulfill the requirements of God's law. For the commandments say, "You must not commit adultery. You must not murder. You must not steal. You must not covet." These—and other such commandments—are summed up in this one commandment: "Love your neighbor as yourself." Love does no wrong to others, so love fulfills the requirements of God's law.*
>
> ROMANS 13:8-10

One way to begin an inventory is by listing how we've broken one or more of the Ten Commandments. Those infractions will be obvious to us. But then we must move on to more difficult things, such as ways in which we have not loved other people.

What are some examples of how you haven't acted in love?

The time we spend on Step Four will lead to specific actions in the Steps that follow. The more time you spend on this Step—expanding your inventory—the more you will benefit later. Take the necessary time for a thorough and honest self-examination.

Study #3: Search Me, O God

This study is based on Psalm 139:1-6, 23-24 (page 775 in *The Life Recovery Bible*). You may want to read the entire psalm several times before working on the study.

1. A HEART EXAM

Some people don't understand how powerful an honest self-evaluation is in recovery. They see the inventory process as something light and superfluous. To think that way, however, they must overlook the word *fearless*. If we are going to be fearless in our self-assessment, we aren't interested in "inventory lite." Instead, we want to enlist the help of God to uncover what is essential to our healing and recovery. A superficial inventory leads to a superficial recovery, which inevitably leads to relapse—and that's *not* what we want. We want *real change*.

King David needed God's help in searching the hidden parts of his heart so that everything within him could be surrendered to the Lord. It's interesting that God can know so much about us and still give us a sense of autonomy. God isn't going to intrude; he waits to be invited. Some ask, "If God knows everything, then why do we need to pray?" Think of a wise parent who knows his or her child has a secret. The parent may even know the secret, but in wisdom, he or she waits for the child to decide when and where to reveal the secret. In this way, the parent preserves the child's sense of personhood. Here's how David describes it:

> O LORD, you have examined my heart
>   and know everything about me.
> You know when I sit down or stand up.
>   You know my thoughts even when I'm far away.

You see me when I travel
and when I rest at home.
You know everything I do.
You know what I am going to say
even before I say it, LORD.

PSALM 139:1-4

God knows you intimately! What does it feel like to know that God cares enough to know everything about you?

What are some things that you are embarrassed to realize God already knows about you? Make a private list. Some of these things will eventually belong in your inventory.

Who has been affected by the things on your inventory thus far?

2. PRAYING THE LIST

When we realize that God knows everything about us, our first thought is probably, "Oh no!" But King David—despite all he had done—did not hide in shame from God. Instead, he experienced God's hand of blessing on his head.

You go before me and follow me.
You place your hand of blessing on my head.
Such knowledge is too wonderful for me,
too great for me to understand!

PSALM 139:5-6

As you review what you have written on your fearless inventory, imagine God in his unfailing love for you, placing his hand of blessing on your head. Write a thank-you note to God for loving you "in spite of . . ."

3. GOD IS MY HELPER

If God knows everything about us, then we can trust him to help us see our blind spots as we work on our inventories. Recognizing that God is a valuable resource, David invited him into his "searching moral inventory" process. Likewise, we need to be willing to ask God to point out everything we need to be aware of in our recovery.

> *Search me, O God, and know my heart;*
>   *test me and know my anxious thoughts.*
> *Point out anything in me that offends you,*
>   *and lead me along the path of everlasting life.*
>
> PSALM 139:23-24

Take some time and read these two verses several times as a prayer. Then wait in silence. Write down anything that God brings to your attention.

As you wait for the Lord to reveal things you have forgotten that need to be dealt with, remember that you are only working on your fearless inventory at this point. Don't get ahead of yourself and worry about what comes next. Just focus on your inventory and write down as much as you can. Thank God for walking alongside you as you work through this Step.

Study #4: The Purpose of the Inventory

This study is based on James 1:19-25 (page 1601 in *The Life Recovery Bible*). Read the passage several times before working on the study.

1. CLEANING HOUSE

One issue we all face in our recovery is *anger*. When it felt as if our lives were going insane, our frustrations grew and our anger leaked out all too often. Some anger is healthy, but the apostle Paul says, "Don't sin by letting anger control you" (Ephesians 4:26). There are ways to express anger without being destructive. For example, we sometimes need the *energy* of anger to enforce our healthy boundaries, but that doesn't mean we have to respond angrily. We feel a healthy sense of anger whenever we experience or witness injustice. Healthy anger always cares as much for the other person as it does for ourselves. But when we lash out in anger or hold on to anger over time, or when we don't really care about the consequences and we just "let it rip," we are using anger in the way that "does not produce the righteousness God desires" (James 1:20). Here's what James says about ridding our lives of the unhealthy, and even sinful, ways we handle anger.

> *Understand this, my dear brothers and sisters: You must all be quick to listen, slow to speak, and slow to get angry. Human anger does not produce the righteousness God desires. So get rid of all the filth and evil in your lives, and humbly accept the word God has planted in your hearts, for it has the power to save your souls.*
>
> JAMES 1:19-21

At times, we have all regretted how we've either expressed our anger or held it inside, allowing it to fuel resentments and bitterness. James invites us to add to our inventories the times and situations when we have expressed anger in unhealthy ways.

Toward whom have you had the most trouble containing your anger? Write the names of those people at the top of the list you just started. Then, next to each name, write a word or two that will help you remember what to add to your fearless inventory.

2. A CALL TO ACTION

James tells us it is time to get serious about our fearless moral inventory. He writes a very practical letter, calling us to work even harder than we have—calling us to greater action.

> Don't just listen to God's word. You must do what it says.
> Otherwise, you are only fooling yourselves. For if you listen
> to the word and don't obey, it is like glancing at your face in
> a mirror. You see yourself, walk away, and forget what you
> look like.
>
> JAMES 1:22-24

What are some of the reasons you are tempted to skip over Step Four?

Why do you think people would do what James suggests—look at themselves in the mirror, then walk away and forget what they saw?

How have you done that in the past?

3. A PROMISE AND A BLESSING

Today is a new day! We are in the process of healing and recovery. We are not going to take a quick inward glance, and then even more quickly walk away and forget what we saw. We are *fearless*, and God promises to bless us if we take our inventory seriously.

If you look carefully into the perfect law that sets you free, and if you do what it says and don't forget what you heard, then God will bless you for doing it.

JAMES 1:25

What blessings have you already experienced on your road to recovery?

How have the Bible studies helped you to anchor your recovery in God's truth?

Take some time to reflect on your progress to this point. Thank God for his faithfulness in responding to you as you have invited him into the journey with you.

STEP FIVE

We admitted to God, to ourselves, and to another
human being the exact nature of our wrongs.

*Confess your sins to each other and pray for each other so that you
may be healed.*
JAMES 5:16

Anna's Story of Recovery: God's Miraculous Answer

It seems as if women enjoy dispensing advice to one another—
information about a good recipe, a great restaurant, a hair styling
product, or the best way to lose weight. Because of this openness and
candor, we see women who are very close to each other, and we hear
a *lot* about women who have *issues* in their relationships with other
women. What's this all about?

I recently read a book that identified two questions that are common among women: "Am I worthy? Am I lovable?" Ironically, we
often look to men to validate us as women, but maybe we actually
want to hear from other *women*, and that's why we can feel threatened or rejected by them. We really need to take a look at the unforgivingness, jealousy, and hurts we carry with us toward and from
other women. If it's true that women want to be validated, loved, and
made to feel safe, could it be we somehow miss these amazing friendships with other women because we constantly worry about whether
they value us too? The "cat fight" stories are not without some basis.

Some women are blessed to have a really great sister, confidante,
adviser, mentor, or other friends who love them—the kind of people

who can help them through *anything*. Making those connections can take years, but the lifelong love of "the sisterhood" can be one of the greatest gifts we receive from God. It's sad to say, but for most of my life, I didn't have any relationships like that. And when I finally did, it was not in the way you would expect.

> *May he grant your heart's desires*
> *and make all your plans succeed.*
> PSALM 20:4

> *You have given him his heart's desire;*
> *you have withheld nothing he requested.*
> PSALM 21:2

> *Take delight in the LORD,*
> *and he will give you your heart's desires.*
> PSALM 37:4

There are many places the Bible tells us that the desire of our hearts should be to seek after God, but when I read psalms like these, I realize that God also wants *us* to have the comfort of what makes us happy. On the other hand, Psalm 51 says that God wants us to have a "broken spirit" and a "repentant heart." That's a tough one.

I can now tell you that, even though it may take many years and go in some seriously roundabout ways, the Lord will give you the desires of your heart. We spend so much time trying to get them for ourselves, instead of waiting for God to handle it. We cry out to him for all the wrong things, because we don't understand the wonderful things he has in mind for us instead.

As a child of older parents, and having grown up with siblings who were selfish and unavailable, I pretty much resigned myself to being somewhat "alone" for the rest of my life. And I was fine with that. My talents were few but good, and I didn't lack for self-confidence. Though I was a "loner" much of the time, it wasn't until I had been married for seventeen years that I realized how alone—and lonely—I really was. I hid it well, even from myself. For most of those years, my beautiful daughters were my treasure.

In my ignorance, I married a man who had a history of going from one woman to the next (along with other hidden addictions). As an overprotected and gullible young woman, I didn't know a charmer when I saw one and had no idea his interest in me was fleeting. My mother warned me not to marry him, as did my pastor, but I "knew what I was doing." Of course, I lost my way and completely ignored God's plan for my life.

For many years, we looked like a happy little family, but behind closed doors (as it always is), a deep sadness permeated our lives. Tom and I were good friends, but never were "married" in any true sense of the word. Through all those years, I was emotionally and spiritually lost, and I lacked the skills to figure out what to do. My parents both died suddenly early in my marriage, and I had no meaningful connection with my siblings. I was alone, period.

In the mid-1980s, when Tom once again became routinely promiscuous, I crawled into a deeper and deeper hole. I can remember lying on the living room floor and crying, "Jesus, where *are* you?" I prayed that God would give me wisdom and hope for the future, friends to walk alongside me, and protection for my girls to survive what I knew was coming in the life of our family. So many people have faced these same challenges, and most are not equipped to even know where to look for help. Inspired by the story of Gideon in Judges 6:36-40, I put a "fleece" before God, asking him to show me, with a big event, what to do. His answer came in many miraculous ways.

My girls had many friends, and I enjoyed getting to know their mothers. We had Girl Scouts, gymnastics, orchestra, neighborhood groups, and softball. Many of the moms and girls were fun to be around, but I really worried about a scared, shy little girl on my daughter Rachel's softball team. She came over to the house for play dates, but I could tell she was an emotional wreck, and so was her mother. They both seemed so afraid and lost.

Eventually, with my husband, the fur hit the fan and our marriage was basically over. My friends at church tried to help, advise, and pray for me. My only prayer was that I would do what God wanted me to do, and I asked him to show me. My pastor sat me down one day and told me the wisest, most powerful thing I ever heard in my adult life: "Anna, your job is to figure out what is wrong with *you* that you have set your life up this way. This whole thing is about *your* problems, not his." My mind was spinning out of control, and I did not know how to take that, or what to do for myself and my girls. My father had taught me to learn from everything, and to listen to what God was telling me, so I tried to be discerning and open.

As the problems continued with my husband, I tried to figure out *who* he was having the affair with. When a good friend filled in some of the details, I immediately thought about the beautiful, sad mom from the softball team. Because my husband previously had been attracted to women in trouble, I was not surprised. But all I really knew about her was that she was a very loving mother.

In the midst of all this, I longed for my own mother to still be alive and for my father's arms around me. I shook my head in sadness that my brother and sister could not advise or help me in any way. They had long since turned away, absorbed in their own dysfunctions.

The deepest hurt during this fearful time was that I was all alone—a feeling that only grew worse when I realized that I had spent half my adult life with this man, feeling alone all the time. My pastor helped me see so many things, and he prayed with me about what I needed. I leaned on the Lord more than ever before, crying buckets, not for my broken marriage, but for my "lost life."

A few days after it all hit, I was sitting tearfully at the softball field when out of the corner of my eye I saw someone rushing toward me. *Oh my gosh, it's her,* I thought. The woman ran up to me, shoved a copy of *Love Must Be Tough,* Dr. James Dobson's book about affairs, into my hands and said, "This book may help you. It is helping my husband." I didn't know *what* to think. By this time, Tom had moved out and was begging this woman to join him.

From that day onward, this woman (who had not left her hus-band, but said she was tempted) showed up *everywhere* I went—not on purpose; that's just the way it worked out. She and I could not escape each other!

When I pulled up at the corner stoplight, there she was in the car next to mine, looking at me with shame in her eyes. Her girls belonged to all the same teams and groups and clubs my girls were in, so we were constantly putting our heads down and pretending the other person wasn't there. When my girls and I went to the shoe store, there she would be, in the same aisle, with her girls. If I went to the grocery store or the department store or ran to the local coffee shop for a latte there she was.

When I saw that look in her eyes again—the same look I had in *my own* eyes—a revelation came to me: *She* was just like *me*. She wanted her own husband to love her, just as I did mine. Oddly enough, I found I could not hate her or blame her for trying to find love. Yes, there were *other* women I had felt wronged by, but not her. This was really weird! I realized I loved her and that I didn't even know her.

I still spent night after night sobbing and crying out to God, ask-ing what to do, how to act—whether to stand up for myself or be humble, to tell my husband not to come home or try to hold our mar-riage together. Somehow, I tried to do *both*, but it just didn't work out.

Now I had a new concern—*what do I do about this woman?* I knew she was still seeing my husband, but I could not mention any of what I was seeing in her to him. Little did I know that she was in love with Tom but still trying to find a way to repair her own mar-riage. I prayed for a "hedge of thorns" to be placed around her mar-riage so she would not leave her husband. Oddly, I prayed this for *her* sake, not because I didn't want my husband to leave me. Honestly, I prayed more for *her* marriage than I did for my own.

My "burning bush" moment with God—when he changed the course of my life and gave me a new mission—came as I drove home one day. As I rounded a corner not far from my house, I saw a petite woman stumbling in and out of the ditch along the roadside. She was sobbing hysterically. As I passed her, I saw who it was in my rearview mirror, and that she was pretty much devastated. I drove on for a while, but then I knew, beyond a doubt, that I was supposed to turn the car around and go back. I didn't know what I was going to say or do, but I felt the Holy Spirit nudging me.

When I pulled my car up alongside her, she kept walking, and I more or less kept a slow pace with her. My window was down and I asked her several times to get into the car. She refused. I could tell we were asking ourselves the same question: "What are we doing here? I am *not* supposed to be with this woman!"

Eventually, she got in the car, and we sat there for what seemed an eternity. Neither of us spoke until I finally said, "What shall we *do*?" She was too hysterical to talk, for so many reasons. We sat staring straight ahead and gradually opened our hearts to each other on a few issues. Finally, I grabbed her hand and we prayed. I offered to get out of both of their lives if she wanted to leave her husband for mine. She adamantly refused, though she also said she was not yet over the relationship with my husband, even though she knew it wasn't what God wanted.

After a while, I drove her to her house, and her husband was astounded when he saw me dropping her off. Truly, she was *just like me*, longing for validation and comfort. What was I doing, providing it?

I'll try to keep the rest of the story short here. More crises hit both homes. My marriage ended, but Kelly and her husband hung in there and kept working on their relationship. She ran from me, but neither of us could forget the other or what she had been through.

Then Kelly lost her teaching position and was out of work for a while. One Saturday morning, at a time when my husband and I had briefly reconciled, I picked up the phone to a whispering, shaky voice: "Anna, I need to talk to you. I have a job offer and it is at *your* school. What do *you* want me to do?"

Lord, what are you doing here? Oh my. All I could do was mumble, "Uh, I guess you need a job, and you should take it."

Kelly worked at my school for a year, having to see me every day, before she was able to transfer to another location. Even though she had drawn my husband away from me, my heart ached for her in some odd way. I knew that God was seriously in this, and I kept myself open to whatever was going on.

When the other shoe hit the floor, through more revelations from Tom about recent affairs, I went straight to Kelly's house, rang the bell, and begged her to let me tell her the truth about him. She looked me in the eye and said, "I hoped you would come, and I know you will tell me the truth. He is beginning to call me again."

We sat for several hours, learning about each other and grieving together about our separate problems. At that point, my husband no longer mattered, but Kelly's safety did. We cried, hugged, and held onto each other's hands as we sat at the dock by her house. I begged her to take care of herself, and she promised me she would. Then we went our separate ways.

The coincidental encounters continued for several years after that, but now she and I were at least able to smile and greet each other. Our girls shadowed each other with orchestra and softball, and when I fell in love with my current husband, Jay, she was the first person I told. I could tell that she and her husband were still on fragile ground, but holding it together.

Through a series of even more providential circumstances, I was involuntarily transferred within the district. Of course, I ended up at Kelly's school. She finally told me that we had to sit down and talk.

We met at a local country club where she thanked me over and over for "saving her marriage." I was honored that she would think that, but all I had done was show her my love and tell her the truth about my ex-husband and what had really happened in our home. To be honest, I knew almost nothing about her marriage.

For some reason, I felt closer to her that day than any other human being I've ever known. We looked each other in the eye and realized that God meant for us to be sisters in some way. We agreed that from then on, we would watch out for each other.

That was more than twenty years ago, and yet it seems like only yesterday. Every moment is still fresh in my mind, and it still amazes me how God intervened and reconciled our lives. What a gift that is.

As my current pastor says, "Persecution can make us leave our comfort zone, and we will only move from that zone (or dysfunction) when we are forced out of it." When troubles come our way, it's hard to "consider it an opportunity for great joy" (James 1:2). But during those years, when I repeatedly read Psalm 51, the one thing I held on to was that having a broken heart was somehow a *good thing*.

The most wonderful blessing of all is that God has given me the "gift of Kelly," my true-blue sister, my confidante, my right arm, my peace, my adviser, my encourager, my comfort in any situation. Today, she is the best friend a person could ever have and more than a sister.

Jay and I have vacationed with Kelly and Dean. We share dinner often and work on projects together. Once in a while, Kelly and I marvel at our story. It's still hard to believe that God would shove us into each other's lives in such a bizarre way, but only he could have done something so impossible and made it work out for good.

We've gone through menopause, worries about our children, job stresses, hair color, problems with relatives, grandbabies, which shoes don't hurt our feet, weight gain (mostly mine), and many of life's daily trials. We speed-dial each other often. When I need advice, I depend on Kelly because I know she has the wisdom to set me straight and tell me the truth about myself.

Kelly often says that people who are hurting will do some very hurtful things, both to themselves and to others. We have to try to help them understand what their hurts are all about. She has so much grace for people that it amazes me.

Our next challenge is a big one: My amazing husband has Parkinson's disease. Through several years of worry and heartache, Kelly has been there for both of us. I spent at least two years crying on her shoulder with fear about it. And Kelly understands it all, because we have "history."

Just over a year ago, Kelly's husband, Dean, started having some odd physical problems. No doubt you can guess the diagnosis. That's right: Parkinson's disease.

Kelly's and my love and our commitment to each other started a long time ago on a softball field, when she handed me a book. I am still kind of in shock about it all. But it all goes back to the fact that God knew the desires of my heart—that I longed for a sister. I had no idea what my pastor from years ago meant when he said that God would "honor" me for leaning on him and trying to do the right things.

STEP FIVE INSIGHT

Doing a fearless, moral inventory is no simple task. It's not something we do in a couple of minutes. But for anyone who is finally willing to face the truth about him or herself, it can be a very productive—though very painful—process. At first, we may have hesitated to write some things down, things we didn't even want to admit to ourselves we had done. But we were *fearless*—we wrote down everything we could think of and hoped no one would ever see our list. And now we come to Step Five and realize that not only must we confess all this to God, but we must also tell another person what we've done.

Isn't there an easier way? Can't we just skip over the part about admitting to another human being the exact nature of our wrongs? Obviously, we've already admitted to ourselves what we have written, and we can confess our sins to God since he already knows everything about us. But if we also have to admit everything to someone else, we'll be *found out*. That person will know who we really are beneath the facade. That's really scary!

Our natural instinct at this point is to keep our inventory secret. Where can we hide the notebook? If we've been fearless and honest, our inventory is a major embarrassment to us. If we admit these things to "another human being," we have too much to lose. Not only will we risk our reputation, but we really may have to give up our favorite *sin* and we'll have to be accountable.

It's interesting to note the progression of "confession" in church history. It began as James intended—fellow Christians confessing to one another (James 5:16). But over time, as church practice became more formalized, confession did as well, until only a clergyman could hear one's confession. In the Roman Catholic Church and the Eastern Orthodox Church, confession was now made to a priest. As part of the Reformation, Protestants eliminated the role of the priest, emphasizing our direct access to God and redirecting our confession to him. However, the Roman Catholic Church, in an effort to combat the teachings of the Reformers, held a council of bishops at Trent to reassert the importance of confessing to another human being, especially to a priest. "If the sick person is too ashamed to show his wound to the doctor," the council stated, "the medicine cannot heal what it does not know."[7]

The bishops had a point. Without confession, there can be no healing. Without healing, our wounds and our sins continue to fester. In Jeremiah 6:14, the prophet says, "They offer superficial treatments for my people's mortal wound. They give assurances of peace when there is no peace." Here's how the *Living Bible* paraphrases this verse: "You can't heal a wound by saying it's not there!" Something about telling another person is the key to our healing. Our reluctance to confess our sins will guarantee that we stay as sick as our secrets.

What else happens if we want to skip the part of the Step that requires us to admit our wrongs to another person? If we avoid this, we will eventually revert to our old behaviors. That is what's called a "relapse." Some people call it an "almost recovery," but it's a recovery that doesn't go very far. Remember, one of the purposes of a fearless moral inventory is to conquer our tendency to deny reality. When we are caught up in our addictions, dependencies, and problems, we continually deceive ourselves. We think that if we would only try harder, everything would be okay. Or if only other people didn't let us down all the time, we'd be fine.

It's only when we confess to another human being that we can break this pattern of self-deception. When we're only talking to ourselves, it's too easy to either understate the exact nature of our wrongs and act as if we don't have a problem or to overstate our problems and remain a victim. We can either trivialize our problems or get so caught up in them that we feel hopelessly trapped. When we don't have the input of another person, we miss the opportunity to see the truth clearly. This is true in every area of our inventories, but probably most true when it comes to our spiritual issues.

How else do we benefit when we admit to another human being the exact nature of our shortcomings—our sins? We experience the healing that comes from confessing to another person. "Confess your sins to each other and pray for each other so that you may be healed" (James 5:16). If we are as sick as our secrets, we can become as healthy as our confessions.

Step Five uses the word *admitted* and the Bible uses the word *confession*, but they mean the same thing. The word for "confess" in Greek is *homologea*, which means, "to speak the same thing." In other words, when we confess, we admit that we agree with what happened. For example, if I lie and really hurt someone, my words of confession must accurately reflect what I did. Confession, as well as admission, means aligning ourselves with the truth.

In the same way, when we confess, we align ourselves with the one to whom we are confessing. When we confess our shortcomings to God (as described in our inventories), we align ourselves with God. When we align ourselves with him, we will experience a growing intimacy with him. When we confess to ourselves the exact nature of our wrongs (as we write our inventories), we align ourselves with ourselves. We become more centered, more of who we really are—accepting the bad parts along with the good. When we confess to another person, we align ourselves with others who can help us grow. We're on the same path together.

When we admit to someone else the exact nature of our wrongs, our confession to God becomes more real to us. If we make our confession to God and then struggle with whether he heard us, our confession to another person will make God's reality more clear. If another person can accept us, and the truth about us, then certainly God will accept us. Confession also forces us to bring another person into our recovery and healing. Isolation is the enemy of recovery and healing.

Confessing our sins to another human being takes us to a new level of willingness and humility, but it can also feel risky. Some of our concerns about confessing our wrongs to another person are legitimate, so when we become willing to tackle Step Five, the first question we need to ask is, "Who do we pick to hear our confession of our sins and shortcomings?" We obviously need to be discerning in choosing this person. For years, priests and pastors were the obvious choice to hear our confessions because they were expected to understand the nature of confidentiality and were not required to report any crimes that might be included in our inventories. Most states now require clergy to be mandated reporters in the same way a teacher or counselor would be. If they hear an admission of a crime, or of child or elder abuse, they are required by law to report it. If criminal acts are part of your inventory, you will need someone who is not a mandated reporter to hear your confession. A trusted friend or your sponsor may be that person.

If there is nothing actionable in your inventory, find someone who is not judgmental, and who understands the nature of confidentiality, to hear your confession. Confidentiality means the person can be trusted not to tell anyone anything about your inventory items. Knowing that what you share will be kept in strict confidence gives you the freedom to share anything and everything with that person.

You probably don't want to choose someone in your family to be your confidant for this Step. In fact, in most cases, family members are *not* the ones you want to confess to. They are not as likely to be understanding, and they are more likely to be hurt by items in your inventory.

It also helps if the person you confess to understands the Twelve

Steps and the recovery process. It doesn't have to be someone who is also in recovery, but he or she must understand what you are doing by taking an inventory, and how important it is for you to share your inventory with another human being.

Don't allow your issues with trust to stop you from confessing to another person, or make you skip this part of the Step. You must trust the other person, and that's a decision of the will that you can make.

Sometimes you will need to confess to more than one person. You may start by admitting your wrongs to one person, but as you go through your inventory, you may realize there are some things you cannot share with this person. Simply mark them and skip over them. If you realize as you confess that you don't feel free to share some of the deeper things with the person you've chosen, share as much as you can and find someone else with whom you can share the rest of your inventory. You don't have to share everything with one person, but you do need to share everything with someone.

Once you have set aside your pride, found someone to confess to, and shared your inventory, praise God for giving you the strength to complete Step Five. Often this is the point that we can really begin to sense and believe that God is changing us. Many people find that from this point forward, they are able to experience more of God's activity in their daily lives.

If we confess our sins to him, he is faithful and just to forgive us our sins and to cleanse us from all wickedness.
I JOHN 1:9

If we confess the exact nature of our wrongs to ourselves, to God, and to another human being, God not only forgives everything we confess, but he cleans us of all the wrong things we have done that we're not even aware of. What a great promise for those who confess!

Allison's Story of Recovery: Sharing My Secrets

I grew up neglected, with no sense of anything being my own. I was conditioned to believe I was worth nothing, that I was a failure, and that everything was my fault. I believed that a girl's only value was as a sex object. I remember wondering as a little girl why I had ever been brought into this world.

In our house, we did not have walls around the bathroom or doors on our bedrooms. My parents' bedroom had a door, but it was clear glass. Even though I don't remember anyone ever watching me in the bathroom, the damage from having no privacy and not being protected as a little girl went deep. Doors protect our dignity and give us a sense of security—and there are things that should only happen behind closed doors. But because of my parents' mentality, my sisters and I were exposed to things that little girls should never see. On top of that, my dad compared us to women on TV, and we had to dress in a particular way to get any form of attention from him. Otherwise, he would leave the room with a disgusted look on his face. From an early age, it was ingrained in me that I would never be enough.

I remember the pinnacle of it all—the day I graduated from high school. I had tried so hard my whole life to measure up, to be everything my dad wanted: choosing the right clothes and wearing my hair long so he would give me some sort of attention. On graduation day, I wore the most beautiful dress I had ever owned, but my dad barely acknowledged me. Even in a beautiful dress I would never be enough.

As the years went on, I maintained an outward appearance that everything was okay so that no one would see who I really was, where I had come from, and what I had seen. I was not going to let myself be rejected like I had been at home. I believed that I was worth nothing more than the damage inside me and that I would spend the rest of my life maintaining the "badness in me" in isolation.

When I was nineteen, I left home to go to Bible school, and there I began a journey that would change my life forever. It took me years of "work that didn't work" for me to seek the right kind of help. I tried it on my own with books and such, but that didn't work. Last year, I went to a New Life weekend, and for first time in my life shared some of my secrets with a group of women. From there, I realized I needed help. It took a while, but last spring I found a counselor who understood me and was willing to walk with me on the journey of digging through my past and learning how to not be defined by it.

Now, the hurts and the memories that used to govern every decision I made are just a piece of me. I have a joy and peace in my life that I had never experienced before. I am learning how to set boundaries and how to use my voice. I now realize that I am not the reason why my home was the way it was. It was not my fault. I realize that I deserve to have rights, and I do have rights.

I recovered from a past that taught me I was nothing, and now that past is a distant memory that no longer sits on my shoulder and defines me. I am learning how to enjoy life. I now have the joy of exploring what I love to do without feeling guilty. I am able to believe, for the first time in my life, that I am not damaged, that the past is over, that I am beautiful and creative, that I am wanted in relationships, that I am valued. I can be me. I can have a voice and not be rejected for it. I can have boundaries and be respected. No, I *deserve* and have the right to be respected.

STEP FIVE BIBLE STUDIES

Study #1: Confession Brings Release

This study is based on Psalm 51 (page 714 in *The Life Recovery Bible*). Read the entire psalm several times before working on the study.

1. HAVE MERCY ON ME, O GOD

King David, the writer of this psalm, needed help in doing his inventory. After committing adultery with Bathsheba and murdering her husband, David thought he could hide everything he had done. He thought he had covered his trail. But God saw it all, and he was not about to let these sins fester in the secrecy of David's memory. So God told Nathan the prophet what David had done, and sent him to confront the king.

Now, you don't just walk up to the ruler of the nation and say, "Hey, King David, you really messed up here!" You could lose your life for doing something like that. So Nathan had to be careful. He had to confront David in a way that would break through his denial. He told a story about an unjust rich man who had lots of sheep but wanted the only sheep his neighbor possessed. So he killed the man and took his one sheep. (You can read the story in 2 Samuel 11:1-12:14.) When David understood what Nathan was telling him, he came out of denial and confessed to God and to Nathan what he had done. Later on, David wrote Psalm 51 to describe his journey of recovery and healing from his sin.

> *Have mercy on me, O God,*
>   *because of your unfailing love.*
> *Because of your great compassion,*
>   *blot out the stain of my sins.*
> *Wash me clean from my guilt.*
>   *Purify me from my sin.*
> *For I recognize my rebellion;*
>   *it haunts me day and night.*
> *Against you, and you alone, have I sinned;*
>   *I have done what is evil in your sight.*
> *You will be proved right in what you say,*
>   *and your judgment against me is just.*
> *For I was born a sinner—*
>   *yes, from the moment my mother conceived me.*
> *But you desire honesty from the womb,*
>   *teaching me wisdom even there.*

PSALM 51:1-6

First, David gives us some great insight into the nature of God, who listens to our confessions. What five things does he tell us about God?

1.

2.

3.

4.

5.

What does David confess about himself in these verses? What would be on his inventory?

The pattern of David's confession fits Step Five, in that he admitted his sins to God, to himself, and to Nathan. In addition, his inventory is written for the whole world to see.

What are some of the things in your inventory that would be difficult to share with another person?

What are some things you could share with more than one person?

2. A CLEAN HEART

After we've spent time writing our inventories, we don't expect to feel clean. In fact, it may feel like we've just dragged ourselves through the muck and mire of the past. But here's David, whom the Bible describes as "a man after [God's] own heart" (1 Samuel 13:14), admitting to two grievous sins—adultery and murder. He violated two of the Ten Commandments! These were not minor or easily overlooked indiscretions. No doubt they haunted David's memory day and night. But in Psalm 51 he comes to God for help in breaking free from the guilt and shame of his past. We can do the same. Every time we remember what we have done, we can also remember God's forgiveness and his cleansing. That's why David asks to be made clean.

> *Purify me from my sins, and I will be clean;*
> *wash me, and I will be whiter than snow.*
> *Oh, give me back my joy again;*
> *you have broken me—*
> *now let me rejoice.*
> *Don't keep looking at my sins.*
> *Remove the stain of my guilt.*
> *Create in me a clean heart, O God.*
> *Renew a loyal spirit within me.*
> *Do not banish me from your presence,*
> *and don't take your Holy Spirit from me.*
>
> PSALM 51:7-11

What does David's phrase "a clean heart" mean to you?

What would it be like for you to have a clean heart?

When have you experienced joy in your life? For David, it seems as if the path to joy goes first through his brokenness. How do you think brokenness leads to joy?

David asks for the renewal of a loyal spirit within him. How does that apply to you? Where have you struggled with disloyalty, either in yourself or in others?

How would you rewrite this passage as a personal expression of prayer?

3. LIPS THAT PRAISE GOD

David makes several important requests and promises in this next paragraph. Underline them as your read these verses.

> *Restore to me the joy of your salvation,*
> *and make me willing to obey you.*
> *Then I will teach your ways to rebels,*
> *and they will return to you.*
> *Forgive me for shedding blood, O God who saves;*
> *then I will joyfully sing of your forgiveness.*
> *Unseal my lips, O Lord,*
> *that my mouth may praise you.*

PSALM 51:12-15

David had to ask God to make him willing to obey him. Where do you still question, or struggle with obeying, what you know God wants in your life?

David's response is to sing of God's forgiveness and to praise him. As you have worked through this step and confessed to God, he has promised to forgive you. Write him a thank-you note for his forgiveness.

4. THE RIGHT SACRIFICE

Before we started our journey of healing and recovery, we thought we knew what we needed to do, or what we wanted God to do for us. Now that we have put God in charge, we are where David was in his recovery. He finishes Psalm 51 with a profound insight into what God wanted from him, and what God wants from us.

> *You do not desire a sacrifice, or I would offer one.*
>   *You do not want a burnt offering.*
> *The sacrifice you desire is a broken spirit.*
>   *You will not reject a broken and repentant heart, O God.*
> *Look with favor on Zion and help her;*
>   *rebuild the walls of Jerusalem.*
> *Then you will be pleased with sacrifices offered in the right spirit—*
>   *with burnt offerings and whole burnt offerings.*
>   *Then bulls will again be sacrificed on your altar.*
> PSALM 51:16-19

The sacrifice described here is a broken and repentant heart. Describe how working through the first five Steps has been the proper sacrifice for you in your healing.

Now think symbolically. Think of the walls of Jerusalem as your personal boundaries. How are you rebuilding your personal boundaries with others?

David mentions what will happen when Jerusalem's boundaries are rebuilt. Life will become the way it was designed to be. As you are rebuilding the personal boundaries in your relationships, describe how your life will be different as you continue the journey of recovery.

Study #2: More Joy!

This study is based on Psalm 32 (page 700 in *The Life Recovery Bible*). Read the psalm several times before working on the study.

1. THE JOY OF CONFESSION

Psalm 90 was written by Moses. In it he describes what happens when we don't align ourselves with God: "We wither beneath your anger; we are overwhelmed by your fury. You spread out our sins before you—our secret sins—and you see them all" (Psalm 90:7-8). According to Moses, "our secret sins" are what ignites God's anger. When we try to hide our sins from God—who knows everything— we experience his anger. It's as if he is saying, "Look, I know it all anyway. Just agree with what I already know—confess!"

How different is David's experience in Psalm 32. Here David has confessed. There are no more secrets. He agrees with God about his sins. Instead of experiencing God's anger, David experiences joy.

> Oh, what joy for those
>> whose disobedience is forgiven,
>> whose sin is put out of sight!
> Yes, what joy for those
>> whose record the LORD has cleared of guilt,
>> whose lives are lived in complete honesty!
> When I refused to confess my sin,
>> my body wasted away,
>> and I groaned all day long.
> Day and night your hand of discipline was heavy on me.
>> My strength evaporated like water in the summer heat.
> Finally, I confessed all my sins to you
>> and stopped trying to hide my guilt.
> I said to myself, "I will confess my rebellion to the LORD."
>> And you forgave me! All my guilt is gone.

PSALM 32:1-5

David compares his life when trying to hide his sin from God to a life "lived in complete honesty." Describe what you experienced when your sins were still secret and unconfessed.

Now that you have acted on Step Five and admitted to God, to yourself, and to another person what was in your inventory, you are promised forgiveness by God. (Remember 1 John 1:8-9!) As difficult as it was to confess, describe the relief you experienced when you were done.

Describe your understanding of what it means to be forgiven by God.

Make a written commitment to yourself to release your guilt into God's hands.

2. RELEASED FROM JUDGMENT

David tells us more about why he experienced so much joy. Not only was he released from his guilt, but he also knows all that God has promised to provide for him.

> *Therefore, let all the godly pray to you while there is still time,*
> *that they may not drown in the floodwaters of judgment.*
> *For you are my hiding place;*
> *you protect me from trouble.*
> *You surround me with songs of victory.*
> *The LORD says, "I will guide you along the best pathway for*
> *your life.*
> *I will advise you and watch over you.*
> *Do not be like a senseless horse or mule*
> *that needs a bit and bridle to keep it under control."*
> *Many sorrows come to the wicked,*
> *but unfailing love surrounds those who trust the LORD.*
> *So rejoice in the LORD and be glad, all you who obey him!*
> *Shout for joy, all you whose hearts are pure!*
>
> PSALM 32:6-11

Remember, David confessed his sins to himself, to God, and to Nathan, and then to the whole world. As a result, he experienced joy instead of what we so often expect—judgment. David reminds us that confession protects us from drowning in the floodwaters of judgment.

How have you felt when you were judged by others? How did it feel when you judged yourself?

There are at least five things that David says we will experience when we have confessed our sins. Underline each one in the passage on page 145, and then write out your experience of the benefits God promises to those who confess.

How incredible that, rather than hide in the darkness of our past, we can have God himself as our hiding place—our place of safety, unfailing love, and acceptance!

Study #3: A Warning—We're Not Finished

This study is based on Isaiah 28:14-22 (page 877 in *The Life Recovery Bible*). Read the passage several times before working on the study.

1. STOP AND LISTEN

Isaiah confronts the arrogance of the leaders in Jerusalem who have become self-absorbed and foolishly self-confident. It's as if they were addicted to their own power, much as we may have been addicted to our own efforts to fix ourselves. Their mind-set was our mind-set— we don't have a problem! Isaiah minces no words as he preaches judgment to them. He warns them that they are not as safe as they believe they are, and if they continue on their path, destruction will come.

Therefore, listen to this message from the LORD,
you scoffing rulers in Jerusalem.

You boast, "We have struck a bargain to cheat death
  and have made a deal to dodge the grave.
The coming destruction can never touch us,
  for we have built a strong refuge made of lies and deception."
ISAIAH 28:14-15

In what way does the attitude of the leaders reflect how we have struggled to fix ourselves—before we admitted we were powerless and started our journey of healing and recovery?

What were some of the lies and deceptions you believed at that time?

What do you think kept you from seeing the truth?

2. THE FOUNDATION STONE

Rather than trying to fix ourselves, we have now turned our wills and our lives over to God. In the midst of Isaiah's message of judgment, he calls on the people to do the same thing. If they do as he says, he gives a promise of what could happen for them.

Therefore this is what the Sovereign LORD says:
"Look! I am placing a foundation stone in Jerusalem,
  a firm and tested stone.
It is a precious cornerstone that is safe to build on.
  Whoever believes need never be shaken."
ISAIAH 28:16

Today, that foundation stone has arrived. The apostle Peter quotes Isaiah 28:16 and identifies Jesus as the promised cornerstone. "You are coming to Christ, who is the living cornerstone of God's temple" (1 Peter 2:4).

Peter says we are the stones in the Temple and Jesus is the chief cornerstone—he's our foundation! Notice the contrast between the lies and deceptions of the leaders confronted by Isaiah and the confidence we can have in Jesus, our cornerstone.

Describe the confidence, safety, and security you have experienced by surrendering your will and your life to Jesus.

3. THE PLUMB LINE OF RIGHTEOUSNESS

All lies and deception involve twisting the truth. To counter the lies and deception of the leaders, Isaiah uses the analogy of a plumb line. A plumb line is a string with a weight attached to one end. When the weight is suspended and the string is held at a point, the plumb line gives a perfectly perpendicular line for the builder to follow, or it will tell the builder where he has deviated from the perpendicular—from the plumb line. Notice how Isaiah suggests the plumb line will be used:

> "I will test you with the measuring line of justice
>   and the plumb line of righteousness.
> Since your refuge is made of lies,
>   a hailstorm will knock it down.
> Since it is made of deception,
>   a flood will sweep it away.
> I will cancel the bargain you made to cheat death,
>   and I will overturn your deal to dodge the grave.

When the terrible enemy sweeps through,
  you will be trampled into the ground.
Again and again that flood will come,
  morning after morning,
day and night,
  until you are carried away."
This message will bring terror to your people.
The bed you have made is too short to lie on.
  The blankets are too narrow to cover you.
The LORD will come as he did against the Philistines at Mount
    Perazim
  and against the Amorites at Gibeon.
He will come to do a strange thing;
  he will come to do an unusual deed:
For the Lord, the LORD of Heaven's Armies,
  has plainly said that he is determined to crush the whole land.
So scoff no more,
  or your punishment will be even greater.

ISAIAH 28:17-22

Lies and deception never measure up to the plumb line of truth. God's anger is measured out to those who place their security in lies. He warns them of what will happen when they fail the plumb line test through their own deceit and trickery. Before we started our recovery, we believed our own lies and deception. Here, the leaders of Jerusalem refuse to align themselves with the plumb line of truth, and they face the consequences.

What do you think God's plumb line of righteousness measures?

Dishonesty and denial are certainly behaviors and attitudes that are rejected by the plumb line. They don't measure up! The plumb line of righteousness in this passage asks us to come out of our denial and dishonesty, both of which are destructive. What a great offer!

Study #4: The Path of Healing and Recovery

This study is based on James 5:13-18 (page 1606 in *The Life Recovery Bible*). Read the passage several times before working on the study.

1. THE PRAYER THAT REQUIRES CONFESSION

The foundation Scripture for Step Five, James 5:16, is part of the Scripture reading for this Bible study. James tells us we need to confess our sins to each other so we can experience healing and recovery. But before he gives us those words, he lays the groundwork by underscoring the importance and power of prayer. We are told to either pray or sing praises.

> *Are any of you suffering hardships? You should pray. Are any of you happy? You should sing praises. Are any of you sick? You should call for the elders of the church to come and pray over you, anointing you with oil in the name of the Lord. Such a prayer offered in faith will heal the sick, and the Lord will make you well. And if you have committed any sins, you will be forgiven.*
>
> JAMES 5:13-15

Happiness versus hardships; prayer versus praise—that's how James simplifies the process. When things are going well in your recovery, give praise. When you are having difficulties, pray. Implicit in this passage is the concept of confession. How are the elders to know how to pray unless you tell them?

How do you give praise when things are going well?

Whom do you ask for prayer when you are having difficulties?

Why do you think James couples the healing of the sick with the forgiveness of sins? Look at Mark 2:1-12 for an example of how Jesus brought these two ideas together.

2. HEALING THROUGH CONFESSION

Now we come to the foundation of Step Five. Be careful not to ignore the plain teaching of this verse.

> *Confess your sins to each other and pray for each other so that*
> *you may be healed.*
> JAMES 5:16

So much of the New Testament focuses on our relationships with others. This verse is one of the most direct statements on the importance of confession and prayer. James makes it clear that our healing—our recovery—comes as we confess our sins and pray for each other.

How would you explain the importance of this verse to someone who wanted to skip Step Five in his or her recovery?

3. THE POWER OF PRAYER

James combines confession with prayer and underscores the importance and power of praying specifically for each other. He gives an example of prayer's power in the experience of Elijah.

> *The earnest prayer of a righteous person has great power and*
> *produces wonderful results. Elijah was as human as we are, and*
> *yet when he prayed earnestly that no rain would fall, none fell*
> *for three and a half years! Then, when he prayed again, the sky*
> *sent down rain and the earth began to yield its crops.*
> JAMES 5:16-18

You can read the full story of Elijah's prayers in 1 Kings 17-19. Elijah confronted King Ahab about the king's rejection of the God of Israel and how he introduced Israel to Baal, the pagan rain god. In his confrontation, Elijah told the king there would be a drought until he prayed for rain. Elijah challenged the gods of King Ahab and his wife, Jezebel. He wanted to show the people that idols made by human hands are powerless.

We also find that Elijah had to hide from King Ahab during those three and a half years because the king was determined to kill him, rather than admit that God was all-powerful and Baal was nothing. Instead of praying for what we believe God wants to see happen in our lives, as Elijah did, we tend to pray for our own comfort.

What things are you praying for earnestly at this time?

Are you praying for another person? Do you know that person's specific needs?

Remember, the promise of Step Five is our healing, our forgiveness from God, and a sense of being centered within ourselves and with significant others in our lives. But even more than that, Step Five is designed to remove the roadblocks in our relationships—primarily with God, but also with ourselves and with others.

STEP SIX

We were entirely ready to have God remove
all these defects of character.

*Humble yourselves before the Lord, and he will lift you up
in honor.*
JAMES 4:10

Beth's Story of Recovery: Healing Is a Choice

I was born Jewish, but I didn't know God at all. I didn't even know
my mother prayed. When I was thirty-four, I became a Christian.

I had no childhood. My dad was extremely selfish. He was a
compulsive gambler, and my mom was in her own little world and
did whatever my dad said to do. They went to the racetrack and on
spending sprees. He took her away from the family. I became the
adult in our home, and my parents were the children.

When my dad was around, there was often trouble. He molested
me at least twice that I can remember, and had an incestuous relationship with my younger sister. Through therapy, I have come to understand that I was too young to have protected her.

My mom told me things that were meant to be between a husband and wife. She screamed at me all the time, and I remember
one day when she made scratches down my arm. We never had any
money because my dad spent it all at the racetrack. He always said
that women were the ruination of all children.

In my family, we had a little bit of everything—alcoholism, anger,
gambling, incest, and everything in between. My family was *beyond*

dysfunctional. My grandfather was given over to a raging anger, and my aunt was an alcoholic. She embarrassed me many times in public. My uncle made a pass at my mom. My cousin exposed himself to me, and nothing was done about it. I also drank alcohol for a number of years, and cried myself to sleep at night.

I never felt safe at home, but I tried to make everyone else feel safe. I was abused physically, verbally, and emotionally. I was in Co-Dependents Anonymous (CoDA) for a number of years, and that helped me tremendously.

As a teenager, I had bulimia. I have also been diagnosed with post-traumatic stress disorder, and I now have asthma, gastroesophageal reflux disease, osteoporosis, scoliosis/kyphosis, and arthritis. I have had two heart attacks, and had a double bypass three years ago. I also suffered from manic depression for about fifteen years, and I couldn't get out of bed for days at a time. I was supposed to be on lithium for the rest of my life, but God healed me.

Were it not for God, I would be in the gutter somewhere, or dead. My sister told me that she would be dead if it weren't for me. In truth, she saved *my* life. I was in a severe depression and was ready to die, and she said, "Beth, I don't want to lose you." That simple statement got me to go to counseling.

By the grace of God, I have learned to put up healthy boundaries. I read the book *Love Is a Choice* years ago, and it helped me tremendously. It prompted me to go to CoDA and to begin counseling. Today, my body bears witness to all I've been through, but I'm still standing and still pressing forward.

STEP SIX INSIGHT

This Step is about preparing for changes in our lives. It's a "pause" in the process of our healing and recovery. Before we can experience behavioral changes in our lives, we first need to experience a change in our hearts. In Hebrew, the language of the Old Testament, the word for *heart* means "the center of our being." If we want to overcome our addictions, dependencies, and problems, we must begin to change at the core of our being. Of course, before we can change our *hearts*, we must become willing to change *at all*.

Willingness to change is the critical point at the center of Jesus' encounter with the man at the pool of Bethesda, described in John 5. This man had been sick for more than thirty-eight years. He probably survived as a beggar but appeared to have no family to support him, except for whoever brought him to the pool in the morning and came back for him at night. It's a wonder he even had that kind of help, for after thirty-eight years he was probably considered a hopeless case—everyone had basically given up on anything changing in his life.

One day, Jesus came to the pool. The man hadn't heard of Jesus; he didn't even know his name. Out of the blue, Jesus walks up to him and asks him the same question being asked in this Step: "Do you want to get well?" It was a question of the will.

Now it may seem like a ridiculous question at first glance—who wants to be helpless, sick, and beg for money every day? But think about it. This was the life he had lived for thirty-eight years—this is what he was familiar with. If he didn't sit by the pool every day, what would he do with his time? Jesus was basically asking him if he was willing to give up his lifestyle.

When you were active in your addiction, or your dependencies, or when you were all caught up in your problems, you may have said you were tired of living that way. But how easy was it to keep doing the same thing every day? Oh yes, you said you were ready for change, but only on your terms, for change can be frightening. It represents the unknown. At least when we're all caught up in our problems, we're in familiar territory. We may be frustrated by our lives, even fed up. We certainly complain about it enough. But it is all too easy to just keep doing the same thing over and over, thinking that, somehow, something might eventually change. But it doesn't.

The man never directly answers Jesus' question. Instead, he offers a valid excuse that at least suggests a willingness to change. He points out that he does not have the means to get down into the pool at the proper moment to receive healing—so he is helpless, yet willing! That's all God needs. Jesus took what the man couldn't do and did it for him.

Step Six simply questions our willingness. There's really nothing else we need to do for this Step. The question is simple and straight-forward: "Do you want to get well? Are you ready for what's next?" In fact, it asks, "Are you *entirely* ready?"

The previous two Steps examined what needs to change in our lives, so why add a step that merely asks if we're ready? *Because the focus is different.* It's not asking if we're *going* to change, as if we're going to do it ourselves. We know that doesn't work because we've tried it in the past. Step Six is asking us if we're ready to do it *right* this time—to let God do the changing!

Still, we may hold back because some of the habits, character traits, lifestyle behaviors, or patterns we have identified in the earlier Steps may have been useful to us. They certainly represent what is familiar, and we may not be certain that we want to let them go. Some behaviors may be so deeply ingrained that they are automatic and we hardly know when we do them. They just seem to be a part of who we are. Do we really have to give them up?

We need to see that this isn't an all-or-nothing step, even though it may feel that way. Remember, it is a step about *willingness*. Are you willing to change? We may respond, "I'm willing, but not yet" for some of the things on our inventory. It's like what the apostle Paul said about his personal journey: "I don't mean to say that I have already achieved these things or that I have already reached perfec-tion. But I press on to possess that perfection for which Christ Jesus first possessed me" (Philippians 3:12). "That perfection" is not what we think of when we think of perfection. Paul is simply talking about his progress toward the goal of excellence—of being everything God wants him to be.

Even if we haven't arrived at a *perfect* readiness, are we at least entirely ready to move forward—to press on to the goal of health, wholeness, and serenity in our lives? In other words, can we at least say that we're ready to start, and that as we press forward, we will face the "not yets" and eventually include them in our readiness for change? Think of it as *generic* readiness—are we willing to at least start cleaning house in our lives and in our character? All we're looking for at Step Six is that *readiness*—Step Seven is the action step.

If Step Six is only about our readiness for change, what could hold us back on this Step? Attitude, for one thing. This is a Step where we are asked to take ownership of our character defects. That may be new for us. Taking ownership means we take responsibility for our lives, our behaviors, and our attitudes—though not the responsibility for *changing* these things, which is now in God's hands.

Frank Buchman, founder of the Oxford Group, the organization at the center of the development of AA and the Twelve Steps, said that we have to give up our defects. It's wishful thinking that God will just take them. When we are willing to give up our defects of character, we become a part of a special process. He said the process is simple: "Sin is the disease (the problem), Jesus is the cure (the solution), and the result is a miracle."[8]

Step Six is a major factor in the continuation of that miracle.

When we were caught up in our problems, taking responsibility was not something we did. Most of us were much better at blaming than at taking responsibility. Now we are being asked to own our destructive thought patterns, the abuse of our bodies, our destructive behaviors, attitudes, and emotions. They are all ours. We own them. We are responsible for them, and for how they have hurt us and others. No one else is to blame. We are to face our fears in these areas of our lives, take complete responsibility for them, and release them to God as he begins to clean the house of our character. We've faced these fears in doing our inventories and in sharing our inventories with another human being. Now we face the fear of releasing these defects and being willing to let God remove them from our lives. What's going to be left? We hope that what remains is very clean and very good. What is left will lead us to serenity in life, not insanity.

Our readiness is also inversely related to the amount of pain our defects have caused in our lives. The more pain our defects have caused, the more ready we are to let God remove them. Defects that have caused less pain may be more difficult to give up. Either way, the key to this Step is for us to have a "broken and repentant heart" (Psalm 51:17). When King David finally faced himself, he realized that nothing had given him the key to success in God's eyes—not his pride, his position in life, or his previous successes. It was only through his brokenness that he was able to experience success in living according to God's standard. God loves us with a faithful love, but his love for us is more fully experienced when we come to him in an attitude of humility, of brokenness. The early developers of the Twelve Steps called this Step the "Step of Repentance." They believed repentance meant turning around and going in a different direction. That's what this Step calls for!

Diane's Story of Recovery: I Was Now the Addict

At the age of twenty, I was a sophomore in college studying for an accounting degree and I was engaged to be married. It was a special time in my life, with every hope out in front of me. I was right on track with where I wanted to be in my life: on a solid walk with Christ, preparing to wed a wonderful Christian man, and looking forward to the life we were planning and pursuing.

While driving to a Campus Crusade for Christ meeting one night, as we did each week, my fiancé, Marty, made a comment to me, a come-on, about wanting to see my body in a certain setting, and in certain detail. He and I had agreed to remain abstinent until our marriage, but we often pushed the envelope to the extreme. Still, I was struck in that moment by the detail of his suggestion. I thought to myself, *He has seen this somewhere before.*

That was my first inkling of his deep involvement in pornography. I would soon discover just how ensnared he had become. Marty's first exposure to pornographic images came when he was in elementary school. While innocently playing in the woods one day, he had stumbled upon a magazine with violent sexual images. He was instantly hooked. Ever since, he had struggled with guilt and shame over his compulsive pursuit of more images through magazines, books, and videos. These behaviors eventually progressed into voyeurism and exhibitionism.

When I found out, I was shocked and confused. I cared for this man and could see and sense his torment of shame and self-hatred. As we began to process what this would mean for us as a couple, we came to believe that these types of behaviors are somewhat normal for a young man who is abstinent until marriage. We anticipated that once we were married and could enjoy a full sexual relationship, our problem would be solved. I naively assumed he would no longer be tempted to look at pornography and other women.

I was wrong.

After making our vows in front of God and our closest family and friends, we began our married life together with all the hope in the world. But, like most addictions, his progressed immediately into riskier and riskier behaviors and caused increasing tension and upset between us.

I was a crazy woman. I threw things at him. I cursed him, multiple times. I made a big production of my anger because I thought if he could see how much he was hurting me, he would want to change and remain faithful to our marriage covenant.

During our first year of marriage, I found a radio show that fascinated me. Several counselors answered phone calls from around the country and offered biblical advice for the problems and challenges of everyday life. I began listening whenever I could. And I began to believe, for the first time, that perhaps I, too, could be helped by a counselor. Especially if the counseling sessions were anything like what I heard on the radio.

The show was *New Life Live*—and I was hooked. Because of *New Life Live*, I sought the help of a Christian counselor as my marriage continued on a downward spiral. About six months after the birth of our second baby boy, Marty and I scheduled our first counseling session. But when our counselor suggested I try recovery meetings for myself, I balked.

"He's the one with the addiction. He's the one who needs meetings!" I didn't understand codependency, or why the counselor thought it would apply to me. I had so much to learn!

Eventually, I took the counselor's advice, and I have been in recovery for twelve years now. I found a very good home in COSA and in Al-Anon. As I always say, I'll still be sitting in my recovery meetings when I'm eighty-three years old because I forever have something to learn, and I now know I have something to give (which is part of Step Twelve).

In recovery, I learned that I must do "the next right thing." As I began to get healthier and healthier each and every day, with the help of my counselor, my sponsor, and my girlfriends who were also in recovery, I developed a more grown-up voice and a firmer set of boundaries for myself. Recovery changed how I valued myself and what I would and would not live with.

I learned that what's right for me is truly what's right for everyone else, too. I learned that if I took care of myself, ate healthy foods, and got enough sleep, I would have a positive effect on my two young boys, and their lives would be improved. I learned that when I spent time connecting with God, my emotional state was more positive, and that had a positive effect on my sons as well.

Still, doing "the next right thing," in my very best effort, took me down a path I did not expect. My husband did not choose recovery, as I did, and after seven years of marriage, we ended in divorce. It was like walking off of a cliff for me. I was unsure if I would survive the heartbreak and disappointment.

Life began to change rapidly. I had to go back to work, my sons began a new preschool, and the three of us moved out of our home and into a new apartment. The boys began spending the weekends with their dad—which left me . . . alone.

I entered a new phase that I never could have anticipated.

I took off my ring, and suddenly—*poof!*—there were men available and knocking at my door. How could this be? I had never experienced attention in this way. I had never experienced my own drive for this type of attention, and it was somewhat surprising to me.

I had hated anything to do with sex for so many years because it was the source of all the sorrow and misery in my marriage. But as a divorcée, I began to discover that flirting and seducing could be really fun. And I began to crave attention and power in this way.

I began dating several very kind and good men at a time, who each treated me like a queen. Eventually I dated just one man for several months. Soon, I became sexually involved with him. This was thrilling for me. It was the most sexual enjoyment I had ever experienced. Yet still, I felt great guilt and shame over living outside of my conviction that sex is reserved for a couple committed to one another in marriage.

Knowing that I truly did not aspire to marry the man with whom I was involved at that time, I ended the relationship, attempting to bring myself back into purity. But then I began another relationship, and before long became sexual with my new guy.

This was my cycle. Eventually, I began a dangerous connection with a married man. This was the scariest and most shame-producing time in my life. I became terrified and soon ended this connection, but not before causing a great deal of damage to both of our families and myself.

I finally began to realize that I was now the addict.

What a blow to my ego. I had criticized my husband for years for his struggle and condemned him for his involvement with other women, and now I was becoming just like him. This was very humbling for me. And in a lot of ways, it was very good for me to get humbled like that. I realized that we are all capable of great darkness apart from a heart surrendered to Christ.

I finally began a new level of recovery. I found Sex and Love Addicts Anonymous one week after a pregnancy scare from my involvement with a boyfriend from high school. I found a group of other women who struggled with childhood trauma, as I did. We were sexualized as young girls and made to feel special in some very sick ways. We had grown up with a radically distorted view of what it means to be beautiful, to be a woman, to be attractive, to be valued.

In recovery, I have found my higher power's perfect love. He cherishes me! By working the program, I know I'm powerless over my tendencies toward darkness but that God can restore me to sanity, and I choose to let him. I take inventory of myself, I make amends and restitutions, and I work continually for conscious contact with my higher power, Jesus Christ, and so I can carry the message of recovery forward.

I am now happily married to a man who honors me sexually and nonsexually. He knows me intimately and celebrates me as an individual with goals and desires. He is a partner with me. We've been married nearly seven years now, and life is beyond good. We walk a path of surrender and reaching for one another and for God. We've been blessed with more children, and we are raising each of them to know the principles of recovery. The message is moving forward.

I thank God for the brokenness, as I learn more and more of his radical love.

STEP SIX BIBLE STUDIES

Study #1: The Big Question?

This study is based on John 5:1-9 (page 1347 in *The Life Recovery Bible*). Read these verses several times before working on the study.

1. THE SETTING

In the time of Jesus, sick people congregated at the pool of Bethesda in Jerusalem, where according to tradition an angel would come and stir the waters. The first one into the pool when the angel stirred the waters would be healed of his or her affliction. We don't know how often this happened, but apparently often enough that a regular group crowded around the pool. They were all hoping for healing.

The man referred to in this passage had been sitting by the pool for thirty-eight years. The pool was "home" to him and probably to many others as well. Someone brought this man to the pool early in the morning, and took him home late at night. This is where his friends were. Sitting by the pool had become his way of life, and without sitting there day after day, he wouldn't know what to do. In his frustration, he told Jesus that there was no one who would put him in the pool when the water was stirred.

> *Afterward Jesus returned to Jerusalem for one of the Jewish holy days. Inside the city, near the Sheep Gate, was the pool of Bethesda, with five covered porches. Crowds of sick people— blind, lame, or paralyzed—lay on the porches. One of the men lying there had been sick for thirty-eight years.*
> JOHN 5:1-5

Prior to starting your recovery journey, how had your addiction, dependency, or problems become a "way of life" for you?

In spite of the painfulness of those problems, what was "comfortable," or familiar, about them?

2. READY, BUT NOT QUITE READY

Now comes the big question from Jesus that forms the basis of Step Six: "Would you like to get well?" It may almost seem like a foolish question until you remember that sitting by the pool had become this man's life. You can imagine all the people sitting and talking about their problems, and about the miracles they had observed in others. They were "comfortable" in their problem setting. It was familiar to them. So Jesus' question is right on—and he asks it of each of us: "Would you like to get well?"

> *When Jesus saw him and knew he had been ill for a long time, he asked him, "Would you like to get well?"*
>   *"I can't, sir," the sick man said, "for I have no one to put me into the pool when the water bubbles up. Someone else always gets there ahead of me."*
> JOHN 5:6-7

What were some of the familiar parts of your addiction, dependency, or problem?

What part of your problem has been the hardest for you to give up?

The man gives Jesus an excuse instead of answering the question. What were some of your excuses? What were some you heard others give?

3. THE UNEXPECTED

What was there about Jesus' voice that enabled this man to do what had been impossible for him? Obviously, the man didn't know who Jesus was. Perhaps the buzz about Jesus healing people hadn't made it to the poolside at Bethesda. Picture the scene: Jesus tells him to get up and walk, and instantly the man, who has been paralyzed for thirty-eight years or more, does what Jesus tells him to do. Wow! He didn't even know Jesus' name! Here's what's exciting—Jesus can work with that same power in our lives today.

Jesus told him, "Stand up, pick up your mat, and walk!"
Instantly, the man was healed! He rolled up his sleeping mat
and began walking!

JOHN 5:8-9

What would Jesus say to you about your addiction, dependency, or problem that might be as startling as what he said to the man by the pool?

What keeps you from believing that Jesus wants to heal you in the same way?

You would think that people would have cheered what Jesus had done. But Jesus healed the man on the Sabbath, which according to Jewish law was *work*. And work was not allowed on the Sabbath. The healed man was also in trouble because he was carrying his mat, which the Jewish leaders also considered work. Unfortunately, there are always people who miss the miracle because they get stuck on a technicality. Don't miss it!

Study #2: Removed, Not Just Improved

This study is based on Romans 6:4-14 (page 1438 in *The Life Recovery Bible*). Read the entire chapter several times before working on the study.

1. NEW LIVES

At this point, our willingness to allow God to remove our character defects is just that—our *willingness*. We often hold on to something because we don't know what will replace it. It's like being on a game show and having to choose between the prize we can see and the one behind the curtain. Step Six asks the question, "Are you willing to give up what you have and what you can see?" Romans 6 is right in the middle of Paul's great explanation of what we have in Christ. In Romans 5, he describes how hopeless and worthless our lives once were, but in spite of our condition, God loved us so much that he sent his Son to die for us so that we could have new life. Now, in Romans 6, Paul gives insight into how we can experience this new life. As you do this study, pray that God will give you understanding about your new life.

> *And just as Christ was raised from the dead by the glorious power of the Father, now we also may live new lives. Since we have been united with him in his death, we will also be raised to life as he was. We know that our old sinful selves were crucified with Christ so that sin might lose its power in our lives. We are no longer slaves to sin.*
> ROMANS 6:4-6

We cannot experience new life until we let go of our old lives. If we have Christ in our lives, letting go of the old life should be a natural step because that life is now considered dead.

What part of your old life is hardest for you to release?

Paul says that the more we identify with Jesus' death, burial, and resurrection, the more we will defeat the power of sin in our lives. How do you try to identify with Jesus' death, burial, and resurrection?

Paul doesn't say we no longer sin. He says we are no longer *slaves*—addicted—to sin. Not only are we in recovery from our problems, but we are also in recovery from sin. The good news is that Jesus broke the power of sin on the Cross. Where are you seeing sin losing its power in your life?

2. DEFECTS REMOVED!

This is a profound passage and one that is hard to fully understand, unless you spend some time with it. You may want to digest the concepts slowly so that you can better understand what Paul wants us to know here.

> *For when we died with Christ we were set free from the power of sin. And since we died with Christ, we know we will also live with him. We are sure of this because Christ was raised from the dead, and he will never die again. Death no longer has any power over him.*
> ROMANS 6:7-9

How do we "die" with Christ?

If we know Christ as our Savior, we know we will live with him for eternity. But how can we live with him today?

3. WHAT HAS BEEN REMOVED?

Paul makes some clear suggestions about how we experience our deadness to sin. We will still sin because we are human. Because God says we are dead to sin, we must live in a way that shows we believe him. Therefore, we live in a way that shows we consider it to be true. But the practical outworking of this reality is now addressed. It's all part of our willingness to have God clean out our lives.

> *When he died, he died once to break the power of sin. But now that he lives, he lives for the glory of God. So you also should consider yourselves to be dead to the power of sin and alive to God through Christ Jesus.*
>
> *Do not let sin control the way you live; do not give in to sinful desires. Do not let any part of your body become an instrument of evil to serve sin. Instead, give yourselves completely to God, for you were dead but now you have new life. So use your whole body as an instrument to do what is right for the glory of God. Sin is no longer your master, for you no longer live under the requirements of the law. Instead, you live under the freedom of God's grace.*
>
> ROMANS 6:10-14

Paul describes our part in experiencing the new life that is promised to us. There are at least five things we are to do. Can you list them?

1.

2.

3.

4.

5.

Which part is the hardest for you to do?

Which parts are you experiencing success with?

We need to review this passage periodically to remind ourselves what humility and willingness are all about. We haven't reached Step Seven—the action Step—yet, so we are only discussing our *willingness*. But what a promise Paul gives us here as we move forward in our recovery! We can have a new life!

Study #3: Ready?

This study is based on Isaiah 55:1-9 (page 909 in *The Life Recovery Bible*). Read these verses several times before working on the study.

1. GOD'S INVITATION

In this passage, Isaiah gives Israel a prophecy regarding comfort and blessing. As we become willing to allow God to change us, we can be reassured that he desires to bless us. The word *bless* is hard to define. It speaks of conferring prosperity or happiness upon someone, but it also includes being honored, approved of, and experiencing divine favor. As we prepare for God to remove our character defects, let's see what Isaiah says about how God wants to bless us.

> *Is anyone thirsty?*
> *Come and drink—*
> *even if you have no money!*
> *Come, take your choice of wine or milk—*
> *it's all free!*

Why spend your money on food that does not give you strength?
Why pay for food that does you no good?
Listen to me, and you will eat what is good.
You will enjoy the finest food.

ISAIAH 55:1-2

What a deal! Everything offered is free. Not only free water, but also free milk and wine. What three words make up the one precondition?

Isaiah deals with more than physical hunger or thirst. He addresses the hunger and thirst of the heart. What does your heart desire from God at this point?

Based on these verses, what do you think God is offering you?

2. BETTER THAN YOU CAN IMAGINE

When we listen to what God wants of us, our first reaction may be defensive, thinking that what he wants is too hard or not something we will enjoy. These thoughts often go back to disappointments we experienced with God in the past. But typically, those disappointments occurred because we tried to tell God what to do. It may be hard to stop and listen, but the request comes with promises. Often, what is hard is resisting the old life; we don't typically find the new life difficult. Isaiah promises that when we come and listen, we will find what our lives can really be.

Come to me with your ears wide open.
Listen, and you will find life.
I will make an everlasting covenant with you.

> *I will give you all the unfailing love I promised to David.*
> *See how I used him to display my power among the peoples.*
>   *I made him a leader among the nations.*
> *You also will command nations you do not know,*
>   *and peoples unknown to you will come running to obey,*
> *because I, the LORD your God,*
>   *the Holy One of Israel, have made you glorious.*
> ISAIAH 55:3-5

This part of Isaiah's prophecy was intended to comfort the people while they were in a strange land. It also is written to help us find comfort. First, God promises an everlasting covenant with us. He speaks here of King David, and how God made an everlasting covenant with him. A covenant is different from a contract. In a contract, I promise to do something if you will do something. In a covenant, the one making the covenant promises to do something regardless of what the other party does or doesn't do.

What does an everlasting covenant mean to you?

God's unfailing love is a major part of his covenant with David, as well as his covenant with us. Because it's a covenant, not a contract, God promises his unfailing love regardless of our actions.

At this point in your recovery journey, describe God's "unfailing love" for you.

In spite of David's sins, God honored him. Isaiah uses the word *glorious* to describe God's plan for David. What word do you want God to use about you?

3. THE BATTLE IS IN THE MIND

Isaiah reminds us that, even though God has made a covenant with us, he is still looking for a response from us. Once we begin to respond, God is very patient with us. But his patience may grow thin if we delay our response. God invites us to respond and to come to him with a willingness to have him help us change our ways. The battle is obviously in our minds—in the way we think—because God's way of thinking is so unlike ours. We must battle to replace our thinking about ourselves and about how to live with how God sees us and how he wants us to live.

> Seek the LORD while you can find him.
>   Call on him now while he is near.
> Let the wicked change their ways
>   and banish the very thought of doing wrong.
> Let them turn to the LORD that he may have mercy on them.
>   Yes, turn to our God, for he will forgive generously.
>
> "My thoughts are nothing like your thoughts," says the LORD.
>   "And my ways are far beyond anything you could imagine.
> For just as the heavens are higher than the earth,
>   so my ways are higher than your ways
>   and my thoughts higher than your thoughts."

ISAIAH 55:6-9

What part of your old life and way of thinking are you having trouble banishing?

Describe how God sees you differently from how you tend to see yourself.

What is hard for you to understand about how God thinks of you?

We battle on two fronts in our recovery. We have to deal with what we hunger and thirst for within our hearts to make certain we go beyond our addictions and problems to the deeper needs within us. And we have to battle with old patterns of thinking that are contrary to God's way of thinking. It's easier than it sounds, for God is ready and able to help us win both battles.

Study #4: The Enemy Lurks

This study is based on 2 Chronicles 32:1-8 (page 576 in *The Life Recovery Bible*). Read these verses several times before working on the study. For the context of these verses, read 2 Chronicles 29-31.

1. THE THREAT

King Hezekiah was one of the good kings in the history of Judah. Everything he did was aimed at repairing the hearts of the people. The Bible says that "he did what was pleasing in the LORD's sight, just as his ancestor David had done" (2 Chronicles 29:2). The kings who preceded him had abandoned the worship of God in favor of idol worship—doing what was evil in God's sight. When Hezekiah came to the throne, he launched the kingdom of Judah on a massive recovery program. First, he cleansed and rededicated the Temple, and then reinstituted the sacrificial system. Next, he had the priests prepare to celebrate the Passover, even though the holy day should have been celebrated a month earlier.

One would think that by honoring God this way, all would go smoothly. But it didn't. In the midst of Judah's recovery, their enemy Assyria invaded the land and prepared to attack Jerusalem.

After Hezekiah had faithfully carried out this work, King Sennacherib of Assyria invaded Judah. He laid siege to the fortified towns, giving orders for his army to break through their walls.

2 CHRONICLES 32:1

What do you think the people felt when they saw the Assyrians invading their land—right after they got things right between themselves and God?

How has your experience mirrored Hezekiah's, with bad things happening once you got serious about recovery?

2. PROTECTING YOUR BOUNDARIES

Hezekiah didn't seem to miss a beat. He didn't get angry with God, nor did he give up by thinking, "What's the use?" After all, when bad things piled on just as he was getting things right with God, he could have thrown up his hands and said, "I give up!" But he didn't. He was serious about the recovery journey.

When Hezekiah realized that Sennacherib also intended to attack Jerusalem, he consulted with his officials and military advisers, and they decided to stop the flow of the springs outside the city. They organized a huge work crew to stop the flow of the springs, cutting off the brook that ran through the fields. For they said, "Why should the kings of Assyria come here and find plenty of water?"

Then Hezekiah worked hard at repairing all the broken sections of the wall, erecting towers, and constructing a second wall outside the first. He also reinforced the supporting terraces in the City of David and manufactured large numbers of weapons and shields. He appointed military officers over the people and assembled them before him in the square at the city gate.

2 CHRONICLES 32:2-6

List the things Hezekiah did to protect the people.

What safeguards have you set in place to protect your recovery journey? Think in terms of boundaries, resources, and supportive people.

3. WE HAVE THE LORD!

After all Hezekiah's preparations, one thing was left to do: rally the people. Not only was Hezekiah a great leader, he was also a great motivator. But his motivating speech wasn't just a lot of positive words—he reminded the people they were not alone, for "a power far greater" than the enemy was on their side. In the same way, when we have turned our lives and our wills over to God, we have "a power far greater" on our side!

Then Hezekiah encouraged them by saying: "Be strong and courageous! Don't be afraid or discouraged because of the king of Assyria or his mighty army, for there is a power far greater on our side! He may have a great army, but they are merely men. We have the LORD our God to help us and to fight our battles for us!" Hezekiah's words greatly encouraged the people.

2 CHRONICLES 32:6-8

How has God helped you thus far in your recovery journey?

How does this account of God's involvement with his people, which lead to their safety, affect your willingness to ask God to remove your character defects? Where do you want him to begin?

Hezekiah and Judah experienced a tremendous victory. The prophet Isaiah helped the king and together they cried out to God for help. "And the LORD sent an angel who destroyed the Assyrian army with all its commanders and officers" (2 Chronicles 32:21). The Assyrian king was forced to return home in disgrace. The people and leaders of Judah certainly had some fear, but they did not give in to their fears, for they knew that God was on their side.

STEP SEVEN

We humbly asked God to remove our shortcomings.

If we confess our sins to him, he is faithful and just to forgive us our sins and to cleanse us from all wickedness.

1 JOHN 1:9

Tina's Story of Recovery: Naming My Addiction Was the First Step

I am the sixth of eight children. My parents loved us and sent us to parochial school, and we went to church every Sunday. My family moved from Indiana to Pennsylvania when I was eleven. It seems like that's when things began falling apart for me. When I was sixteen, my twenty-year-old brother, Doug, committed suicide by drug overdose. I thought it was an accident until I learned the truth twenty-nine years later. Before Doug's death, I had already gotten involved with a married man with two young children.

I tried my first drink when I was fifteen, and I drank fast to get drunk. At first, I would feel a great sense of ease and comfort, but then I would throw up or pass out. I always had regrets afterward. I soon moved on to other substances that I thought I could control, like pot and speed. By twenty-three I was pregnant, and when I was six months along, I married the father. The pregnancy was difficult, resulting in a premature birth at twenty-eight weeks. This was due to my physical makeup, not to drugs or alcohol. By then, I had been clean for a while.

During the delivery, the doctor fractured my baby's skull with the forceps. As a result, my daughter was severely disabled—always in diapers, confined to a wheelchair, unable to walk, talk, roll over, or sit up. She had to be spoon-fed and occasionally needed a feeding tube. My husband's lack of character added to the difficulties, but that's another story.

Three and a half years later, I had another premature baby. My son spent his first three months in the hospital but was healthy, strong, and intelligent.

My daughter was the purest soul I have ever known, and she touched so many lives without a word. I learned to give of myself to her, and she was entirely dependent on me. Remembering Jesus' words—"whatever you do to the least of these, you do to me"—helped me to be selfless. Gabrielle passed away when she was seven, due to complications of her condition. My husband left for a week with a friend to help him "deal with her death," leaving me alone with my son, who was two weeks from his fourth birthday, neither of us knowing yet how to grieve.

Sometime after the death of my daughter, I started drinking again. I don't remember the exact circumstances.

When my son was ten, he showed me a large bruise on his chest one day and said my husband had punched him for talking in school. He said, "Don't tell Daddy I told you, or he'll get me worse." Then he asked, "When are you going to make him stop?"

I said, "Right now," and we took a ride to the police station. I had my husband arrested, and he was convicted of child abuse. My "self-employed," stay-at-home husband was finally out of the house, never to return. We divorced a year later, and he made no effort to reconnect with our son—not even attending the parenting classes required by the court to regain visitation rights.

My drinking progressed, though only at home and on week-end nights since I was now a single mother with an angry son who blamed me for "making Daddy go away." I was promoted to manager at work, which meant more responsibility. Then I made a terrible choice to move in with a man I had known for fifteen years. He was an alcoholic, and if I hadn't been drinking myself, I never would have chosen to be with him. The new living arrangement only increased the tension between my son and me, and my drinking soon progressed to every night. Meanwhile, my son was getting in fights every day at school and things were bad.

When my company decided to close my branch and consolidate operations in Massachusetts, I was faced with the prospect of being out of work, with no college education, or moving five hundred miles to keep my job. I decided to move. At this point, I was still blaming other people for my problems, and I wanted to get away and make a fresh start—a so-called geographical cure.

After two weeks in Massachusetts, I decided I didn't have a drinking problem. After all, I was an adult, I only drank at home, and I wasn't hurting anybody. I was on my way to the liquor store one day when my son, now fourteen, begged me not to buy any beer. I chose to buy the beer anyway, proving that alcohol was number one in my life, even over my son, whom I dearly treasured. But I couldn't see it at the time.

By the time my son was seventeen, he had problems of his own. He went to court on a drug charge, and the judge told him he could start with a new record if he could stay clean for six months. He couldn't do it, and he knew he needed help. By order of the court, he went to a teen boys' residential home for substance abuse treatment. The program also required parental involvement. It was there that I learned about recovery, though I still didn't think my problem was that bad. If people knew about my life, they would understand. I just thought no one understood my situation.

I had to supervise my son at all times when he was home on earned leave. If he was home more than twenty-four hours, he had to attend an Alcoholics Anonymous meeting, and I went with him. It was there that the seed of recovery was planted in my heart. It took months, but the message finally got through to both of us. By the time my son graduated from the program, neither one of us wanted it to end.

A month or so later, I was laid off from my job after twenty-three years. I was terrified of the future and called one of the counselors at the treatment home. She told me to "go to a meeting." I knew she meant an AA meeting, but I didn't understand why, since that wasn't my immediate problem. Nevertheless, I trusted her and went.

When I arrived, I saw someone from the treatment home there. Revelation! I hadn't realized the staff members were all in recovery themselves. He said, "So, are you one of us?" I said, "I guess I am," though I still wasn't fully convinced. But in that meeting, when I raised my hand and said, "My name is Tina, and I am an alcoholic," something clicked in my head. I said, "That is the first time I've said that and meant it."

Looking back, I can see that I had the gift of desperation—and I truly consider it a gift, for nothing else could've pushed me out of my own way on the path to surrender. My pride, anger, and self-sufficiency were what had carried me thus far.

Naming my addiction—and *meaning* it—was my first step on the road to recovery. I began to reach out for help. I jumped in with both feet and haven't looked back since. I joined a group, got a sponsor, and ran with the fellowship of AA for eighteen months. I felt accepted, loved, and welcomed. But after those months, the fellowship of AA wasn't enough to keep me sane or sober. It wasn't working for me anymore. I practically grabbed a fellow by his lapels and said, "This isn't working. I need help!" He said, "Oh, yes, eighteen months. That's about when it happened to me. You need to do the work, the Twelve Steps of recovery."

For a year and a half, I had been staying sober on what I knew as the Five Suggestions: (1) join a group; (2) get active; (3) get a sponsor and use her; (4) get on your knees every morning and ask God for help; and (5) out of common courtesy, get on your knees at night and thank God for his help. I have since learned that I am in a Twelve Step recovery program, not a Five Suggestions program—though I continue to practice the Five Suggestions as well. Going to meetings and not drinking were not enough to keep me sober. I had to change or I would drink again. I knew it.

The more I learned about the disease of alcoholism, the more I understood myself and my family members. This helped me in the process of forgiving everyone. Until I went through the recovery process—the Twelve Steps, one by one, as laid out in *The Big Book* of Alcoholics Anonymous—I was not going to stay sober or sane. Step Four revealed my character defects, the pattern of choices in my life, and why I made those decisions (usually based on fear, pride, selfishness, etc.). I became *willing* to allow God to remove these character defects, and I humbly asked him to remove them. I also saw my part in my resentment toward others. By making amends to those I had harmed, I cleared myself of the burden of holding on to those resentments. Acceptance is now a reality of life for me, past and present. "Not to regret the past nor wish to shut the door on it," as the AA *Big Book* says.

By the grace of God, I have not had the desire to drink since I admitted I was an alcoholic nearly seven ago. One day at a time, I am being transformed into a new person: physically, spiritually, and emotionally. Character growth is the key to recovery.

I surrendered to the fact that I cannot have alcohol in my body without it taking control of me—I am powerless over it. Further, I admitted that my life is unmanageable without God in control of it. I have become accountable for my choices, ceasing to blame people, places, and things for my actions. By working through and living the Steps, I live a life that is amazingly peaceful and productive.

Although I thought I always believed in God, I did not know how to practically apply that knowledge in my everyday life. Now, with Jesus Christ as my Lord and Savior, I actually *rely* on God and *trust* him with all my cares and concerns. Every time I help a newcomer to the program, I am being used by God as a tool to bring someone else the gift of faith and recovery.

I am now married to a good Christian man, who recently celebrated twenty years of recovery. My son is now twenty-five and is living on his own. Not long ago, my son, my husband, five of my husband's family members, and I all got baptized together in

Chesapeake Bay. Praise God! We are active participants in our local church and love our Christ-centered lives together. I want people to know that recovery is available to *everyone*—one day at a time, with the help of God and the Twelve Steps. By the grace of God, I have a recovery story of my own.

STEP SEVEN INSIGHT

Step Seven proves the wisdom of working the Steps *in order* from the beginning. Some people want to jump in anywhere that strikes their fancy. But when they do, their recovery becomes stilted or tainted. A haphazard approach to recovery is similar to a builder constructing a home by starting with some beautiful carpet. If carpet is the first material used in construction, some pretty ugly consequences will result. Yes, looking at the carpet over the grass and dirt on a vacant lot could be quite attractive. But without the foundational steps and structures underneath and around it, the carpet is doomed to become a soggy, sun-bleached mess. In the same way, it is no better to start the Steps out of order than to roll out carpet to start a house.

This is especially true for Step Seven, which is the culmination of Steps Four through Six. In Step Six, we moved deeper into the heart of our problems and recognized that the pathway out begins with a *readiness*, or *willingness*, to have our defects removed. Before we could be *ready* and *willing*, we had to undertake a fearless moral inventory in Step Four, and then take that inventory and admit the truth of it to God, to ourselves, and to another person. Those necessary Steps brought clarity to our lives and became the foundation for the rest of our journey. They lead to Step Seven, where the *willingness* of Step Six becomes a request that God remove our defects.

We take a huge step when we finally ask God to do something specific in our lives. *Asking* God to move is far beyond *allowing* God to move. *Allowing* God is surrender. *Asking* God is a humble petition. When we have humbled ourselves enough to see that God is the *only* answer to our need for growth, maturity, and a sober life, then we can humbly ask him to remove the character defects from our lives. *Asking* is a request for a better life that *gives* rather than *takes*. *Asking* opens the way to a life of slowly but surely growing into mature men and women who can be used by God. It is the first request on a path to a blessed life.

A Common Trap

When we ask God to remove our shortcomings and defects, we must be certain not to fall into a common trap that eliminates our growth potential. That trap is expecting God to fix us *instantly* or take away all of our problems. The truth is, God has a very different plan. God's plan will involve other people, tough experiences, and hard decisions. We will need every bit of God's plan to change us from people with potential into people who grow, relate, and achieve the way God wants.

Sometimes we see miraculous breakthroughs that appear to be instant healings or changes. For some people, the desire to lust or the craving for sugar or the quest for alcohol disappears instantly. While we celebrate these amazing miracles, we also find ourselves somewhat jealous, wishing God would do the same for us. But what actually happens in those "instant change" scenarios?

These radical changes in urges and cravings are real. We have seen this time and time again. One fellow struggler, who drank about a fifth of vodka every day, woke up one morning, filled the sink with water, saw his reflection in it, and asked God to heal him. His desire for alcohol immediately left and never returned. The urge was gone, but what was left? He was not given instant character or delivered into maturity. His family was not instantly healed of all the resentment and bitterness that had built up over the years. Each of these developments would take additional time and work. The reduction or elimination of desire was a *gift* to allow the work to begin, but it was not the completion of growth and recovery.

Some who have had their cravings lifted think they have license to teach or counsel others. But these "instant change helpers" don't do well because God does not deal with each person the same way. "Instant change" advice comes from an empty well and quenches nothing. We often see relapses and failures as a result of not understanding what happened in the instantaneous change and what did not. The end of the desire was a *gift*, but it was also an *invitation* to do the work that leads to a life of wisdom and maturity.

One pastor had an "instant healing" that turned out very badly. He had developed a problem with alcohol, sneaking drinks out of sight of his family and the members of his church. After almost wrecking his car one night, he fell to his knees and asked God for a miracle. God instantly removed his desire to drink, and he was sober from that day forward. But there was a problem. Rather than being humbled by this gift or overcome with gratitude, he became prideful. He thought he knew everything about recovery and that God had done a total work of healing in every part of his soul. But the character defects and shortcomings that had led to his drinking were still there. Rather than becoming a recovery expert, he became an arrogant scold, teaching that anyone with real faith could experience what he had experienced. The inevitable result was *emptiness*.

If you preach and teach transformation but have not experienced it yourself, emptiness of the soul will take over and drive you to try to fill it. This pastor had lost his desire to drink, but he started to become energized by women who were not his wife. He loved their adulation. He became drunk on his position and how people viewed those in authority. Before long, he crossed the line with a woman from his church. When she confessed their encounter, his world came crashing down around him.

It did not have to be that way. He could have seen the lifting of the urge to drink as a gift of *clarity*, enabling him to go to work on himself with God's help, without the distraction of uncontrollable urges. Instead, he saw God's healing as an *entitlement* and thought he now had all the answers. He tripped over himself and his character defects and shortcomings, rather than taking God's gift as an opportunity to get to work—which is exactly what *we* need to do.

Doing the Opposite

Somehow, you have come across this book at this particular time. There is a reason. It was not an accident. It was a gift. That gift is an invitation to grow deeper and richer in your relationship with God. In order to move in that direction, you must ask God for help in removing the obstacles—those character defects and shortcomings that trip you up—and be willing to do what will bring light and direction into your life.

God's plan is often a work of *opposites*. He challenges us to rely upon him and ask the Holy Spirit for the power to do the opposite of what we are accustomed to do. We argue with our impulses and humbly ask God to give us the strength to move in the opposite direction. We have not thought well of groups in which people share the intimate details of their lives. We've often characterized "those folks" as losers who just want to moan and groan about their problems. Now we have to stop ridiculing them and do the opposite— become part of them.

Once we're there, in the domain we never dreamed we would experience, we begin to feel the freedom to open up a little. We encounter people who are transparent, and their openness calls us to be transparent. We hear others talk of problems worse than ours and how they overcame their adversities. Their stories give us hope that if we continue to come back again and again, we might not be so lonely, and we might discover new ways to win in the midst of pain and struggle. Over and over, *opposite* becomes our goal.

Perhaps our fears have kept us locked up inside, even locked up in our homes, not venturing into the cruel world. Asking God to rid us of this fear will require some very uncomfortable moves in the opposite direction. We will move toward people and new experiences and stretching our boundaries rather than staying locked inside the walls of predictability. If we cannot come out of hiding on our own, we ask someone to lead us and guide us and be there for us. If one other person is not enough to move us beyond our fears, we seek out another. If we need six months of meetings and six months of counseling with a trained therapist, we move in that direction. Ever since we made the bold move of asking God to help us get rid of our defects, he's been calling us in the opposite direction.

If we have control issues and feel the need to direct other people, we do the opposite—keeping our mouths shut when we're tempted to speak. Rather than jumping in with demands or judgment, we stop ourselves and look to God first. We hold our tongues and ask God to give us peace and serenity as we allow others to be less than perfect—or maybe even completely wrong. We realize that our attempts at running the lives of others have produced a lot of results, but authentic intimacy is not one of them. We stop juggling the events of our lives on our own and pursue the opposite—living in authentic, connected community with others. *Hope* becomes the action God calls us to—which is often, or most likely, the opposite of what we have done before.

Sometimes God heals us through opportunities for opposite action. When I (Steve) was in my twenties, I managed a hospital group with a facility at the top of Big Bear Mountain. After a meeting one day, I made my way down the hill, hoping to avoid rush hour traffic. A few miles into my homeward commute, I came upon an accident between an eighteen-wheeler and a car that looked as if it had been flattened by a can crusher. Dust from the accident was still in the air. I was the first on the scene. The truck driver was walking around talking to himself, repeatedly raking his hands through his hair in anguish. He had failed to check his brakes before making the trek up and down the mountainside. When they went out on the way down, he swerved from lane to lane in an attempt to reduce his speed. Unfortunately, he veered into oncoming traffic at the exact moment when three people in a Volkswagen Rabbit convertible were coming around a curve on the uphill side. The collision forced the small car under the truck, bending the windshield downward and decapitating the two people in the front seat.

I walked to the car and discovered the lone survivor in the back seat. I could have offered comfort while waiting for an ambulance or helped the truck driver or others who were traumatized by the scene. But when other motorists stopped to help, I got into my car and drove down the hill to beat the traffic. When I arrived home in good time, I realized that I had walked away from where God could have used me. My shame was so great that I didn't tell anyone about the incident for more than thirty years. I saw how my impulsiveness, ego, drivenness, and cowardice had caused me to run, and I was too ashamed of my defects to share the story.

It wasn't until years later, on a New Life Ministries trip in Israel, that I felt compelled to do the *opposite* and tell my story to the one hundred forty people who had come on the trip. I confessed that I had been too preoccupied with my own life to stop and help others in need. A great burden of shame lifted off my back. But that was not the end of the story.

The very next day, as I was walking through a market, a woman in my tour group became extremely ill and needed an ambulance. I contacted a tour guide, and help was summoned. I waited with the woman for the ambulance to arrive, then got into the ambulance and went to the hospital with her. Once there, I filled out the papers for her and offered my credit card to get her admitted. When there was no room available for her, I stayed by her side in the lobby while she deliriously talked and sang to herself.

Eventually, a room was found and the tour operator arrived and took over. He told me to go back to the group and that he would help the woman from there. During the cab ride back to the hotel, I was struck by the reality of what had happened. One day after I had told the story of leaving the scene of an accident, God provided an opportunity for healing and restoration. By doing the opposite of what I had done thirty years earlier, I found release from my shame. God does things like that. He provides opportunities for us to do the opposite of our usual behaviors and uses those experiences to heal us.

Some of our healing experiences may be painful. Some of our problems have developed as a result of avoiding pain at all costs; in fact, our addictions, no matter how they manifest, may actually be addictions to comfort. We may eat or have sex or gamble or control or drink or sniff or shoot up or swallow a pill all in search of instant comfort. The problem is, these ways of seeking comfort have caused us more *dis*comfort than the original problem. By simply doing what came naturally, rather than doing the opposite of our human desires, we ended up in *deeper* pain and now have to face even *more* pain to find our way out. *But pain is not always harmful.* Pain can be the most helpful element in a struggler's life. In the healing process, it is vital that we be willing to face the pain.

Our desires, beyond comfort, relate to *freedom.* We want to be able to do what we want to do when we want to do it. In many respects, we are like adolescents, doing everything we *can* do rather than doing the things that are best for us. In our pursuit of freedom and independence, we have chained ourselves to deadly dependencies that rob us of fulfilling lives and may eventually rob us of life itself. In that light, the pain of recovery, which may seem unbearable, becomes the pain that releases us from the *real* pain.

The Courage to Take Action

A news story from August 2011 exemplifies the courage it takes to endure immediate pain to gain a future. A logger in Colorado went into the woods to load up some trees to cut for firewood. As he detached a six-ton trailer from his truck, it fell and pinned his foot. When he realized he was trapped and that no one was near enough to hear his cries for help, he used his pocketknife to cut away his boot and assess the damage to his foot. Concerned that he might soon go into shock from the injury, he made a courageous and difficult decision. He took the knife and began cutting off his toes. Already in pain, he continued cutting until he was completely free. Then he wrapped his detached foot in a shirt and drove himself to get help. Though doctors were unable to reattach his toes, the man survived and expects to be able to return to work. He endured great pain, removed the things that stood in the way of freedom and life, and then went to a place where he could be helped.

Imagine the logger's fate if he had prayed, "God, if you want me to live, remove this six-ton trailer from my foot." People pray prayers like this all the time, waiting for God to do what God is waiting for them to do. The man could have prayed for superhuman strength to push the trailer off of his foot. He could have prayed to be free of pain while he severed his toes from his foot. Or he could have waited and prayed that someone would come to help him. There is nothing wrong with any of these prayers. It would be natural to pray them, and I would imagine this man prayed every one of them while asking God to remove the horrible obstacle in his way.

But prayer was not the only thing the man was willing to do. He was also willing to act. He had courage. Courage is the willingness to do what needs to be done when it needs to be done, no matter the cost. The logger needed courage, and we need it too. We need the courage to do more than just ask God to fix or heal or change something in our lives. We need to be willing to mobilize all the courage we have to do our part in order to get the needed result, even if the price is severe pain. Courage and the willingness to endure pain are true barometers of our intentions, according to the Bible.

> So then, since Christ suffered physical pain, you must arm
> yourselves with the same attitude he had, and be ready to suffer,
> too. For if you have suffered physically for Christ, you have
> finished with sin.
>
> I PETER 4:1

What an amazing verse. Other translations reverse the order a bit and say that until we are willing to experience pain, we are not truly finished with sin. For us, we are not truly finished with our home remedies, our self-selected comfort producers, our best-friend-turned-jailer, until we are ready to experience the pain of severing our ties with whatever we have come to depend on, whatever has put us in such poor conditions, whatever we have used in our worship of the god of comfort. We must find the courage to endure the pain that will free us and lead us to ultimate, eternal comfort.

The Humility to Ask God

Step Seven sounds so simple—"We humbly asked God to remove our shortcomings"—that it would be easy to overlook the importance of each part. If we miss the part about humility, for example, we miss a major piece of the Step. Humility means that when we ask God to remove our shortcomings and defects, we are willing to do what he prescribes, in the way he prescribes.

Bill W., one of the founders of AA, provides some insight into Steps Six and Seven in *The Big Book* of Alcoholics Anonymous:

> I humbly offered myself to God, as I then understood Him,
> to do with me as he would. I placed myself unreservedly
> under His care and direction. I admitted for the first time
> that of myself I was nothing; that without him I was lost.
> I ruthlessly faced my sins and became willing to have my
> newfound Friend take them away, root and branch.[9]

> My Creator, I am now willing that you should have all of
> me, good and bad. I pray that you now remove from me
> every single defect of character which stands in the way
> of my usefulness to you and my fellows. Grant me strength,
> as I go out from here, to do your bidding. Amen.[10]

Bill W. helps us to understand that Step Seven is not just about *asking*. It is also about being humble enough to willingly *do* whatever is required. He also points us to the *purpose* and *meaning* of all of this recovery talk and these recovery Steps. He points us to the *missional* life—that is, becoming *available* to God to be used for his good purpose. We work on our character so it does not stand in the way of our usefulness. Humbly asking God to remove our shortcomings ultimately prepares us to go out and do the work of God. Simply put, God saves us so we can go out and save others. (More about that in Step Twelve.)

For now, we need to evaluate whether we are willing to ask God to remove our defects, even if it means hard and painful work. If we are not willing to ask, perhaps it is time to reread and ponder our searching and fearless inventory from Step Four before we move into or beyond Step Seven.

If we confess our sins to him, he is faithful and just to forgive us our sins and to cleanse us from all wickedness.
I JOHN 1:9

This passage is a great motivator for Step Seven. It reminds us that God is on our side, and that he wants the best for us. Because God wants the best for us, he is willing and faithful to forgive our sins and our shortcomings. All we have to do is *confess* our sins to him. Making a full and honest confession to God assumes that we are also asking him to deal with our sins. This *confessional petition* asks God to take the crummy stuff in our lives and look beyond it. If our confession is not combined with a request for forgiveness, then there isn't much reason to confess. Why admit our faults if we're not willing to have them corrected? But many of us miss that vital point in this hopeful verse.

Often, we find the most difficult person to forgive is ourselves. We may have confessed to God and to another human being, and yet still experience great guilt and shame over our offenses. But John tells us that God will forgive us and cleanse us if we confess. We need to accept that forgiveness and cleansing. We need to confess with the expectation of total forgiveness and banish the notion that we need to feel worse about what we have done. When we meet God, are we hoping to be rewarded for feeling bad about our failures? If that's what we're on a path to do, congratulations will come—but it will be Satan who congratulates us. He has us right where he wants us—ruminating and obsessing about how our sins prevent us from pleasing God or being used by God. No, if we confess our sins to God, we need to be ready to accept *everything* he offers us, which includes total forgiveness, complete cleansing, and freedom from our chains and bondage.

Step Seven seems like an easy one at first glance. It looks like we're just making another request, like the thousands of other pleas, demands, questions, and supplications we have offered to God in the past. But it's not so simple to *prepare our hearts* to ask in the right way, with humility and expectation. And it's also not easy to live out what Christ has done for us. We need to ask and then live as if what we asked for is already a reality—that we are truly clean, fully forgiven, and able to live completely free in Christ, ready to take the next step for a deeper and richer life with our fellow strugglers. We clean up the mess we have made of our relationship with God so that we can move forward and clean up the mess we have made with other people. Step Seven increases the quality of our insight into ourselves so that we can increase the quality of our relational lives.

To move forward, we take the defects we have discovered in our souls and humbly lay them before the Creator of the universe and the source of our salvation and transformation. We humble ourselves before almighty God and ask him to remove these shortcomings. We want a better life, and we want to grow *toward* him rather than stagnate in the foolishness of our self-obsession. We want new tools and new insights, and we are willing to do whatever God wants us to do so that we may become who he wants us to become. And though it is only natural to want lightning-quick change in our lives, we must expect that the removal of our shortcomings will take a lot of time. It will also require the help of other people, because it is through other people that God does some of his toughest work. We ask God to remove our defects, and we wait willingly for challenges, hardships, and pain to be used as the heavy equipment needed to bring change.

STEP SEVEN BIBLE STUDIES

Study #1: Humility or Humiliation?

This study is based on Luke 14:7-14 (page 1316 in *The Life Recovery Bible*). You may want to read Luke 14:1-14 several times before working on the study.

1. SOME PRACTICAL ADVICE

Humility does not seem to be a natural part of human behavior. Based on what Jesus said in Luke 14, it's more common for us to seek the place of honor in social situations. Some people seek the praise of others in an overt way. They seek to build themselves up in the eyes of others. Others are more covert—we don't see what they're doing until later—but their intentions are the same. Either way, to some degree, we all have to fight the urge to make ourselves look good.

The opposite—acting in humility—is something we have to learn. So when we read in Step Seven that we must *humbly* ask God to remove our shortcomings, we know we must be *intentional*, not simply following our natural tendencies. On the other hand, could we *arrogantly* ask God to remove our shortcomings? Maybe if we were trying to clean up our lives on our own and merely giving lip service to God. But then we would be like the person Jesus mentioned who sought the seat of honor, only to be humiliated by being asked to move to the foot of the table. Notice how clearly Jesus spoke:

> When Jesus noticed that all who had come to the dinner were
> trying to sit in the seats of honor near the head of the table, he
> gave them this advice: "When you are invited to a wedding
> feast, don't sit in the seat of honor. What if someone who is
> more distinguished than you has also been invited? The host
> will come and say, 'Give this person your seat.' Then you will
> be embarrassed, and you will have to take whatever seat is left
> at the foot of the table!"
>
> LUKE 14:7-9

In what ways have you "sought the seat of honor"—to make your-self look good—in the past?

Has this ever backfired on you, as in the story told by Jesus? What happened? How did you handle it?

Have you ever acted in humility and then been honored? How did that feel?

2. TRUE HUMILITY

Humility is an interesting word. It's not the kind of thing you can write a book about, describing how you achieved it. Bragging about humility doesn't make any sense. Seeking to be recognized for our humility leads only to false pride, the very antithesis of true humility. True humility affects our behavior, since it comes from the heart.

> *Instead, take the lowest place at the foot of the table. Then when your host sees you, he will come and say, 'Friend, we have a better place for you!' Then you will be honored in front of all the other guests. For those who exalt themselves will be humbled, and those who humble themselves will be exalted.*
> LUKE 14:10-11

Write your own definition of humility.

Describe how your definition fits with the example Jesus gave—the opposite of seeking to be exalted.

What has your recovery journey taught you about humility so far?

Describe an example of how you have demonstrated humility in your recovery.

3. A STEP BEYOND HUMILITY

Jesus then expanded his definition of humility to include acts of service to others.

> *Then [Jesus] turned to his host. "When you put on a luncheon or a banquet," he said, "don't invite your friends, brothers, relatives, and rich neighbors. For they will invite you back, and that will be your only reward. Instead, invite the poor, the crippled, the lame, and the blind. Then at the resurrection of the righteous, God will reward you for inviting those who could not repay you."*
> LUKE 14:12-14

Humility isn't just about seeking or not seeking a place of honor at an event or seeking or not seeking the praise of others. Humility has more to do with our *attitude* toward other people, especially those who have no ability to repay us for our actions. Humility is expressed in acts of service to others.

If we let Jesus' reference to "the poor, the crippled, the lame, and the blind" symbolize anyone who has needs and who can't pay us back, who in your life is an example of this kind of person?

Make a list of the kinds of actions you could take that would fulfill what Jesus talks about in this passage.

Our definition of humility now includes two ideas. First, we don't seek the praise of others, either directly or indirectly. Second, we do seek to give to and care for others who have no way to repay us.

Study #2: An Expression of Joy at Forgiveness

This study is based on Psalm 103:1-18 (page 750 in *The Life Recovery Bible*), a psalm of David. Read these verses several times before working on the study.

1. THE JOY OF FORGIVENESS

Many of the psalms begin with a complaint, with a request that God destroy the enemy, or with some other negative theme. But even though these psalms begin with negative themes, the writer always ends up praising God for his love and faithfulness. Psalm 103 is different; joy and praise are woven throughout the passage from beginning to end.

We need to meditate more often on the "praise psalms" like Psalm 103. When we are struggling with our problems, it seems so much easier to be negative and complain. We can easily relate to the negative themes in so many of the psalms. But that only keeps us stuck where we don't want to be. Our lives are healthier when we admit the negative but focus on the positive—on what is *good* in our lives—and on being grateful for what God has done. A spirit of gratitude is essential to our healing and recovery. Perhaps the main focus of our gratitude is the recognition that we have been forgiven.

> *Let all that I am praise the LORD;*
>   *with my whole heart, I will praise his holy name.*
> *Let all that I am praise the LORD;*
>   *may I never forget the good things he does for me.*
> *He forgives all my sins*
>   *and heals all my diseases.*
> *He redeems me from death*
>   *and crowns me with love and tender mercies.*
> *He fills my life with good things.*
>   *My youth is renewed like the eagle's!*
>
> PSALM 103:1-5

Since you started your recovery journey, what are some of the positive things God has begun to fill your life with?

David is also joyful about the negative things that God has taken away. At this point in your life and in your recovery, what are some of the negatives that God has removed?

2. THE GIFTS WE RECEIVE FROM GOD

David tells us about other things that God wants to add to our lives. Many of them are abstractions, such as our not being punished for our sins and not being dealt with harshly. David certainly had his share of negatives. For twenty years, he had to run and hide from King Saul, who had every intention of killing him. David hid in the barren wilderness, just as we have hidden in our addictions, compulsions, and dependencies. He had to take care of himself, as well as the small army of men who traveled with him. This was not the life he expected when he was anointed as king. David complains in many of his psalms, but he always proclaims God's goodness and faithfulness by the end. He always rejoices as he sees God at work in his life. In this psalm, his heart is full of gratitude.

> *The LORD gives righteousness*
> *and justice to all who are treated unfairly.*
> *He revealed his character to Moses*
> *and his deeds to the people of Israel.*
> *The LORD is compassionate and merciful,*
> *slow to get angry and filled with unfailing love.*
> *He will not constantly accuse us,*
> *nor remain angry forever.*
> *He does not punish us for all our sins;*
> *he does not deal harshly with us, as we deserve.*
> *For his unfailing love toward those who fear him*
> *is as great as the height of the heavens above the earth.*
> *He has removed our sins as far from us*
> *as the east is from the west.*
>
> PSALM 103:6-12

There have certainly been ups and downs since the beginning of your recovery journey. But as you consider this psalm, stop and take time to be grateful for the good things that have happened in your life.

What unexpected blessings from God have you experienced at this point in your healing and recovery?

David refers twice to God's "unfailing love," yet if you read the story of his time running for his life, he probably didn't have a continual awareness of God's unfailing love. It was seen only as he looked back.

> Look back over the time of your recovery and list the ways in which God has shown his unfailing love to you.

Notice the last phrase in this passage, the primary example of God's unfailing love: "He has removed our sins as far from us as the east is from the west." There are two things to contemplate based on this statement: (1) our sins are removed from God's presence and from us as well, and (2) our sins are removed an infinite distance. We cannot define how far it is from the east to the west, and that's how far God has taken our sins from us.

> What does it mean to you that God has taken your sins from you and separated them from you an infinite distance?

> What are some things from your inventory that you need to believe God has removed from you?

3. A NEW RELATIONSHIP

Many people don't have good relationships with their earthly fathers. They may have been abusive, controlling, or simply not there. Some fathers are present in the home, but not involved. David's father forgot he even had a son named David. When the prophet Samuel came to anoint the next king, he told Jesse to assemble his sons.

After determining that none of the seven older boys was to be chosen, Samuel asked if there was another son. Only then did Jesse say, "There is still the youngest, . . . but he's out in the fields watching the sheep and goats" (1 Samuel 16:11).

David must have worked through his father issues (as shown by what he says in Psalm 103). But if your relationship with your father is problematic or unresolved, you may need to envision the image of a wonderful grandfather or the father of a friend to understand what David says here.

> *The LORD is like a father to his children,*
>   *tender and compassionate to those who fear him.*
> *For he knows how weak we are;*
>   *he remembers we are only dust.*
> *Our days on earth are like grass;*
>   *like wildflowers, we bloom and die.*
> *The wind blows, and we are gone—*
>   *as though we had never been here.*
> *But the love of the LORD remains forever*
>   *with those who fear him.*
> *His salvation extends to the children's children*
>   *of those who are faithful to his covenant,*
>   *of those who obey his commandments!*
>
> PSALM 103:13-18

David tells us that God knows us and knows our weaknesses, and that he is careful in how he treats us. If humility includes the idea of accepting our weaknesses, where are you still struggling to be strong?

When David says we are like the grass that is here and then gone, his purpose is not to emphasize the temporary nature of our lives. Instead, he's drawing a contrast between our short lives and the length and breadth of God's love for us—it remains forever. Write God a note, thanking him for his infinite ability to love you.

Study #3: The Promise of Recovery

This study is based on Isaiah 49:8-13 (page 903 in *The Life Recovery Bible*). Read these verses several times before working on the study.

1. FROM DARKNESS TO LIGHT

In Isaiah 49, God promises to restore Israel to its land and its heritage. The book of Isaiah can be divided into two parts—before and during Israel's exile in Babylon. Chapters 1–39 addressed the people prior to their defeat and capture. It is filled with warnings, which the people ignored. Chapters 40–66 were written around the time the people were taken captive and relocated. The prophet Isaiah sought to comfort the people and remind them of God's love. During this time, the people of Judah and Israel had lost everything and were living in a strange land. In their minds, God had abandoned them. All was hopeless. But Isaiah sought to show them that God was still there, and that there would come a time when they would experience a restored relationship with him.

When we were acting out our addictions or dependencies or were lost in our problems, it may have felt as if God had abandoned us.

Now that we are in recovery, we can find interesting parallels between what God promised Israel and what he has for us in our recovery journey.

This is what the LORD says:
"At just the right time, I will respond to you.
*   On the day of salvation I will help you.*
I will protect you and give you to the people
*   as my covenant with them.*
Through you I will reestablish the land of Israel
*   and assign it to its own people again.*
I will say to the prisoners, 'Come out in freedom,'
*   and to those in darkness, 'Come into the light.'*
They will be my sheep, grazing in green pastures
*   and on hills that were previously bare.*
They will neither hunger nor thirst.
*   The searing sun will not reach them anymore.*
For the LORD in his mercy will lead them;
*   he will lead them beside cool waters.*
And I will make my mountains into level paths for them.
*   The highways will be raised above the valleys."*

ISAIAH 49:8-11

God's timing is often not our timing. As you look back on your recovery journey, what things happened "at just the right time" for you?

Isaiah used the phrase "come into the light" to speak to those in darkness. He emphasized the extreme contrast between darkness and light. How would you describe your recovery journey as a "coming into the light"?

2. A NEW FREEDOM

In Isaiah 49:8-13, the prophet reminded the people of God's faithfulness. They would one day return to their land. And when they experienced the recovery of all they had lost, they would rejoice. When they returned to the Promised Land, Isaiah reminded them, it would be a time of great joy. At this point, though, they were to focus on God's faithfulness and remember that he is the giver of comfort.

> *See, my people will return from far away,*
> *from lands to the north and west,*
> *and from as far south as Egypt.*
> *Sing for joy, O heavens!*
> *Rejoice, O earth!*
> *Burst into song, O mountains!*
> *For the LORD has comforted his people*
> *and will have compassion on them in their suffering.*
> ISAIAH 49:12-13

How has the Lord comforted you during your recovery process?

How have you thanked him?

Those who walk in the light enjoy freedom. John tells us that Jesus is our light and that "his life brought light to everyone" (John 1:4). So for us, walking in the light means walking with Jesus.

Study #4: A Prayer for You

This study is based on Ephesians 3:14-19 (page 1513 in *The Life Recovery Bible*). Read the third chapter of Ephesians several times before working on the study.

1. A PRAYER FOR GROWTH

When we surrender our wills and our lives to God, we become a part of all the people over the ages who have followed God and who know and love Jesus. If that is true, then it's also true that when the apostle Paul prayed for the Ephesians centuries ago, he was also praying for us. We need what he prayed for just as much as those who first read his letter. We continue to need strength for the journey, as well as direction and an experience of God's love. Here's how Paul prayed for us:

> *When I think of all this, I fall to my knees and pray to the Father, the Creator of everything in heaven and on earth. I pray that from his glorious, unlimited resources he will empower you with inner strength through his Spirit. Then Christ will make his home in your hearts as you trust in him. Your roots will grow down into God's love and keep you strong.*
>
> EPHESIANS 3:14-17

Strength for the journey, especially inner strength, is essential. Where do you need to be strengthened today?

God's resources are unlimited. Write him a list of what you would
add to Paul's prayer for your life today.

2. FILLING OUR NEEDS

God's love for us is unfathomable. In his letter to the Romans, Paul
says that "when we were utterly helpless. . . . God showed his great
love for us by sending Christ to die for us while we were still sinners"
(Romans 5:6-8). Paul also says we might be willing to die for a really
great person, but not for someone described as a helpless sinner. Yet
that is exactly what Jesus Christ did. We don't have to clean up our
act for God to love us; we clean up our act *because* he loves us. There's
a big difference between those two. Here's how Paul described God's
love for us:

> *And may you have the power to understand, as all God's people*
> *should, how wide, how long, how high, and how deep his love*
> *is. May you experience the love of Christ, though it is too great*
> *to understand fully. Then you will be made complete with all*
> *the fullness of life and power that comes from God.*
> EPHESIANS 3:18-19

Describe as best you can what you believe about God's love for you,
as shown through the sacrifice of Jesus Christ.

The more we understand the love of Christ, the more complete we
become through the "life and power that comes from God." What
an incredible promise! It's time to put away our self-condemning
attitudes and bask in the reality of God's unfailing love for us!

STEP EIGHT

We made a list of all persons we had harmed and
became willing to make amends to them all.

Do to others as you would like them to do to you.
LUKE 6:31

Miranda's Story of Recovery: Everything Is Different Now

My name is Miranda. I am a believer in Jesus Christ, and I struggle
with codependency. One year ago, I was at the lowest point in my
life. I was depressed, guilt ridden, abused, hurting, alone, and hopeless. I honestly didn't think I was going to make it. I had let my
life get so awful that I really couldn't even move. You know how
you have those dreams where someone is chasing you and you can't
run or scream? That was my waking life. I was paralyzed and didn't
know what to do or if there was any chance that things would ever
get better.

I really can't explain how things changed so much this past year,
but everything is different now. Today, I have a peace inside me that
defies explanation. I look around at what I have and I can hardly
believe how far I've come. My boys are happy and healthy; I have my
dream job, a wonderful home, a supportive church family, the best
friends I could ever imagine, an amazing family, and a Savior who
loves me. It is almost unreal, and I feel so blessed. Honestly though,
my life has been hard, and according to the statistics, I shouldn't
be here and shouldn't have the job or the family I have. There is no
logical reason why I have made it as far as I have—only by the grace

of God. He has always been with me, guiding my steps (when I let him) and watching over me. His grace has changed everything. I'll tell you why I say that.

My parents both had very difficult childhoods. My dad grew up on the streets, his mom was an alcoholic, and he never knew his dad. He basically raised himself and took care of his mom. He never had a normal childhood—not even one normal day, so it's no surprise he didn't know how to be a dad. When I was growing up, he never told me he loved me or showed me affection. He wasn't there for my sports events or special days. He wasn't there to protect me from the world or to tell me everything was going to be okay. He didn't know how to do these things, or even that he was supposed to. The things that every little girl needs to feel safe and protected in the world were kept from me. My dad loved me, in a serious and disciplined way, and he spent time with me, but it always involved rigid rules, correct grammar, and the expectation of perfection. Everything was about discipline; tenderness, fun, laughter, and having a good time weren't part of the deal between my dad and me.

My mom had an equally hard childhood. Her mom was married several times, and she, too, never knew her dad. She wasn't given the time or attention she needed, so she found it in all the wrong places. When she was teenager, she met an older man, married him, and ended up pregnant with my big brother at seventeen. The man she married was very abusive. He beat her all the time in front of my brother. My brother told me stories of how he watched our mom get beaten so hard that she passed out, and then her husband used her face to wipe her blood off the kitchen counter. There were many similar stories, but you get the idea. My mom finally mustered the courage to leave after many years of abuse, and that's when she met my dad. Their marriage lasted nine years.

My childhood was pretty normal during my parents' marriage. I don't have any negative memories, only memories of camping, going to the zoo, happy birthdays, and happy holidays. Everything was good for a while. Then my mom walked out. There really wasn't a good reason, except that she had never gotten help or healed from the abuse she had endured. She wasn't close to God, and when you don't have God to rely on, there is always an aching in your soul for something or someone to fill that void. My dad couldn't meet all of her needs, so she went looking for something else to fulfill her.

I can't even count the number of men my mom had in and out of our lives from the time I was nine until I was seventeen. I can remember one day taking seven messages for her, all from different men. She eventually married one of them and settled down for about five years, until he no longer filled the emptiness inside of her. Then it was back to the same old thing—one relationship after another.

I am very fortunate I was never physically or sexually abused by any of the men in my mom's life. I realize that is something that happens all too often when a woman has a lot of men around her daughters. Nevertheless, my mom's sexual escapades hurt me deeply, as I was often aware of what was going on. She also had little time for me and never seemed to care about what I was doing. I was alone a lot and learned how to take care of myself. I became the caretaker of our home—cooking, cleaning, and even buying groceries as a teenager when I had money. I basically raised myself and became desperate for a normal family.

After my parents' divorce, my dad followed a similar path to my mom's—in and out of relationships, though not as many as my mom. He would get serious with someone for a few years, but then they would break up and he would start fresh with someone else. This pattern lasted until after I was married; he is currently on wife number four. I always felt as if I was in the way when it came to my dad—like an inconvenience. I felt bad for him when he had to drive over to pick me up every other weekend. I felt bad that he had to pay my mom child support when he hardly had enough money to support himself. I felt bad for everyone, and I felt responsible for all that my parents went through.

I guess that's where my codependency began. As a little girl, I was responsible for taking care of the household with my mom, and I felt responsible for all of my dad's emotions as well. It's no wonder that I jumped into several abusive relationships myself. I always thought I could help everyone, that I could fix them. That's what life was like for me. I really had no boundaries and let everyone treat me as they pleased. I did not have any standards of my own. I didn't know I was important enough to be treated kindly. I didn't expect people to treat me the way I treated them.

I accepted Jesus Christ as my Lord and Savior when I was thirteen. I found an amazing church and youth group and put all of my trust in Jesus. My relationship with him helped me through so many times. I read the Bible, spent time in prayer, and believed with all my heart. After an amazing week at church camp, I got baptized, and it seemed as if my life was heading in a good direction.

The only problem was that I was broken inside and had two broken parents. We never really stood a chance. Even though I had Jesus in my life and wanted to live my life right for him, I had a very big, empty hole in my heart that I didn't even know was there.

As a teenager, I fell in love with a boy and wanted to spend my life with him, but he cheated on me. All I wanted was a family, and I was working hard to find one with any guy who would have me.

After my first relationship ended, I quickly moved on to the next. I fell in love with Tony immediately. He seemed to have things together, more than I ever had. He liked me, and we spent every day together for the first few months. I'm not sure exactly when our relationship went bad, but my obsession for him to love me and always stay with me seemed to fuel the fire. When Tony started cheating on me early in our relationship, it devastated me, but not enough for me to leave him. In fact, it didn't matter what he did; I loved him and just wanted him to stay with me. I allowed Tony to treat me any way he wanted without recourse. He did give me one wonderful thing, though. At the age of seventeen, I conceived my first son. He's now a teenager himself and one of the loves of my life.

Back then, though, life was hard. When I was three months pregnant, Tony had an affair with my best friend and tried to force me to have an abortion. When I refused, he tried several other things to try to cause me to lose our baby. Thankfully, those attempts failed, and I gave birth to a healthy little boy not long after my eighteenth birthday. I knew the life I was living was wrong, but for some reason I just couldn't stop. I needed the validation of a man so badly that I let sin rule my life. I was a desperate, broken girl, now trying to take care of another life, and I had no idea what I was doing.

Though I still tried to make things work with Tony, he continued to tear me down, calling me worthless and no good. He told me that no other man would ever want me because I had a baby. I guess I believed him, because I stayed. He left me on Mother's Day, the day our son turned six weeks old. I wish I could say that was the last of it, but unfortunately, things went back and forth for a couple more years. My relationship with Tony lasted four years in total, and he was verbally and emotionally abusive and left me terribly scarred emotionally. One day, I finally had enough and ended things. He was heavily into drugs, he didn't want anything to do with his son or me, and he was unable to help us financially.

After ending things with Tony, I turned my life back over to God. I moved to California with my parents and began going to college. I also began attending church again and decided I would try to get things right this time. I made myself all sorts of promises, especially this one: "I will never let a man treat me like that again." I really wanted to make a good home for my son. I loved him so much, and he brought me so much joy. The problem was that I still had a gaping hole in my heart, and I thought it could only be filled by a man who loved me. Even as a rededicated Christian, I couldn't see that I already had what I needed in Jesus. I just continued to make bad relationship decisions.

Over the next two years, I had several relationships—one that resulted in a broken engagement; another in which I fell head over heels but then messed up; and then my current relationship with my husband, Nathan, whom I married after only three weeks. Yes, I met my husband one night at a bar and we got married three weeks later. He was my fairy tale, my knight in shining armor. He was everything

I wanted, everything I needed, and he filled the holes in my heart from all the neglect and hurt I had from my past. We were crazy in love—for a while—and for a while I had everything I had ever wanted.

I married a Marine, a man who wanted to have a life with me and was willing to raise my son. The problem with marrying someone you've known for only three weeks is that you really know nothing about him. We began fighting immediately—and I mean immediately, starting with a huge fight on our wedding night. A life of chaos ensued, getting worse and worse as time went on. I'm not blaming my husband for the terrible life we had. He, too, came from a very broken childhood. We were both desperately looking for someone to fill the gaping holes in our souls—someone who would meet our every need, fix all our problems, and give us the love we'd never had.

Three days after our wedding, Nathan left for Japan for six months, but that only meant our fighting continued over the phone. But we loved each other, and I didn't think too much about it. I was never going to get divorced like my parents had, so there was no reason to think much about it. When Nathan returned, I quickly got pregnant with my second son, Jimmy. Two weeks after Jimmy was born, Nathan left for Iraq. This tour wasn't too bad, only four months long, and we were able to stay in touch. I sent him a picture of our son every day, and he called home at every opportunity. He returned shortly before his enlistment in the Marine Corps ended, and we decided to move back home to Arkansas.

Things were very hard for us for many years; we had brutal fights with a lot of verbal and emotional abuse. I really had no boundaries and was so desperate for love that it didn't matter to me how I was treated. My only requirement was that he stay with me, which he did. Even when he probably should have left, he never did. In response to his verbal abuse, I abandoned him emotionally and put my boys and everyone else before him. I never gave him the love he deserved as my husband, and he never gave me the tenderness I deserved as a wife. We were both totally messed up.

Shortly after our move to Arkansas, he joined the National Guard and was quickly deployed, this time for fifteen months. This deployment was brutal for both of us, but it gave us a break from our fighting. I had a miscarriage right before he left, but I managed to finish college and graduate with an accounting degree. I found a job at an accounting firm and worked full time, while also raising two kids on my own and trying to prepare for my husband's return from war.

During my final semester of college, when my older son was in first grade, we found out he had cone-rod retinal dystrophy (CRD), a progressive disease that leaves a person legally blind with the probability of completely losing his or her vision. This really broke my heart. My son's vision was diagnosed at 20/400, with a severe color deficiency and limited peripheral vision. This was the first time I was unable to do something to help my child. I wanted to take away the disease for him so badly, but there was nothing I could do.

After my husband's return from war, our marriage continued to get worse. We were like the perfect storm, two broken people trying to make a life together, but without the right tools. We both were Christians and believed in God, but it wasn't enough. Our lives were hell together.

I don't know what happened to the promise I had made to myself not to allow someone to treat me so badly. I don't know why we stayed together for so long. I guess we both had pledged that, because our parents' divorces had been so devastating for us, we would never do that to our children. Also, we both loved God and knew that he hated divorce. It wasn't until things started getting really physical that I knew I had to do something. Our kids had witnessed many years of terrible screaming and horrible threats, but they had never before seen Nathan hit me. In the final days, it was like a nonstop horror movie. What's sad is that I never once thought I deserved to be treated better. I thought this was just how life was; dysfunction was all I had ever known. I was so insecure, so low, so depressed that I could not see the truth. I never demanded to be treated better, and neither did Nathan.

I remember the beginning of the end of my abuse. I will never forget how I felt that day or how desperate I was. I was on the back porch, devastated and full of fear after Nathan had hit me. With my eyes full of tears and my voice barely above a whisper, I looked up to the sky and said, "Jesus, save me." It was then that he started the real change in me. I had believed in Jesus since I was thirteen. I trusted him for everything. I just didn't know who I was. But calling out to him for help that day led to my new life.

I knew things had to change. I was terrified of my husband, almost to the point of being paralyzed, but Jesus gave me a psalm that helped me begin to move toward a better life.

> *Have mercy on me, O God, have mercy!*
>   *I look to you for protection.*
> *I will hide beneath the shadow of your wings*
>   *until the danger passes by.*
> *I cry out to God Most High,*
>   *to God who will fulfill his purpose for me.*
> *He will send help from heaven to rescue me,*
>   *disgracing those who hound me.*
> *My God will send forth his unfailing love and faithfulness.*
>
> *I am surrounded by fierce lions*
>   *who greedily devour human prey—*
> *whose teeth pierce like spears and arrows,*
>   *and whose tongues cut like swords.*
>
> *Be exalted, O God, above the highest heavens!*
>   *May your glory shine over all the earth.*
>
> *My enemies have set a trap for me.*
>   *I am weary from distress.*
> *They have dug a deep pit in my path,*
>   *but they themselves have fallen into it.*

My heart is confident in you, O God;
  my heart is confident.
    No wonder I can sing your praises!
Wake up, my heart!
    Wake up, O lyre and harp!
    I will wake the dawn with my song.
I will thank you, Lord, among all the people.
    I will sing your praises among the nations.
  For your unfailing love is as high as the heavens.
    Your faithfulness reaches to the clouds.

Be exalted, O God, above the highest heavens.
    May your glory shine over all the earth.
PSALM 57

This psalm helped me to see that I could hide in the shadow of God's wings, that he loved me, and that he would protect me. I had never understood that God loved me. I thought love was only discipline or doing for others. I never understood that I was God's beloved daughter and that he cared about me. I never understood that he did not want me in an abusive relationship and that he did not choose that for me. I understood the legalistic side of God, but not God the loving Father. I have a Father in heaven who loves me.

I knew I had to do something about my life, so I sent an e-mail to the pastor of the church I attended: "I know I'm not a member of your church, and I don't always attend, but I need help with my marriage. If we don't get help, it won't last one more day."

Thankfully, he responded quickly with an amazing answer—the name and phone number of a mature Christian counselor. I called her and began seeing her almost immediately. I truly believe that God has worked through her. I know she's not the one who saved my life, but God used her to help save my life. Through her counseling, I began to see all of the lies I had believed about myself, my family, my children, my marriage, and God.

Having God (as I now know him) in my life, along with my counselor, my recovery program, and my small group of girls from the Step study has turned my life around more than I could ever share in a brief testimony. I cannot believe the joy and the peace I have. I cannot believe what I have been missing my whole life. If only I had known it would be this easy. Before, I was totally isolated; now I have so much support and love in my life that my life is a constant song of joy. Things do not always go my way, and they are not always easy. I still have a lot of problems and I'm separated from my husband, but in the midst of everything, I have peace, and things are always better than they were.

During my weekly visits with my counselor, I share my thoughts and feelings and she guides me into truth. She has taught me that I am not worthless, that God does not want horrible things for me, and that I am good. I doubted myself every day of my life until I was taught differently. I'll never forget what my counselor told me one day when I was really down on myself for the way I had lived my life and what I had put my children through. She said, "Miranda, if my parents taught me only to speak Spanish, would I be upset with myself—or would anyone else be mad at me—for not knowing English? We only know what we have been taught. We cannot live our entire lives speaking one language and then expect to be fluent in another language the next day. It takes time to learn a new language, and it will take time to retrain yourself into healthy habits." She was so right, and she has helped me so much. I cannot adequately express how much Christian counseling has helped me.

My Step study has been just as valuable in my healing process. It has given me two powerful tools that have helped me turn things around. I actually get up every morning and smile. I have peace within me because I am no longer desperate for something that can never truly fill me. I'm not saying that a healthy relationship would not be wonderful—I would still like to have one of those someday—but my happiness is no longer found in *needing* one. The foundation of my security is in God. I love to serve him, I love to sing to him,

I love to worship him, and I love knowing he is with me. All that I need I have in him. He was always with me before, but I couldn't see him because I didn't know who I was. I am a daughter of God, with all the rights and privileges. I belong to God and I trust in him. I now know that I don't have to be an enabler, a people pleaser, or a doormat. I am worth more than that. My worth comes not from what I do, but from *who I am.*

I am nowhere near perfection; I'm still in recovery and dealing with the effects of my bad decisions. But I have hope. I take things one day at a time and remember that I am not in control. God is. I must act in faith and trust that he will be with me, guiding my steps.

I've discovered that the Twelve Steps really are the key to healing and lasting change. I follow these Steps and reread them to remember how I should live. Every principle is important and vital to a changed life. From Step One (realizing my life was unmanageable), to Step Two (believing that I matter to God), to Step Three (choosing to commit my life to God), to Step Four (honestly examining my life), to Step Five (confessing my faults), to Steps Six and Seven (submitting to every change God wants to make in my life), to Steps Eight and Nine (making amends), to Step Ten (admitting when I am wrong), to Step Eleven (spending time with God daily), to Step Twelve (bringing this good news to others), these principles are truly life changing.

One more thing: I would never have come this far if not for my amazing friends. I have so many wonderful people in my life who give me support and listen to me anytime I need to talk or vent. I also have a faithful accountability partner who keeps me grounded and supports me continually, even if I call her twenty times a day. She always reminds me that I have to take things one day at a time or one moment at a time. We are all works in progress.

The healthier I get, the healthier my family and everyone else around me becomes. It has been amazing to see both of my parents grow and change just because of my growth. When I stopped enabling and started loving people like Jesus did, it affected everyone, even my children.

STEP EIGHT INSIGHT

If you have lived detached and isolated from others until now, Step Eight is the first of three Steps that will change your life. If you're one who has a difficult time looking other people in the eye, or if you feel self-conscious about the life of rebellion you have lived, this Step will begin to unchain you from your past and release you into current, confessed-up relationships. Step Eight leaves the past where it should be—in the past—and begins to move us out of ourselves and into healed and restored relationships. And it all begins with a list.

Lists are valuable tools in completing the requirements of the Twelve Steps. In Step Four, we listed all of the shortcomings and defects we knew about ourselves. Now we need to make a list of people who have been affected by those shortcomings and defects. This will be a list of people we know we have harmed. This is our trail of tears, our confession that we have damaged and hurt people who expected more from us. Our lists may contain the names of people to whom we have done horrible things that cannot be undone or taken back. But it is also a list of *potential restoration*. More than anything, it is a list of hearts that may be healed and restored when we honestly seek to make amends for what we have said and what we have done.

When we start this list of people we have harmed, the names of certain people will naturally jump to the top because it is so easy to recognize the hurt we have caused them. The abused and the broken are obvious entries. We realize we are thieves, and we take note of those we have robbed—whether we stole their money, their innocence, their love, or their time.

Some people's names will be on our lists because our sin against them, or the impact of our sins, is so large that it cannot be ignored. When I (Steve) sat down to make my list, the first name was not difficult to recall. It was a young woman I had gotten pregnant and taken to abort our child. I put her name at the top of my list because my time with her was the most regrettable time of my life. Forcing her to have an abortion was the most terrible thing I had done.

We will also need to contact people who might not be as obvious—those who have felt our rejection or abandonment. We may have slighted them or intentionally put them out of our lives because we refused to accept them for who they are. We may have judged them and shared those judgments with others. No matter how big or small the offense, we are to write the names of those who most likely do not think fondly of us or of their time with us.

Step Eight is a tough way of carrying out Luke 6:31: "Do to others as you would like them to do to you." Wouldn't we all love to get a call from someone who hurt us and hear him or her express regret and remorse? Wouldn't we love to know that, in the end, this person was not gloating over what was done to us, but instead wanted to make it right? Most likely, such restitution has rarely happened in our lives because so few people can humble themselves enough to admit they were wrong, let alone be willing to make amends to those who paid the price for their actions. Since we reached a place of humility in Step Seven, we begin the process of making a list of those we have harmed.

Once our lists are complete, we must once again exercise our will. Each entry may come with a host of excuses for why we should not make amends. In our unwillingness, we will create invalid reasons for why it would not be helpful to make amends. But this Step concludes with a very significant word: *all*. Our willingness to make amends must encompass *every* entry on our lists. Later we might discover some valid reasons that it wouldn't be wise or helpful to make contact or amends, but for now we are called to be *willing* to make amends to *everyone* we have harmed.

Willingness might be easier if we only had to say we were sorry or ask for forgiveness. But the Step requires far more than a simple *request*. We must become willing to make amends—to make things right—with the people we have harmed. And because we are human, we find it is so much easier to express regret than to take the steps needed for true restitution. If our infraction involves the theft of money, for example, apologizing is obviously not enough.

Willingness to make amends requires restitution and repayment of what was taken. We cannot say we are willing to make amends until we have counted the full cost of making things right with *everyone*. In the case of money, that means paying back what we can, when we can.

Willingness is a huge word in the recovery process. We cannot work any of the Steps without being willing. And we cannot work any of the Steps *well* unless and until we have come to the place where we are willing to do whatever it takes, not just what is comfortable. It's not easy to be responsible, consistent, and dependable when addiction and dysfunction have prevented us from maturing as other adults have matured. But when we commit to something and do not back away from the commitment, our character is built and maturity increased. Often, what is so difficult to imagine or accomplish will be the very thing God uses to catch us up, grow us up, and create in us a clean heart. All of this begins with our complete and total willingness.

> *You will always harvest what you plant. Those who live only*
> *to satisfy their own sinful nature will harvest decay and death*
> *from that sinful nature. But those who live to please the Spirit*
> *will harvest everlasting life from the Spirit.*
> GALATIANS 6:7-8

Simply put, we reap what we sow. Making our lists is *not* sowing. Making our lists is *preparing the seed* to be sown. We will sow our seed in the next Step, and what we reap will be the amazing experience of *restoration* and *reconciliation*. But first we must make our lists.

When developing our lists, we must be careful about a couple of things. One is *rationalization*. We can rationalize a lot of people off our lists by focusing on what they did to us or comparing their horrible act with our merely crummy act. Don't give in to rationalization. Do what responsible list-makers do and focus on the impact of *your own* behavior on that person. What happened and what was the result? If the result or impact of what you did or said was anything less than helpful in developing the other person into a better human being, you need to consider that person for the list.

This standard is important because it helps us work through our natural denial. It may be easy to deny or minimize the impact of our behavior or our words on other people. If we include not only the names of those whose lives we have damaged but also those whose lives we have not improved, then we will be more likely to include all those who need to be on the list. We can also, in moments of clarity and sanity, remove from the list people who were not damaged by our behavior—but it's better to have them on the list and then take them off than to never consider them.

Another caution is against *defensiveness*. It is easy to focus on and obsess about who should be contacting *us* and to decide that the other person should be the one to make the first move. We have to get beyond our naturally defensive thoughts and focus on our own responsibility. We must concentrate on our own behavior and not delve into the depths of the other person's responsibility. Thus, we make amends for the ten dollars we stole even if the other person has stolen one hundred dollars from us.

As tough as they are, these are the principles we must follow in the list-making process. They will move us toward the willingness to make amends instead of allowing us to refuse to do so based on what is owed to us. Even if we're *not yet* at the willingness stage, we need to make the list. Even if we never intend to make amends, we need to make the list. Making the list is the next step in the process toward both *willingness* and *making amends*.

Kathy's Story of Recovery: Praying for Continual Awareness

Being raised in a Christian home, I first came to realize my need for salvation at the age of seven. On a few successive Sunday mornings, several of my friends had walked forward in church to "make a decision for Christ." I asked my parents what this meant, and they explained it to me in terms I could understand. That's how I became aware of my need to ask Jesus Christ for forgiveness and to accept that he died to pay for and save me from the punishment of sin. I was baptized at the age of twelve, when I came to realize that Jesus gave me the power to live my life in victory over sin, according to his death and resurrection.

The next major decision in my life came at nineteen, in the spring after I graduated from high school, when I married my college-aged sweetheart. We were from the same faith, church, school, and community background. Our first child was born five years later, followed by three more, all about three years apart. It was an exciting time, though with some hard relationship trials as well.

As our family grew over the years, I developed some unhealthy relational habits, including a negative attitude that grew from my sense that I was somehow entitled to a happy, problem-free life. I was immature and did not have the relational skills I needed to deal with life at such a fast and busy pace. Consequently, I had little understanding of the people closest to me.

Over the years, we moved our family a few times, and for a while, life seemed to get better. Then some problems that I thought had been resolved began to show up again, with increasing frequency. I sought help for myself, but it seemed too little, too late. I had isolated myself from close, Christian fellowship for the sake of "family commitments" and my marriage, which had become like a god to me. It was not a healthy way to think or live, and I was reaping what I had sown. I thought I was doing the right thing, but now I understand that I needed other skills and habits of living. Codependency and trying to please myself and others only made things worse.

Brokenhearted, and in what felt like a crisis to me, I left my family and put myself in the care of a church I had been attending. I finally admitted I could no longer bear life on my own, and I believed that only a power greater than myself (God) could restore sanity to my life and my situation. I didn't want to leave my husband and kids, but I felt there was no other way to start to heal. I was tired, hurt, and angry.

Seeing the exact nature of my wrong, and admitting it, was a struggle for me. During the next year and a half, I met with a New Life counselor and joined a Twelve Step group, where I found a sponsor who worked through the Steps with me for the first time. My wounds were fresh, and these women helped me as I began to understand my codependent behaviors and my selfish, people-pleasing ways. I am still learning how I need to grow to correct those habits and behaviors. Making amends to my family meant getting help for myself so I could become a more mature Christian and love them, with God's help.

Admitting our sin as the sin that God sees is never easy, and I try to excuse it many times. I do this with others by not learning and practicing loving confrontation, or I speak too boldly and come across as harsh, insensitive, or selfish, which pushes other people away. This will be an ongoing process for me, but now I am praying for continual awareness. To be entirely ready for God to remove these character defects in me, I've had to learn from the pain I experience when I sin. I believe I become humble more quickly when in pain, but I pray for gentle correction.

As I become aware of the harm I bring to others, whether through my words or my actions, my desire is to express my love in ways that are meaningful to them and to ask for their forgiveness. My marriage did not survive the separation, which lasted more than a year, but by God's grace I look forward to thriving in the principles of recovery and restoration for the rest of my life. My prayer is that I will keep short accounts with others and that others will be aware of the opportunity to learn and practice these principles with me as I continue my journey.

STEP EIGHT BIBLE STUDIES

Study #1: Living in Grace

This study is based on Romans 12:9-21 (page 1448 in *The Life Recovery Bible*). Read the entire chapter several times before working on the study.

1. LET'S NOT PRETEND

Our addictions, dependencies, and problems can cause us to isolate ourselves from other people. When we're dealing with problems, it's natural to want to be alone. *If I'm alone, I can work things out on my own.* Of course, it doesn't work; we are simply left alone with our problems.

There's a good reason why being alone doesn't work. We're wired to connect with other people. That's part of God's design for our lives. A lot of research shows how unhealthy isolation is for us—physically, emotionally, and spiritually. That same research shows that when we have supportive people in our lives, we live healthier and longer. People who live successfully, live in relationship with others. When we come to Step Eight, we are asked only to *prepare ourselves* for repair work in our relationships. Once again, we have a Step that does not require action, but does require willingness.

> *Don't just pretend to love others. Really love them. Hate what is wrong. Hold tightly to what is good. Love each other with genuine affection, and take delight in honoring each other. Never be lazy, but work hard and serve the Lord enthusiastically. Rejoice in our confident hope. Be patient in trouble, and keep on praying. When God's people are in need, be ready to help them. Always be eager to practice hospitality.*
>
> ROMANS 12:9-13

These verses include ten things that Paul says we must be willing to do in our relationships. Let's look at each one and evaluate our willingness to practice these relational skills:

1. "Don't just pretend to love others. Really love them. . . . with genuine affection." What part of this principle is difficult for you?

2. "Hate what is wrong." Are you willing?

3. "Hold tightly to what is good." How consistently do you do this?

4. "Delight in honoring each other." What are some ways you can do this?

5. "Never be lazy, but work hard and serve the Lord enthusiastically." What part of this principle is hard for you?

6. "Rejoice in our confident hope." What does this mean to you?

7. "Be patient in trouble." When do you have difficulty with patience?

8. "Keep on praying." How regularly or consistently do you pray?

9. "When God's people are in need, be ready to help them." Whom could you help?

10. "Always be eager to practice hospitality." In what ways can you practice hospitality *eagerly*?

2. GRACE-FILLED LIVING

Paul doesn't stop with these ten things—that was just the first paragraph. Now he adds seven more things that God expects from us if we are living our lives surrendered to him. And he ups the level of difficulty. Some of these are not going to be easy, but remember, right now we are working on a *willingness* step.

> *Bless those who persecute you. Don't curse them; pray that God will bless them. Be happy with those who are happy, and weep with those who weep. Live in harmony with each other. Don't be too proud to enjoy the company of ordinary people. And don't think you know it all!*
>
> *Never pay back evil with more evil. Do things in such a way that everyone can see you are honorable. Do all that you can to live in peace with everyone.*
>
> ROMANS 12:14-18

As we did with the first ten, let's evaluate seven more things that we are to incorporate into our lives.

1. "Bless those who persecute you. . . . pray that God will bless them." This goes completely against our natural response. How do you struggle with this one?

2. "Be happy with those who are happy." Give some examples of how you do this.

3. "Weep with those who weep." Who needs your support and empathy right now?

4. "Live in harmony with each other. . . . Do all that you can to live in peace with everyone." Which person is the hardest for you to live in peace with?

5. "Don't be too proud to enjoy the company of ordinary people." Describe how this applies to you.

6. "Never pay back evil with more evil." Give some examples of when you have returned evil for evil. How can you change this in the future?

7. "Do things in such a way that everyone can see you are honorable." With whom will this be the most difficult task to accomplish? What makes it so hard?

3. PARADOXICAL LIVING

Several of the things Paul has listed seem *paradoxical* and contrary to common sense. But then, a lot of what works in relationships is paradoxical. Paul now confronts us with the most difficult thing he wants from us—and it is completely paradoxical. No one would suggest that we could do this in our own strength.

> *Dear friends, never take revenge. Leave that to the righteous*
> *anger of God. For the Scriptures say, "I will take revenge; I will*
> *pay them back," says the LORD. Instead, "If your enemies are*
> *hungry, feed them. If they are thirsty, give them something to*
> *drink. In doing this, you will heap burning coals of shame on*
> *their heads." Don't let evil conquer you, but conquer evil by*
> *doing good.*
>
> ROMANS 12:19-21

Paul has already asked us to love our enemies and to bless them and pray that God blesses them. But now he wants us to go even further—he wants us to actively show love to them. We are to feed them and give them something to drink. In other words, our actions must now be consistent with our blessings and our prayers.

Who will be most difficult for you to act kindly toward in the way Paul is asking us to in these verses?

How would you explain what Paul means when he says we are to "conquer evil by doing good"?

No one is expected to live out these principles perfectly. But they are to be our goal. When we relate these verses to Step Eight, we are reminded that our goal at this point is *willingness*. As you review this passage, keep one central question in mind: *Am I willing to do this?* Where you find yourself hesitating, take some time to understand your resistance. Stick with the process until you can honestly say you are willing.

Study #2: Being Responsible

This study is based on 1 Thessalonians 4:3-12 (page 1540 in *The Life Recovery Bible*). Read these verses several times before working on the study.

1. CONTROL YOURSELF

When Paul wrote this letter, the culture in which the Thessalonians lived was much like our culture today. Sexual mores were loose—almost anything was deemed okay. In some of the pagan religions, prostitution was a legitimate part of worship, and many of those who were in the Thessalonian church had practiced that form of worship before their conversion. Unrestricted sexual expression was considered natural. Like a lot of people today, the people in the church wanted to know why certain forms were wrong. Here's Paul's answer:

> *God's will is for you to be holy, so stay away from all sexual sin. Then each of you will control his own body and live in holiness and honor—not in lustful passion like the pagans who do not know God and his ways. Never harm or cheat a Christian brother in this matter by violating his wife, for the Lord avenges all such sins, as we have solemnly warned you before. God has called us to live holy lives, not impure lives. Therefore, anyone who refuses to live by these rules is not disobeying human teaching but is rejecting God, who gives his Holy Spirit to you.*
>
> I THESSALONIANS 4:3-8

Paul says that these expectations are not man-made. Rather, God expects us to live in holiness and honor.

Three times in this passage, Paul tells us we are called to holy living. What do you think Paul means when he uses the terms *holy, holiness,* and *holy lives*?

Based on this passage, how is sexual purity part of living a holy life?

Paul associates "holiness" with "control" of our bodies. In your own words, paraphrase what Paul is saying.

2. LIVING IN LOVE

Part of living responsibly is living in relationship. Prior to beginning our recovery, many of our behaviors were rooted in isolation. Now Paul reminds us not only to love each other, but that God himself is the one who teaches us to love each other. How has God done this?

In Isaiah 54:13, God promises to teach all our children and that the result of his teaching will be peace. God has now fulfilled his promise through the sacrifice of Jesus on the cross. And remember, Jesus died for us when we were still his enemies (see Romans 5:8). With that sacrificial act of love as a backdrop, Paul reminds us to live in community and to love one another.

> *But we don't need to write to you about the importance of loving each other, for God himself has taught you to love one another. Indeed, you already show your love for all the believers throughout Macedonia. Even so, dear brothers and sisters, we urge you to love them even more.*
>
> 1 THESSALONIANS 4:9-10

What are some lessons in loving that God has shown you since you began your recovery?

When is it difficult for you to love others? What makes it so difficult?

When Paul urges us to love even more, he implies that our ability to love others is a growth opportunity—we can always do it better. Toward whom, and in what situations, do you still need to grow in your ability to love others?

3. THE QUIET LIFE

Paul now adds to his description of living responsibly: We are to live quiet lives. He seems aware that our lives and the lives of those around us were chaotic when were active in our addiction, dependencies, and problems. One of the goals of recovery is that the chaos will subside and life will become quiet and peaceful. We will begin to experience a greater degree of serenity in our lives.

> *Make it your goal to live a quiet life, minding your own*
> *business and working with your hands, just as we instructed you*
> *before. Then people who are not Christians will respect the way*
> *you live, and you will not need to depend on others.*
> I THESSALONIANS 4:11-12

Describe some of the chaos you lived with prior to beginning recovery.

Now describe some of the ways you are living a more "quiet life."

Now that we are living more responsibly, our goal is to live more honorably, lovingly, and peacefully as well. Part of living responsibly is being *willing* to make amends to those we have harmed.

Study #3: The Power of Words

This study is based on James 3:1-12 (page 1603 in *The Life Recovery Bible*). Read these verses several times before working on the study.

1. CONTROLLING THE TONGUE

One common childhood myth is "sticks and stones may break my bones, but names will never hurt me." We knew it hurt if someone hit us with a stick or a stone, but we also knew it hurt when someone called us a bad name. James goes beyond mere name-calling to say that all words are powerful—for good or evil. In fact, he says a loose tongue is one of the most difficult things to control. When we review our inventories, we will probably see a number of areas where we need to make amends related to speech.

> *Dear brothers and sisters, not many of you should become teachers in the church, for we who teach will be judged more strictly. Indeed, we all make many mistakes. For if we could control our tongues, we would be perfect and could also control ourselves in every other way.*
>
> JAMES 3:1-2

Why is it so difficult to control our words?

When have you been hurt deeply by something someone said about you?

Review your inventory and look at the amends you need to make that are related to things you said. What made it so hard to control your words in each situation?

2. THE POWER OF LITTLE THINGS

"It was just a small thing," we might say. Yet often it seems that the smallest things can cause the biggest hurt. James draws several comparisons that show the truth of this statement. We can control a horse with a small bit, turn a huge ship with a tiny rudder, and start a major forest fire with a tiny spark. Likewise, a single word can ignite all sorts of wickedness, corruption, and pain.

> *We can make a large horse go wherever we want by means of a small bit in its mouth. And a small rudder makes a huge ship turn wherever the pilot chooses to go, even though the winds are strong. In the same way, the tongue is a small thing that makes grand speeches.*
>
> *But a tiny spark can set a great forest on fire. And the tongue is a flame of fire. It is a whole world of wickedness, corrupting your entire body. It can set your whole life on fire, for it is set on fire by hell itself.*
>
> JAMES 3:3-6

Describe a time when something you said "set your whole life on fire."

Were you able to repair the situation? Why or why not?

James observes that the fire of the tongue is set by hell itself. How does this relate to the situation you just described?

3. THE UNTAMABLE TONGUE

As James continues his description of the power of our words, it almost sounds as if taming the tongue is a hopeless task. But then he draws another analogy that goes deeper. He sees our words as an expression of our hearts. Recovery is a heart issue even more than a tongue issue. If we treat only the symptom—what we say—without dealing with the source—our damaged, corrupted hearts—our attempts to tame our tongues will never work. We have to go deeper. Perhaps James had Jesus' words in mind: "The words you speak come from the heart—that's what defiles you. For from the heart come evil thoughts, murder, adultery, all sexual immorality, theft, lying, and slander. These are what defile you" (Matthew 15:18-20).

People can tame all kinds of animals, birds, reptiles, and fish, but no one can tame the tongue. It is restless and evil, full of deadly poison. Sometimes it praises our Lord and Father, and sometimes it curses those who have been made in the image of God. And so blessing and cursing come pouring out of the same mouth. Surely, my brothers and sisters, this is not right! Does a spring of water bubble out with both fresh water and bitter water? Does a fig tree produce olives, or a grapevine produce figs? No, and you can't draw fresh water from a salty spring.

JAMES 3:7-12

How has your tongue revealed the attitude of your heart?

James makes the case that our little tongues can cause great problems. But then he ties everything to the heart. How would you describe this concept to someone who didn't understand?

In what ways are your *heart* and the concept of *willingness* connected?

Recovery is not a superficial journey; it's hard work. And just as the bit controls the horse and the rudder controls the ship, there is something that controls the tongue. For the horse, it's the rider; for the ship, it's the pilot; for the tongue, it's the heart.

Study #4: Internal Changes

This study is based on Luke 19:1-10 (page 1324 in *The Life Recovery Bible*). Read these verses several times before working on the study.

1. THE RICH LITTLE MAN

This story records an actual event in the life of Jesus; it is not one of his parables. To really understand the interaction between Zacchaeus and Jesus, it is important to know how the people of that day viewed tax collectors like Zacchaeus. We might compare him to the most corrupt politicians of our day. If you feel utter contempt for those people, you have a sense of how the people around Jesus felt toward Zacchaeus. Tax collectors were despised, in part because they represented the Roman emperor, but even more so because they were corrupt. Zacchaeus had profited greatly from his corruption. For Jesus to call him out and announce that he was going home with him—that would have grabbed everyone's attention.

Jesus entered Jericho and made his way through the town. There was a man there name Zacchaeus. He was the chief tax collector in the region, and he had become very rich. He tried to get a look at Jesus, but he was too short to see over the crowd. So he ran ahead and climbed a sycamore-fig tree beside the road, for Jesus was going to pass that way.

LUKE 19:1-4

There must have been a hunger in Zacchaeus's heart for change, for he was determined to see Jesus. When you think of Jesus, what more do you want to learn about him?

We don't have to climb a tree to learn more about Jesus; we have the four Gospels that describe him and his life here on earth. As you've read several stories told by Jesus, and now this story, what impresses you most about him?

2. SPECIAL ATTENTION GIVEN

Jesus had a way of doing the unexpected. Zacchaeus only wanted to catch a glimpse of Jesus; but when Jesus saw him, he called him by name. Here is a little man, despised by everyone, and yet Jesus knows his name! How did Jesus know? Was Zacchaeus's reputation that well-known? Or did Jesus just know? From what we've seen in other passages in the Bible, we would conclude that Jesus just knew these things because he is the Son of God. For example, Mark 2:8 says, "Immediately Jesus knew in his spirit that this was what they were thinking in their hearts, and he said to them, 'Why are you thinking these things?'" (NIV). But notice the reaction of the crowd to Jesus' openness to Zacchaeus:

When Jesus came by, he looked up at Zacchaeus and called him by name. "Zacchaeus!" he said. "Quick, come down! I must be a guest in your home today."

Zacchaeus quickly climbed down and took Jesus to his house in great excitement and joy. But the people were displeased. "He has gone to be the guest of a notorious sinner," they grumbled.

LUKE 19:5-7

Whenever something good happens, someone will complain. Who has been resistant to the changes you are making in your recovery?

Why do you think the people grumbled about Jesus and Zacchaeus?

Why do you think people are bothered by the Steps you are taking in your recovery?

3. A CHANGED MAN

Now we come to the "willingness" part of this event. Without a word of judgment or a challenge from Jesus, Zacchaeus states his willingness to change and make amends. He didn't have Steps Eight and Nine of a Twelve Step program to tell him what was next—he simply was willing to change out of gratitude for how Jesus accepted him. By law, if Zacchaeus claimed he had made a mistake, he only needed to add 20 percent restitution for what he had taken. But if he had stolen from people, the law said that restitution was to be four times what was taken. Zacchaeus not only admitted his sin and declared his willingness to make amends, but he also made no attempt to defend his past behavior. Luke comments at the end of the passage that this was why Jesus came to live on earth—to seek and save those who were lost, those whose lives needed healing. The same is true of Jesus today—his interest is not in those who are self-righteous, but in those who are aware of their needs and are willing to open themselves to do whatever God wants them to do.

> *Meanwhile, Zacchaeus stood before the Lord and said, "I will give half my wealth to the poor, Lord, and if I have cheated people on their taxes, I will give them back four times as much!" Jesus responded, "Salvation has come to this home today, for this man has shown himself to be a true son of Abraham. For the Son of Man came to seek and save those who are lost."*
>
> LUKE 19:8-10

Why do you think Zacchaeus was so willing to make amends?

What was there about meeting Jesus that changed his life?

If Jesus were standing in front of you, what would he notice in your life that would cause him to say, "This man (or woman) has shown himself (or herself) to be a true child of recovery and healing"?

So much of Zacchaeus's willingness came from his gratitude. To the general public, Zacchaeus was a pariah in his town—someone to be hated and avoided. But Jesus didn't avoid him. In fact, he treated him with love and respect, inviting himself to Zacchaeus's home. Jesus, by his acceptance, opened a spring of gratitude inside Zacchaeus that released a spirit of willingness. When we understand how Jesus accepts us *just as we are*, we can also experience this spring of gratitude and spirit of willingness. (For a review of what Jesus has done for us, read Romans 5:6-11.)

STEP NINE

We made direct amends to such people wherever possible,
except when to do so would injure them or others.

*[Jesus said,] If you are presenting a sacrifice at the altar in the
Temple and . . . someone has something against you, leave your
sacrifice there at the altar. Go and be reconciled to that person.
Then come and offer your sacrifice to God.*

MATTHEW 5:23-24

Debbie's Story of Recovery: The Classic Middle-Class Family with a Secret

My first memory of being molested by my father is when I was five
years old. I was the youngest of three, with two older brothers. They
would have been nine and ten at the time. I also had four male cousins who lived near us. Growing up riding motorcycles, camping, and
fighting with the boys gave me a male mentality to some extent. I
remember at a young age wishing I were a boy because I thought it
would give me more power over people and I wouldn't be touched
by my dad anymore.

By the age of twelve, I was drinking alcohol, smoking weed, and
experimenting with pills. I gradually became sexually active with
boys my age. Sometime within that year, my mom caught my dad
on top of me in my room. I thought, *Finally, someone else knows. It's
over!* I was wrong. My mom buried herself even more in her work
and acted as if what she'd seen had never happened.

With my hormones flaring and my mental state deteriorating, I was a mess by the age of thirteen. My parents moved us from the only place we had lived to a small hick town, population three hundred. My brothers didn't stay long, moving back to our hometown to live with our cousins. Left alone two-thirds of the time, with whiskey and beer in the house and weed at my fingertips, I numbed my miserable life.

My parents provided shelter and financial support. They very seldom argued and never physically fought, but they also never saw each other more than an hour or two a day (if that) during the week. We were the classic middle-class family with a secret. I worked at a convenience store from the age of thirteen to seventeen, which supported my drug habit.

Feeling displaced and alone, I wasn't able to process the severity of what had happened to me and how it would affect my life without proper help. I don't remember a lot of the times that I was molested— I learned to fade my mind to other things until it was over—but it didn't end until I was seventeen and moved out of the house.

Over the next several years, I gave birth to three girls, with an abortion between the first two, and by then I was convinced that God hated me. I loved my daughters tremendously, but I was not the right person to be raising girls. I wasn't equipped.

When I got pregnant with my youngest daughter, I married the father. (My two older girls had different dads, who were not in the picture at that point.) When I was seven months into my pregnancy, my eldest brother and two of his friends were murdered. My life had just begun to get bad.

My husband and I became connected with a biker club, and with it, all the meth we could handle (and then some). My two older girls had to go live with my parents—which was pure insanity—but my youngest stayed with us. I honestly don't know which was worse. My husband and I eventually divorced, and my dad passed away two years later, after three or four years in a nursing home. He had landed there after a failed suicide attempt when I found out he was molesting my two older girls and reported him to Child Protective Services.

When I was forty, I finally stopped smoking dope. But still I pushed my daughters away because I didn't know how not to not hurt them. The following spring, after many failed attempts at reconciliation, I started going back to church. One of the last people I had gotten high with was released from prison that summer and sent me a *Life Recovery Bible*, which is a tremendous tool.

I started going to an addiction class once a week at my church. I thought I was going because I still craved dope, but I soon realized the class was for my unacknowledged alcoholism. Even though I drank bourbon and cola every day, I never thought I was an alcoholic. I started having night terrors again (which I'd had occasionally while growing up), and they increased in frequency until they came almost every night. I prayed the Lord's Prayer and other prayers until the terror subsided. I had my last drink on November 24, 2008, had my last night terror the next night, and was delivered from alcohol addiction on November 26. I praise God for that. I haven't had a real nightmare or scary dream since.

I have forgiven my mom and dad, and I asked forgiveness from all three of my girls. We now have the mother-daughter relationships we had missed out on. I'm a grandma three times and expecting another any day now. I know now that God loved me through everything; the enemy is the one who hates me. And whether or not anyone else forgives me, I know I'm forgiven by God.

I used to be a liar, a murderer, a poor excuse for a mother, an alcoholic, a drug addict, a sex addict, and more, but I'm in a new skin now. Though it took some time to get used to it, I like it.

I left out so much of my life experience, but I think most addicts can fill in the blanks—whether it be with deceit, self-loathing, confusion, lack of self-esteem . . . and the list goes on.

Laura's Story of Recovery: I Needed a Process of Self-Examination

I grew up in a typical middle-class home in the suburbs of Philadelphia. My dad was an economist and my mother a homemaker and community volunteer. Our family's dark secrets revolved around mental illness—we were all very lost people.

After years of therapy, my Christian counselor explained that my father was a sociopath. My mother told me that she became pregnant with me when my dad raped her on a date. When she refused to have an abortion, he took her down to the jewelry store to pick out a ring. To say he was emotionally unavailable would be an understatement. When I was a child, he wouldn't hold me or even talk to me. After I graduated from college, I asked him one time why he had never spoken to me. He said, "You never had anything intelligent to say until you were educated."

My dad was emotionally abusive to my mother and me, and to anyone else who crossed his path. I saw him strike my mother only once, but I suspect there were other occasions, and he threatened to kill us several times. He also exaggerated our failures and made up lies about us to our relatives, coworkers, neighbors—to anyone who would listen to him. For example, even though I was a very good student, he gave me a real complex about my lack of mathematical abilities. He had a master's degree in mathematics and economics from Penn State, and as he put it, "I just can't understand how a child of mine is so stupid in math." His lack of faith in me really limited my perception of what I could handle in college. In addition, he cheated on my mom throughout their marriage and even insulted me by asking my boyfriends if they would like to go out and pick up "a real woman" some night.

My counselor also told me that my mother has classic bipolar disorder, though her fears have never allowed her to go to a doctor for treatment. Her mood swings are incredible, but mostly she stays depressed. Even though it has been two years since my father died, she constantly talks about all the abuse we suffered from him. When I was growing up, I could never challenge her because I felt so sorry for her. However, after years of counseling, I realize she is just as controlling and abusive as my dad was.

My mother emotionally and physically abused me with her "good intentions," and she will tell you today that all my success is due to her strict discipline and moral standards. My mother thought nothing of calling me a whore and slapping my face in front of the high school football team as they walked past after practice. Or beating down the door to the band room to accuse me of having an affair with the band director (a complete figment of her imagination).

My mother pushed me to be competitive and independent in order to succeed in life. Though it was unusual in the 1960s, I went to pre-kindergarten, kindergarten, and started grade school early, because my birthday technically fell on the first day of school. It was as if she lived through me, always reminding me that my life would be different due to the opportunities she had never had.

My life was programmed to be performance-based, and I went along with it because I saw education as a way out of my chaotic childhood. My mother lectured me incessantly about how children and men would ruin my life, but my career would always be there for me. Later, I learned the truth in Psalm 118:8: "It is better to take refuge in the LORD than to trust in people."

When I entered middle school, my parents became involved in the occult and the New Age movement. Before this, they were professed atheists and forbade my involvement in "organized religion." It became normal to have witches and weirdos sitting in our living room channeling spirits during séances, having out-of-body experiences, and participating in other physic phenomena. My mother even told me that she believes I am the reincarnation of her mother, who died when my mother was six.

As one who grew up amid occultist practices, I never saw anything but madness and destruction come out of it. There was a period when my father was losing his ability to walk, and he threatened several times to kill my mother and shoot himself due to his beliefs in reincarnation. He felt that if he could end his life he could be reborn and get a new body that could walk again.

I thought my parents had totally lost their minds, but I had to admit that some of the things I saw were definitely not a hoax; there was supernatural power present, but it wasn't from God. These experiences prompted me to begin my journey to find the real God, not the counterfeit. (I now know this was the Holy Spirit directing me.) Proverbs 16:9 states, "A man's heart plans his way, but the LORD directs his steps" (NKJV).

My first boyfriend was concerned about my salvation, so we started attending church with his family. My parents weren't happy about that decision, but my mother liked the idea that we would be chaperoned because she feared I would become pregnant.

Then I got saved. I knew the gospel was real, and I wanted to be God's child. My boyfriend's family helped me hide my baptism from my parents—and I thought I got away with it, until a year later when the pastor mailed my baptismal certificate to my house. I was making arrangements on the phone for my parents to pick me up from college after my freshman year when my mother mentioned the certificate. I knew I was in trouble. She told me she had torn it to pieces. My parents both expressed their disappointment in me, and for the entire summer, my father treated me like I had become pregnant.

During my senior year in college, my boyfriend got another girl pregnant. I was devastated. A friend and fellow band member asked me out to talk about it, and then he drugged and raped me. I had now lost my virginity, which I had been saving for my future husband, and my friend just blew it off like it was casual sex for him. For some reason I didn't report it as a sexual assault, but now that I thought I had nothing special to offer anymore, I started sleeping with every new boyfriend.

After I graduated from college and began my career, I bought my first home. Over the next ten years, I had several long-term engagements, but each one ended in betrayal. When my latest fiancé told me he was expecting a baby with another woman, I decided I was done with romantic relationships and would be taking a long sabbatical.

Even my career, which my mother had said would always be there for me, failed me when I was laid-off, and I had to take in a roommate and work four jobs to pay my mortgage. With all the unresolved emotional conflicts and layers of loss and stress, my health declined. At night I would lock my jaw, eventually cracking seven of my teeth completely through the roots. I had to have them all pulled and the severe infection treated. I developed hypothyroidism, lost my eyebrows, gained seventy-four pounds in one year, and had to have my thyroid gland removed. My disillusionment with my identity, based on worldly relationships, success, status, career, and my physical appearance, caused me to take a closer look at God to learn more about him.

I had attended church only occasionally in college. To tell you the truth, I just couldn't relate to all the hugging and emotions with groups like Campus Crusade for Christ. Back then, I was intimidated to walk into a church with my lack of Christian upbringing. So I started listening to Christian radio and eventually gained enough courage to visit a few churches. I gradually felt comfortable enough to attend regularly, and I began to get involved and seriously study the Bible. I admit I had a hard time seeing practical applications to life because a lot of church people speak "Christianese" and the Bible was difficult to read and understand. But when I started reading Proverbs, and then Psalms, I found a wealth of reason and truth, which encouraged me to keep reading.

I prayed and asked Jesus to help me find a good man. I married Darrell when I was thirty-seven.

I initially came into recovery to support my husband's recovery. My motivation for what I call life recovery is that I finally understood that if I didn't allow God to initiate the healing process in me, he was never going to be able to use me fully according to his will. Without him, I would always remain broken. My favorite Scripture verse is Psalm 17:15: "I shall be satisfied when I awake in Your likeness" (NKJV).

I like to tell newcomers that recovery works because it is the biblical way to healing and restoration. There are no other options. It is comforting to know that I am finally on the right path after all my searching for a way out of my pain. By the way, have you ever noticed that God does not fix what is not broken?

I discovered in working through the Steps that in order to escape denial in my life, I needed a process of self-examination to determine whether I was motivated by worldly values or God's grace. By completing a spiritual inventory (which is Step Four), I could see my life choices and turning points written out on a timeline, which gave me hidden insights. I noticed I had been blaming myself for the sins of others—especially in my childhood, for which I have no responsibility. Also, I have deeply regretted how I strayed from the Christian lifestyle and obedience to God when I was first saved. The inventory revealed that I had only been exposed to Christianity for a couple of months before I found salvation. How much could I really have absorbed from a brief period of church sermons? Enough to know I wanted salvation, but not enough to become a mature Christian. Hebrews 5:14 says, "Solid food is for those who are mature, who through training have the skill to recognize the difference between right and wrong." I had heard God's Word proclaimed, and now I needed to develop a habit of putting it into practice.

Coming from a secular perspective, my understanding of God was mainly a decision of whether I would go to heaven or hell when I died. It took me a while to realize that Christianity is a way of life and a daily relationship with Jesus. Due to my dysfunctional relationship with my earthly father, I had tremendous difficulty relating to God as my Father (whom I should trust and go to for guidance). I couldn't pray to God to just take my pain away and make it better or blame it on a lack of faith; I needed to do the hard work and go through the healing process just like the Bible instructs: "Let us examine our ways and test them, and let us return to the LORD" (Lamentations 3:40, NIV). "Confess your sins to each other and pray for each other so that you may be healed" (James 5:16). That is essentially what we do in recovery.

I had been working on forgiveness and restitution for a long time before I was able to forgive my parents and set up appropriate boundaries with them. A priest once told me, "You must respect your parents, but you are not responsible for their salvation." At first that confused me, because I knew I was the only Christian they had contact with and I thought, *How is this going to happen?* Well, God told me, "You're not the messenger," so I had to turn it over to him.

Two years after Darrell and I moved to North Carolina, my parents wanted to follow us. I actually asked God not to bring them down unless he was going to save them. Miraculously, God placed good Christians in their path, and my father got saved three months before he died!

My mother attends church now. She still believes in reincarnation and thinks Jesus was only a prophet, but the Holy Spirit is working on her. I got sick during Christmas one year, and my mother actually called to tell me she had been praying for me all week. That is a miracle—in my entire life, I've never heard her pray for me!

I have found that service and giving to others is what gets me out of depression. It keeps me balanced. Plus, I want to give back to others to help them along their path to recovery. I want to encourage you to complete the Twelve Steps so you can help others in the future.

STEP NINE INSIGHT

In Step Eight, we mentioned the time when I (Steve) paid to abort my own child after getting my girlfriend pregnant. This action was at the top of my list when I came to Step Nine in my recovery. When I called her to make amends, the conversation revolutionized my thinking. I realized that in addition to paying for the abortion, I had pressured her into having it. I asked for her forgiveness and she gave it, which brought resolution to the most troubling issue in my life. Because she was still alive and I was able to track her down, it was possible to contact her to make amends. But even if I had not been able to find her, or if she were no longer alive, I at least could have told *someone*.

Before talking to my former girlfriend, I had never told anyone about that abortion, but I had always felt guilty about it. When I was able to confess, my troubling problem was resolved through forgiveness.

Sometimes we never find resolution because we are unwilling to confess the reality of our sin. Is there an area we avoid talking about? Is there a shameful event we have never confessed? Until we do, we won't have full resolution. Unless we confess our wrongs to at least one other person, we will find our healing incomplete. If we can talk, write, phone, text, or e-mail the person we have harmed, we need to do so. If the person is dead or cannot be located or contacted, we need to at least tell some other person to get the secret out. Finally, if we cannot make amends directly to the person we harmed, perhaps we can make amends in another way.

This Step includes a qualifier—"except when to do so would injure them or others"—that can wrongly be used as an excuse not to make amends rather than as protection for those who have been hurt. It can allow us to walk away from life-changing opportunities, for ourselves and others. Let's say we have been unfaithful to a spouse and believe that to reveal the affair would cause an immediate breakdown of the other person and result in divorce. We could declare to ourselves that our spouse must be spared the reality that would probably ruin our marriage and might even cause him or her to commit suicide. Or we could take an approach that would lead to ultimate healing.

If the person we have sinned against is too weak or sensitive or wounded and may be hurt further by our confession, then perhaps this is not the right time to confess. Nevertheless, we can begin to work toward when the right time will be. And when the time comes, we do not necessarily have to tell the truth one-on-one, alone. We may need the help of a counselor to make the process go as well as possible. This person can help us identify all the areas in which we need to accept one another. The counselor can teach us the language of forgiveness and give direction. The resolution might not be quick, but it will happen at the most effective time possible.

If we use "any hurt or pain at all" as a condition of whether or not we make amends, we will fail to resolve the guilt and shame that eats away our serenity. We must realize that not all hurt is harmful. Not all pain is damaging. Just as a needle might hurt us in order to deliver a vaccine that could save our lives, the truth may be painful but could be necessary for healing.

If we have stolen from people, it will be painful for them to learn that they don't have the kind of friendship and security they may have thought they had with us. But it is not our place to protect other people from the truth. They are entitled to know that they have been betrayed. If we don't tell them how we deceived them, we leave them vulnerable to others who may want to cheat them. We must proceed with what will be painful for them and uncomfortable for us.

This is a very tough Step, but in some ways it makes more sense than any other. At least its purpose is easier to understand than that of many other Steps. Quite simply, it is not enough in every case for us to apologize for what we have taken from others without offering to make restitution. It might be enough if they accept the amends but do not want further contact. It might be enough just to say we're sorry if there is no tangible way to make it right. But more often than not, there is a way to make amends that includes complete restitution.

The simplest example would be if we had stolen ten dollars from someone. How foolish to think that an apology alone would make things right. We need to give back the ten dollars with interest, and we know it. The same principle applies in many other areas that are not as easily quantifiable. One person did this by simply following the wishes of the person he'd hurt. Here's Kevin's story.

Kevin had been unfaithful to his wife, Darla, by meeting a woman at a local hotel for repeated sexual encounters. He went from feeling justified in what he was doing to feeling responsible to get himself out. So he stopped the relationship and attended an Every Man's Battle workshop. When he did, he was prompted to make things right with his wife. Whatever she wanted from him, he was committed to give it. Upon returning home, he confessed what had happened in an act of full disclosure. It was not easy for Darla to hear that her marriage was just a mirage. She was devastated—but she was also a very bright woman.

She asked Kevin if he would be faithful to her for the rest of his life. She asked if she had anything further to worry about. She wanted to know that he was fully committed, no matter what. Of course, he assured her that he was determined to change everything and to never cheat on her again. Then she did the unexpected. She demanded that he make restitution for what he had taken from her. He said he would do anything he needed to do to make it right.

That's when she told him that she wanted everything they owned in common to be transferred to her name alone. If he was sure he would never have another affair and never leave, then he should not mind going to the courthouse and signing everything over to her. She wanted him to sign a quitclaim deed that would place all of their assets in her name alone. She wanted to be in control of everything.

It was a very tough request, but because of how much he had stolen from her and how he had humiliated her, he was willing to humble himself and do exactly what she requested. In an effort to make restitution, he signed everything over to her.

But Darla wasn't finished yet. She told him that his hairy chest had always bothered her, and she asked him to shave it. He agreed. And she requested that he get braces to fix his crooked teeth. Again, he agreed. That began the recovery of their marriage. Because Kevin recognized how he had humiliated Darla by his actions, he became willing to humble (and even humiliate) himself in order to make amends and restitution to a level that would be meaningful to her. They both agreed these steps were necessary, and they maintained open communication as they worked to rebuild all that they had once had—and more. Restitution made all the difference when it came to seeking and receiving forgiveness and making things right.

Darla and Kevin succeeded in identifying very tangible things that Kevin could do to make amends. But for many people it is difficult to either come up with a way to make restitution or find a way to ask for it. It takes communication and patience for two people to work through their differences and resolve the damage and the pain. It takes creativity and effort to make it all right. There is also a caution for those who have been hurt.

It is important that forgiveness not be withheld until a person makes restitution. Otherwise, neither may ever happen—forgiveness nor restitution. The expectation of restitution can derail a person's recovery. Begin the forgiveness process as if restitution will never happen. Even if you ask for it and the person cannot deliver on your request, don't withhold forgiveness. In Matthew 5:23-25, Jesus clearly shows how important this step is to God:

> *So if you are presenting a sacrifice at the altar in the Temple and you suddenly remember that someone has something against you, leave your sacrifice there at the altar. Go and be reconciled to that person. Then come and offer your sacrifice to God. When you are on the way to court with your adversary, settle your differences quickly. Otherwise, your accuser may hand you over to the judge, who will hand you over to an officer, and you will be thrown into prison.*

Here is the God of the universe, who deserves and demands our worship, telling us that there is something even more important than our worship—a clean slate in our relationships. If we know that someone has something against us, God wants us to find a way to be reconciled to that person. Then we can come and worship God with a clean conscience. Reconciliation, restitution, and making amends are very high priorities for God. We would be remiss to neglect their importance. They are not optional or merely suggested. We need to do whatever we can to make things right with the people we have harmed, as long as doing so will not wound them or someone else more deeply.

Completing restitution and reconciliation has untold benefits. Life is lighter. We can *feel* the forgiveness God has given us. Happiness

can actually seep in where regret used to live. Restitution and reconciliation mean that we tie up loose ends and deal with unfinished
business in life. These are the boldest moves we will make in recovery,
and the results will be bold as well. Remember, we reap what we sow.
When we sow restitution, we reap reconciliation, connection, and
the restoration we never dreamed.

Neil's Story of Recovery: The Connection between Confession and Healing

During the summer of 2002, I was sick and tired of being sick and
tired, and I was also longing for a real connection with God. I had
tried countless times to feel close to God, but I felt as if I couldn't
read the Bible enough or pray consistently enough to make a lasting
difference. At one point, I felt impressed to do a forty-day fast. I
made it seven days before I began to have physical problems. When
my doctor suggested I end the fast, I felt I had failed. I wasn't strong
enough; I wasn't committed enough. I couldn't even succeed in
knowing God the way I thought he wanted me to. Ending the fast
was the most devastating defeat I had experienced to that point in my
life. Unfortunately, it wouldn't be the last—or the worst.

Fast-forward to 2008. I was still sick and tired of being sick and
tired, and I was still longing for a real connection with God. This
time, though, I knew what was standing in the way of that connection: my unwillingness to confess past adulteries to my wife. I had
known this for several years. I had confessed my sin to God hundreds
of times. I had been trying very hard not to fall back into those sins
again. And yet, there was still that area of disobedience that was ruin-
ing the possibility of the kind of relationships God desired for me to
have with my wife, my kids, and with him.

I was convinced that confessing to Angela would end our marriage and fracture my relationship with my kids. And yet I knew that
the only thing I could do to find peace and restoration was to bring
out into the open the sins I had committed, dating back to 2002.

One night, after settling the kids into bed, I sat down with my wife and said, "I have something to tell you." By the look on her face, she knew it wasn't good. "I committed adultery. I'm so, so sorry."

It was horrible to see the pain and hurt my confession caused, but it was not as terrible as what my wife had experienced for the past six years because of my sins. At the same moment I felt the heaviness of my sin being thrust upon my wife through my confession, I experienced the lifting of the weight of my sin and disobedience. It was the first step toward healing.

I believed my marriage would be over. God hates divorce, but he has given the spouses of adulterers the option to leave the marriage or stay. I thought, *My kids are going to be from a broken home, just like me, and it's all my fault.*

On top of that, I knew I would lose my job. I was a pastor.

You may have heard the old saying, "Confession is good for the soul." Actually, there's a word missing. It's an old Scottish proverb that reads, "*Open* confession is good for the soul."

Proverbs 28:13 says, "People who conceal their sins will not prosper, but if they confess and turn from them, they will receive mercy." Our sins build barriers between ourselves and others, including God.

> *Confess your sins to each other and pray for each other so that you may be healed.*
> JAMES 5:16

I had never seen the connection between confession and healing before. Jesus Christ saved me from my sin, and God used Angela to open my eyes to my hurts, hang-ups, and habits. I don't say that to take anything away from the redeeming work of Christ in my life. But if my wife had left with the kids for her parents' house the next day like I thought she was going to—and like *she* thought she was going to—I wouldn't be able to admit that I am a recovering sex addict.

I had no clue. I thought I was just a horrible sinner, which I was; but without open confession, I wouldn't have discovered and connected all the dots that contributed to my sexual addiction. I wouldn't have *faced the truth*. Without facing the truth and understanding my history, I most likely would have been doomed to repeat it.

Open confession is where the healing begins!

On my healing journey, I have learned that I am a narcissistic egomaniac with an inferiority complex. And I had deep emotional scars based on what I perceived as my inability to please my dad.

My mom left our family when I was thirteen, which created a great fear of abandonment in me. It came out in the difficulty I had with trusting people. I also learned to lie about my actions, thoughts, and feelings, because I thought if I were truthful, someone might not like what I said or did and leave me. I have battled depression most of my life. In recent years, medication has balanced my moods and contributed to better anger management.

From a very early age, I viewed women as sex objects. I used pornography as a teenager and dishonored almost every girl I dated. I was obsessed with sex. My heroes were Sam "Mayday" Malone from *Cheers* and leading men in the movies who always got the girl (or girls).

As I got older and got more involved in the church, I told myself I was too "spiritual" for pornographic materials—but paranoid about getting caught was more the truth. So, I became sneaky about it, finding soft porn in catalogs, chick flicks, and news stories, and letting my mind fill in the blanks. I used these and other things in an attempt to medicate the pain in my life. There are chemicals released in the brain by sexual stimuli that give the person a "high." Sex addicts are really drug addicts; it's just that the chemicals are naturally produced.

My choices to commit adultery were the worst of many sinful choices I made to medicate the pain in my life. Thankfully, God promises us "victory over sin and death through our Lord Jesus Christ" (1 Corinthians 15:57).

And you will know the truth, and the truth will set you free.
JOHN 8:32

There is no condemnation for those who belong to Christ Jesus.

ROMANS 8:1

All have sinned; . . . yet now God declares us "not guilty" . . . if we trust in Jesus Christ, who in his kindness freely takes away our sins.

ROMANS 3:23-24, TLB

No more guilt doesn't mean no more sorrow. In my case, even though I had regret for my sins, there was more sorrow than ever before.

It also doesn't mean no more responsibility or consequences. I lost my job as a pastor, and my family reaped what I had sown. We had to leave our church and their friends behind. At that time, all they knew was that their lives would be forever changed because of sinful choices I had made in the past.

Everyone was hurt; everyone was angry—and rightfully so. It was all my fault. It's healthy and right to take ownership and responsibility for our own sin. It becomes unhealthy when it leads to shame, the feeling that we are worthless or defective as human beings. I lived in that lie for years. That's the kind of blaming I needed to stop.

My wife had no part or responsibility in my decisions to commit adultery. It was never her fault. I was a sex addict long before I knew her. Unfortunately, I was in denial all those years and too proud to ask for help when I made poor choices in this area of my life.

My relationship with God has been healed. I now know God loves me. Before, I had never really felt that he did. How could he, with everything I had done? I could never please him. Sound familiar? Another lie from the enemy. But God does love me and always will love me; I know it and believe it.

Since I confessed and began a new life of radical honesty, I no longer shoulder the weight of the sin of my lies and the hard work of remembering my lies. Confession has simplified my life and given me such freedom.

Angela never really knew me before. I wouldn't let her, because

I thought if she did she wouldn't want to be with me. That was another lie I believed. Angela knows me now, everything about me. She doesn't like it all; some of it she hates, and rightfully so.

I was finally willing to risk it. It doesn't always work out that way for everyone, but I truly believe that if one of the consequences was, or ever becomes, the end of our marriage because of my sins, I wouldn't regret my confession and the healing God has done in me.

Pain is inevitable for all of us, but misery is optional. In *The Living Bible*, Psalm 32:3-5 says, "There was a time when I wouldn't admit what a sinner I was. But my dishonesty made me miserable and filled my days with frustration. . . . My strength evaporated like water on a sunny day until I finally admitted all my sins to You and stopped trying to hide them. I said to myself, 'I will confess them to the Lord.' And You forgave me! All my guilt is gone."

Today I am winning the battle of sexual addiction, with God as my helper. Job 31:1 says, "I made a covenant with my eyes not to look with lust at a young woman." I have made that covenant and included *all* women.

A turning point for me in my recovery was when I realized my recovery was and is for *me*—not for Angela, not for our marriage, and not for our kids. Along with that came the awareness that I was living completely to please Jesus Christ in my recovery and no one else. Owning my recovery and embracing it gave me the ability to accept and answer any question or accusation from my wife or others about my thoughts and actions.

I have confessed my adultery to our kids, and we are teaching them that the "rules" of dysfunctional families—don't talk, don't feel, and don't trust—are unhealthy.

Angela and I are learning new communication skills and are learning to share our real true feelings without the fear of rejection.

I am enjoying God and his presence in my life.

STEP NINE BIBLE STUDIES

Study #1: God's Support of Us as We Make Amends

This study is based on Genesis 32:3-12 (pages 47–48 in *The Life Recovery Bible*). Read these verses several times before working on the study. You can also read verses 13-21 to see what Jacob did to try to make amends.

1. A FIRST ATTEMPT

In Step Nine, we are called to *action*. Step Eight dealt with our *willingness* to make amends; Step Nine calls us to actually make amends when possible. Jacob leaves home because his brother Esau threatens to kill him for stealing their father's blessing, which was meant for Esau, the firstborn. Those were violent times, and there is little question that Esau means what he said. Jacob's mother sends him to live with her brother, a journey of several days away.

After Jacob has been there for twenty years, God tells him to go back home. Halfway there, Jacob remembers why he left home in the first place—because of Esau's threat on his life. So Jacob seeks to make amends to his brother. First, he tells a messenger to go and meet with Esau and to use a specific wording in his greeting: "your servant Jacob." What does that mean? Well, the blessing that Jacob stole from Esau was the family birthright, which gave the elder brother preeminence after the death of the father. By stealing the blessing, Jacob won the right to rule over Esau. What Jacob wants to say now is something like this: "Remember that blessing? Forget about it! I'm your servant!"

Next, Jacob sends messengers to Esau, who is living in the region of Seir in the land of Edom. He tells them:

> *Give this message to my master Esau: "Humble greetings from your servant Jacob. Until now I have been living with Uncle Laban, and now I own cattle, donkeys, flocks of sheep and goats, and many servants, both men and women. I have sent these*

messengers to inform my lord of my coming, hoping that you
will be friendly to me."
GENESIS 32:4-5

I don't think Jacob was willing or ready to make amends with Esau, but circumstances forced him to act. He couldn't return home unless he made amends.

Fortunately, unless circumstances intervene, we make direct amends when we are ready. What do you think Jacob experienced as he realized he had to make amends with Esau?

With whom are you not ready to make amends?

With whom are you ready to make amends?

2. WHEN MAKING AMENDS GETS COMPLICATED

When we seek to make direct amends, there is no guarantee we will be well-received. Some people may be so hurt by our past behavior or so skeptical about our recovery that they don't really want to hear our amends. That's okay. We need to, and can, give them the time they need to respond. In Jacob's situation, his efforts went from difficult to terrifying. Instead of a "welcome home" from Esau, the messenger reported that Esau was bringing an army to confront Jacob. Jacob fully believed he was preparing to meet a brother bent on revenge. So he made some preparations for what appeared would be a battle. He divided his entourage into two groups and sent them ahead on two different paths in the hopes that at least one group, which included his wives and children, would survive.

> *After delivering the message, the messengers returned to Jacob and reported, "We met your brother, Esau, and he is already on his way to meet you—with an army of 400 men!" Jacob was terrified at the news. He divided his household, along with the flocks and herds and camels, into two groups. He thought, "If Esau meets one group and attacks it, perhaps the other group can escape."*
>
> GENESIS 32:6-8

Describe what you think Jacob felt when he got news that his brother was bringing a small army to meet him.

When you look at the difficult amends you need to make, how can you prepare to cover any contingencies?

3. SEEKING GOD'S HELP

Once Jacob had done what he could do on a human level, he turned to God. How different Jacob's approach is compared to what we often did before we surrendered everything to God. Typically, when faced with a crisis, most people begin by making demands of God. After all, in our self-sufficiency, we think we know what is going to fix the crisis. When God doesn't act as we demand, we get frustrated and angry with him.

Jacob's petition shows us how to come to God when faced with a crisis. It is a wonderful example of how we are to pray. First of all, in his prayer, Jacob exhibited a humble spirit based on his total dependence on God for the outcome. For example, he prayed, "I am not worthy of all the unfailing love and faithfulness you have shown to me" (Genesis 32:10). Second, Jacob appealed to God based on God's relationship with him, his father, and his grandfather. Third, he reminded God of the promise God made to him twenty years before, when Jacob first left home (see Genesis 22:17 and Genesis 28:3-4 for the promise God made to Jacob). Finally, he reminded God that God was the one who told Jacob to return home. Notice these four things as you meditate on Jacob's prayer.

> *Then Jacob prayed, "O God of my grandfather Abraham, and God of my father, Isaac—O LORD, you told me, 'Return to your own land and to your relatives.' And you promised me, 'I will treat you kindly.' I am not worthy of all the unfailing love and faithfulness you have shown to me, your servant. When I left home and crossed the Jordan River, I owned nothing except a walking stick. Now my household fills two large camps! O LORD, please rescue me from the hand of my brother, Esau. I am afraid that he is coming to attack me, along with my wives and children. But you promised me, 'I will surely treat you kindly, and I will multiply your descendants until they become as numerous as the sands along the seashore—too many to count.'"*
>
> GENESIS 32:9-12

How did you pray when you faced a crisis prior to beginning your recovery?

Which of the four characteristics of Jacob's prayer is most difficult for you?

If we come before God with humility, we can ask for his help in those difficult areas, especially as we begin to make direct amends. Write a prayer that expresses your humility in requesting God's help with making direct amends.

Study #2: Time to Heal

This study is based on Hosea 3:1-5 (pages 1098-1099 in *The Life Recovery Bible*). Read Hosea 1, as well as these verses, several times before working on the study.

1. AN UNFAITHFUL WIFE

Hosea was a prophet during a very chaotic time in the history of ancient Israel. His contemporaries included Amos, Jonah, Micah, and Isaiah. In the book of Hosea, we get a glimpse of his personal life, which is used to illustrate God's relationship with Israel. At the beginning of the book, God says to Hosea, "Go and marry a prostitute, so that some of her children will be conceived in prostitution. This will illustrate how Israel has acted like a prostitute by turning against the LORD and worshiping other gods" (Hosea 1:2).

Then Hosea was told to name his children to illustrate God's relationship with Israel. The first one was named Jezreel, because God said, "I am about to punish King Jehu's dynasty to avenge the murders he committed at Jezreel" (Hosea 1:4; you can read about this event in 2 Kings 9-10). Hosea's first daughter was named Lo-ruhamah, which means "not loved" (Hosea 1:6), and a third child, a son, was named Lo-ammi, which means "not my people" (verse 9). Through the names of Hosea's children, God sent a message to the people of Israel that his patience with them was running out.

Then God told Hosea to change the names of his second and third children, dropping the word Lo so that Ruhamah now meant "the ones I love" and Ammi now meant "my people" (Hosea 2:1).

Sometime later, Gomer left Hosea and returned to her life of prostitution. Her life crashed and she sold herself into slavery. God now tells Hosea to go and bring Gomer back to the marriage.

> *Then the LORD said to me, "Go and love your wife again,*
> *even though she commits adultery with another lover. This will*
> *illustrate that the LORD still loves Israel, even though the people*
> *have turned to other gods and love to worship them."*
>
> HOSEA 3:1

Here we have an example of God's unfailing love in action. How does God's instruction to Hosea illustrate God's unfailing love?

How does the example of Hosea and Gomer make God's unfailing love more personal to you?

2. A TIME FOR HEALING

Hosea had to buy back his wife, Gomer. The Bible doesn't tell us why, but Gomer had probably accumulated debt that she couldn't pay and was living as a slave to pay it off. The price Hosea paid to redeem her was about half of what a slave sold for in those days, suggesting that Gomer wasn't worth much at this point. Her life of addiction and dependency had brought her to the bottom. Hosea obeyed God's command, even though it was probably a very difficult and humiliating thing to do. Notice, however, that when Hosea redeemed Gomer from slavery, they didn't resume their marriage immediately. A time of testing and healing needed to come first. It was as if Hosea told Gomer she had relapsed and now needed to restart her healing and recovery. Only then would they be husband and wife again. As before, God used Hosea's relationship with Gomer to illustrate his relationship with the people of Israel.

> *So I bought her back for fifteen pieces of silver and five bushels of barley and a measure of wine. Then I said to her, "You must live in my house for many days and stop your prostitution. During this time, you will not have sexual relations with anyone, not even with me."*
>
> *This shows that Israel will go a long time without a king or prince, and without sacrifices, sacred pillars, priests, or even idols! But afterward the people will return and devote themselves to the LORD their God and to David's descendant, their king. In the last days, they will tremble in awe of the LORD and of his goodness.*
>
> HOSEA 3:2-5

Hosea set a boundary with Gomer when she came home. It probably wasn't a comfortable one, but it was a necessary one. What boundaries have you experienced in your recovery?

What boundaries have been the most difficult for you?

When you look at the last part of this passage, what promise does it hold for you as you are faithful in your recovery journey?

Through Hosea, God tells the people that there will be difficult times—times when it feels as if nothing is happening. But we are to be patient with the healing process, for there will also come a time when we look with awe at what God has done!

Study #3: Motivated by Love

This study is based on Luke 6:27-36 (page 1299 in *The Life Recovery Bible*). Read these verses several times before working on the study.

1. GOING AGAINST OUR INSTINCTS

Making direct amends is not easy. In fact, with many of the people on our list, we would just as soon let it go and hope they forget what we did. But that's not going to lead us to our recovery and healing. If it were easy, we wouldn't need the Twelve Steps to direct our journey. In this passage, Jesus once again calls us to live differently. He begins with eight paradoxical injunctions that will require God's help. After meditating on these eight principles, evaluate your amends list to see who fits each of the principles.

> But to you who are willing to listen, I say, love your enemies! Do good to those who hate you. Bless those who curse you. Pray for those who hurt you. If someone slaps you on one cheek, offer the other cheek also. If someone demands your coat, offer your shirt also. Give to anyone who asks; and when things are taken away from you, don't try to get them back. Do to others as you would like them to do to you.
>
> LUKE 6:27-31

Which "enemies" are you to make amends with? How can you love them?

Which people on your list "hate you"? How can you "do good" to them?

Which people on your list "curse you"? How can you bless them anyway?

Who on your list has "hurt you"? Can you pray blessings for them?

Does it feel as if anyone on your list has slapped you? How can you "offer the other cheek also"?

Who has taken things from you? How can you give them more, breaking the cycle of revenge and hate?

Who needs something from you? Can you respond?

"Do to others as you would like them to do to you" is the Golden Rule we hear about so often. How does it relate to making direct amends?

2. CHOOSING TO LOVE

Again, as when we looked at humility, we are asked to make amends without expecting anything in return. Jesus calls us to a radical lifestyle so that our lives will stand in bold contrast to the world's standards. We can read the passage on page 268 and say, "Oh, yeah, that would be nice. But no one can live like that today." That's exactly the point Jesus is making. In our own strength, we can't live out these principles. But when we live in relationship with God, we are called to live differently.

> *If you love only those who love you, why should you get credit for that? Even sinners love those who love them! And if you do good only to those who do good to you, why should you get credit? Even sinners do that much! And if you lend money only to those who can repay you, why should you get credit? Even sinners will lend to other sinners for a full return.*
>
> LUKE 6:32-34

How does this passage relate to making direct amends?

From a human standpoint, loving and giving in this way is an impossible way to live. How can you personally develop a healthy dependence on God to help you live in such a selfless way?

3. A NEW WAY TO LIVE

Here, Jesus continues with his "impossible" expectations. If we lend without expecting to be repaid, we are not really lending—we are giving. We are often told to give within the family without expectation, but Jesus establishes this type of giving as a general principle.

Then comes the clincher: When we live this way, we are not acting like everyone else, but "as children of the Most High."

> *Love your enemies! Do good to them. Lend to them without expecting to be repaid. Then your reward from heaven will be very great, and you will truly be acting as children of the Most High, for he is kind to those who are unthankful and wicked. You must be compassionate, just as your Father is compassionate.*
>
> LUKE 6:35-36

If God the Father is compassionate, even to those who are unthankful and wicked, how does this define his compassion toward you?

How can you develop a compassionate lifestyle?

Compassion is an attitude that flows from the heart. Jesus says that when our hearts realize that the Father loves *us* this way, we can show compassion out of the fullness of our loved hearts, even to those who don't deserve it. After all, that's really the point of making direct amends. We don't do it for the sake of someone else; we make amends so that our own hearts can experience recovery and healing and be more compassionate and loving.

Study #4: Being Sensitive

This study is based on 1 Corinthians 10:23-11:1 (pages 1467–1468 in *The Life Recovery Bible*). Read these verses several times before working on the study.

1. CAREFUL LIVING

When we first read, "Don't be concerned for your own good but for the good of others," we may think that Paul is encouraging us to be codependent. But we need to understand why he says what he says. In Paul's day, almost all the meat sold in the meat market was offered to idols when it was slaughtered. Many of those who had become believers had left the worship of idols. They did not want to fall back into their old ways of living. To them, eating meat that was offered to idols was offensive—like they had never left their pagan religious practices.

In contrast to those believers, some weren't bothered by eating meat that had been offered to idols, and they made the point that God did not forbid them to do so. They weren't concerned about this issue, so they shopped openly in the market that sold meat offered to idols and maybe even invited some of the more sensitive people to barbecues at their homes, thinking, *So what if it was offered to idols?*

> *You say, "I am allowed to do anything"—but not everything is good for you. You say, "I am allowed to do anything"—but not everything is beneficial. Don't be concerned for your own good but for the good of others.*
>
> I CORINTHIANS 10:23-24

Think of those who were sensitive to the issue of eating meat that had been offered to idols. What is a similar sensitivity in your experience or in the experiences of those around you?

How do you respond to these sensitivities?

With verse 24 put in context, how does being concerned "for the good of others" differ from being codependent?

2. SENSITIVITY TO OTHERS

One of the principles from this passage relates to making direct amends. We need to be sensitive to what other people may have experienced when we were caught up in our problem behaviors. As we look back, we may think our actions were not problematic. However, they may have been problematic for someone else. Paul suggests that we be very sensitive to how our behavior affects, or affected, someone else. Sensitivity and understanding are so important when we come to this Step. Making direct amends requires a sensitive spirit.

> *So you may eat any meat that is sold in the marketplace without raising questions of conscience. For "the earth is the LORD's, and everything in it." If someone who isn't a believer asks you home for dinner, accept the invitation if you want to. Eat whatever is offered to you without raising questions of conscience. (But suppose someone tells you, "This meat was offered to an idol." Don't eat it, out of consideration for the conscience of the one who told you. It might not be a matter of conscience for you, but it is for the other person.) For why should my freedom be limited by what someone else thinks? If I can thank God for the food and enjoy it, why should I be condemned for eating it?*
>
> I CORINTHIANS 10:25-30

In looking over your list of amends, where does Paul's principle of being sensitive to other people apply?

How will you handle those amends?

3. THE SENSITIVITY PRINCIPLE

In summary, Paul gives us two principles that should guide our lives in recovery. First, we are to consider everything we do and every attitude we have to see if our motivation is to glorify God. If we take this principle seriously, we see that God is interested in every facet of our lives, from the smallest attitude to the largest behavior. Second, we are not to give offense to anyone. Paul adds that he wasn't perfect on this, but he worked at it. Then he makes a very bold suggestion: "Imitate me, just as I imitate Christ." What a way to live—to be able to suggest to those around us that they live as we live! We can only do that if we are working to please Christ in every way.

> So whether you eat or drink, or whatever you do, do it all for the glory of God. Don't give offense to Jews or Gentiles or the church of God. I, too, try to please everyone in everything I do. I don't just do what is best for me; I do what is best for others so that many may be saved. And you should imitate me, just as I imitate Christ.
>
> 1 CORINTHIANS 10:31-11:1

How do you respond to Paul's two principles?

Which is harder for you—glorifying God in everything or not giving offense in anything?

Describe some areas of your life where you would be comfortable saying, "Imitate me."

Where are you still working on the "imitate me" process?

These two principles are at the heart of what Paul believes. He repeats them in several places in his letters. He wants us to think about every area of our lives so that we can purposely glorify God in each area. He wants us to live in such a way that we do not create conflict with our fellow believers. Sounds like a recipe for serenity!

STEP TEN

We continued to take personal inventory, and
when we were wrong, promptly admitted it.

If you think you are standing strong, be careful not to fall.
I CORINTHIANS 10:12

Sharon's Story of Recovery: Sometimes the Only Way *Out* Is *Through*

I guess you can say that life for me started with violence. When my mother was fifteen, she became pregnant from a sexual assault. Her decision to keep me was very brave. Even in the midst of the "free love" 1960s, being unmarried and pregnant carried a stigma. She was shunned and lost most of her friends, whose parents did not allow them to associate with her. She continued high school but had teachers who tried to fail her due to her circumstances. I went to her graduation on her shoulders.

I was raised by young adults, and our home was mostly a party destination. The man my mother married was an alcoholic and very violent. We never knew peace or when the next blowup would occur. My little brother was born as a result of this marriage. There were times my mom told me to carry him down the street to safety while she received a beating from my stepfather. There was drug abuse, violence, and all of the dysfunction that comes with that type of lifestyle.

After my mother divorced her husband, our lives were a procession of boyfriends with similar addictions and issues. We were beaten and abused sexually and mentally. I was given marijuana as a child by my mother. As a teenager, I continued abusing drugs, which became a numbing device for me to deal with the pain of my past. I also perpetuated the cycle of my mother's life, becoming involved in many codependent and abusive relationships. That was just normal for me; I could never dream or fathom there was a way out. I didn't have the tools to make healthy decisions or choices. The people who were supposed to care for me were predators. As a result, I married the same man three times, only with a different face.

Looking back, I can see that God had his hand on my life from the very beginning. He had a plan, a hope, and a future for me. I can remember from the earliest age my desire to go to church. My family never went, but they didn't discourage me from going. I just hitched a ride with any family I could. I didn't care where they went. I think I've been to every kind of church—mainstream, cult, or otherwise. I just wanted to find out about God. Finally, in my late teens I accepted Jesus. I had no idea who he was or what to do with him; I just knew that sin was not fun anymore. In my early twenties, I found a mentor who taught me about the redemptive work of the Holy Spirit and spiritual warfare. I can tell you firsthand that we do have an enemy of our souls, and it was a fight for my life and the lives of my two children.

I wish I could say that once you give your life to God, everything in the past just disappears and life is set right again, but I would be lying. You have to work through your baggage, just like the time when Jesus walked through the middle of a crowd of people crying out for his blood in his hometown. Sometimes the only way *out* is *through*. But with God you have a major ally, for "greater is He who is in you than he who is in the world" (1 John 4:4, NASB). Many times, my enemy has looked behind me, seen Jesus standing there, and fled. I am no longer alone or helpless.

Through many years of wise counsel, I now walk in freedom. When people hear my story, they are amazed at how much God has brought me through. They would never know it by looking at me. I have a happy marriage to a godly man. My children are both believers in their twenties. I am on staff at a local church. I have a good relationship with my mother and have forgiven her. I realize that she was also operating in her own brokenness. She is now a believer as well. I am also a cancer survivor and am in remission, which is another miracle story.

When I first picked up *The Life Recovery Bible*, I felt as if it was speaking my language. On its pages are help and encouragement for the broken, the addicted, the hopeless. People like me. It is a wonderful resource.

STEP TEN INSIGHT

We can be tempted to act as if this Step does not exist. We hit bottom, see where our problems have driven us, give up our favorite addictions, make amends for all the damage we've done, and then never integrate the inventory and confession principles into our lives. We can be tempted to settle for a Nine Step recovery. But when our recovery is vibrant and we are growing, we will continue to look deeply into our lives and evaluate the impact of our behavior on those around us. We will continue to review our defects, and where they have hurt other people, we will admit it and do what we can to make it right.

Working through Step Ten requires that we know where to work and where to look for the areas that need our attention. When we see patterns and frequent repetition in our behaviors, we realize these are symptoms indicating that our recovery is lacking in some way. If we neglect or refuse to monitor our behavior, review our defects, and make amends when necessary, we may have stopped drinking, abusing, controlling, eating, pleasing—but we have short-circuited our recovery and are not really living the life we could. We may have given up our compulsion, addiction, or obsession, but that's about it. Beyond that one accomplishment, life is not much better than when we were using or abusing—especially for our friends and family, the people who have to live with us. There's a big difference between *stopping* a negative behavior and *starting* a life that has a positive impact.

Conducting an ongoing inventory and making amends when neces-sary is crucial to leading an impactful and fruitful life.

The first principle of an ongoing, effective recovery is *honesty*. We must embrace the principles of *transparency* and *authenticity*. That means we stop acting like magicians, creating illusions to convince people that things are not as they appear. We refuse to allow our lives to be governed by fraud, double-dealing, or trickery. We work to root out any kind of deceit because we know that godly character has no need for deception. Proverbs 23:23 challenges us to "get the truth and never sell it." That includes the truth about ourselves.

Another area to review is the level of *striving* in all aspects of our lives. Are we striving to earn favor with God? Are we demanding of others because we are striving to achieve something beyond our capacity? Are we so perfectionistic that we exhaust ourselves trying to get everything just right so we will look good and feel in total control? Sometimes, when we can't accomplish the impossible, we procrastinate—achieving the exact opposite of what we want. When our striving turns inward, we end up struggling to do nothing more than break out of our stagnant state.

In our striving, we become pressured by what we "ought to do" or by what others *tell* us we ought to do. Life becomes a tyranny of "the shoulds," as we continually strive to *do* more, *be* more, or meet some incomprehensible demand that never subsides. Striving holds us hostage while we victimize those around us, always wanting more and never feeling like it's enough.

Psalm 46:10 clearly tells us what God thinks about striving: "Cease striving and know that I am God" (NASB). When we stop trying to do things on our own, we renew our commitment to sur-render. We once again decide to turn our wills and our lives over to God. We *quit* living in an obsessive way and *return* to a life of seren-ity. Our lives once again become focused on what God can do in spite of us, instead of on our own failed attempts to achieve goodness. We remember that God is in control, and we *allow* him to be in control of every element of our lives.

When we get off track in our recovery, we start judging other people—especially those who have hurt us or been insensitive to us. But James asks, "What right do you have to judge your neighbor?" (James 4:12). If Jesus did not come into the world to condemn it (which he did not), where do we get the idea that it is *our* job to do it for him? Our judgment of others places us above Christ and his role on earth. When we find ourselves in this condition, we need to look at *why* we are trying to establish ourselves as superior to others. Usually it's because we're trying to compensate for our own deep sense of inferiority.

Comparing ourselves to others starts us down the road to judgmental conclusions. We move from accepting ourselves to self-evaluation and self-rejection. We often think we have good reason to feel bad about ourselves. If someone betrays us, it is easy to feel that we were not good enough to foster loyalty. Our sense of inferiority demands that we elevate ourselves in some way. So we begin to view ourselves as better than others because we were the *victim* of betrayal rather than the perpetrator. But other people's mistakes do not justify self-righteous judgment and condemnation from us.

The first sober alcoholic I (Steve) ever heard speak was a woman named Gertrude, when I was still in grade school. I loved to listen to her, and I practically memorized her entire story. I remember how she talked about being judgmental of others. She had been raised with a significant amount of wealth and looked down on drunks and drug addicts. But after some time in recovery, her attitude changed, and she even opened her home to numerous alcoholics and addicts who needed a place to sleep. She said she no longer looked down on alcoholics and addicts, but now she had to conquer her tendency to look down on people who looked down on people.

It seems that the more we lose our surrendered hearts, the more negative we become about life. We display pessimism to others, and our lives look and feel as if we are running out of hope. We start to fear the future because we see only the negative potential in it. We take God out of our lives while realizing we cannot rely on ourselves, and we end up stuck without a future we can look forward to or a present that is easy to endure. Our ongoing inventories need to include a checkup on the level of negativity we put out. It is not a stretch to assume that the more negative we are, the more afraid we are of what lies ahead. God is not the originator of that fear.

> *For God has not given us a spirit of fear and timidity, but of power, love, and self-discipline.*
> 2 TIMOTHY 1:7

This verse points out that the source of our fear is Satan—or our own hearts, when they are not surrendered to God. If we leave God out of the equation and don't allow him to be in control, it's easy to wander into an unhealthy state. First we become fearful and timid, and then we become powerless, unloving, and undisciplined. Our lives once again become unmanageable. When we lose our love for others, we become negative about them and pessimistic about life. We get so caught up in our resentments and bitterness and grudges that we lose ourselves and our self-control. If we don't stop the downward spiral brought on by fear, we will relapse.

When we reverse the trend toward fear, our lives take on the characteristics described in Ephesians 4:32: "Be kind to each other, tenderhearted, forgiving one another, just as God through Christ has forgiven you." When we get beyond our self-obsession, we become free to offer grace and tranquility to others who need a break. Kindness, tenderness, and forgiveness are the "*ness*-cessities" of a life of serenity. When our ongoing inventories reveal that we've strayed from the path of kindness, tenderness, and forgiveness, it's time to reassess our progress and do what we need to do to get back on track.

When we take an inventory, reviewing our flaws and areas of vulnerability, we need to admit our shortcomings and make amends. We also need to repair the broken places in our recovery plan so that we see a decrease in the unhealthy parts of our lives. The following are some questions we can ask to determine what might be missing in our recovery:

1. Am I exercising on a regular basis? This keeps me alert, reduces my stress, relaxes me, and gives me a sense of accomplishment.
2. Is my eating helping me or hurting me? I need to eat nutritious food to stabilize my moods and give me energy to stay on task and think clearly.
3. Am I getting enough rest? Sleeping seven or eight hours a night will help my mind and body function at their optimal efficiency.
4. Does my life include too much negative influence and not enough support? Do I need to correct a lack of accountability and an overabundance of negative influence? Do I need to set some new boundaries with people who are unhealthy or overwhelming for me?
5. Am I growing by working the Steps, going to meetings, and getting involved in a Bible study or other things that can help me build character?

"If you think you are standing strong, be careful not to fall" (1 Corinthians 10:12). The best way to avoid falling is to take a regular inventory. And when we're wrong, humbly admit it and make it right.

Amy's Story of Recovery: A Wardrobe of Masks

I am a believer in Jesus Christ and am in recovery from the effects of abuse, eating disorders, and codependency with all its typical attributes—especially anger, pride, and controlling behaviors.

I grew up in an intact, but quite shame-based, family consisting of my mother, father, and younger brother. My grandmother died when my mom was only six, and my mom was raised by a large extended family. My father grew up in the lawless hills of Appalachia and was drafted to fight in World War II while still in high school. Married after the war, my parents waited quite a while to have children. When I finally came along, I was a colicky baby, and the parent-child bonding process was difficult. Plus, my parents had really wanted a boy. The notice about my birth in the local newspaper even said I was a boy. My mother was told not to have any more children, but she did anyway because she and my father wanted a boy so much. So, from the very beginning, I felt I was not the wished-for child. That was a lie, but it felt true.

From my earliest memory, I remember thinking I was bad. I don't recall ever feeling good about myself. I was raised in a strict evangelical church where spirituality was performance-based. I accepted Jesus as my Savior when I was six years old, but I believed God was mad at me most of the time and that my eternal destiny in heaven was in continual jeopardy. My parents did not want me to face eternal damnation, yet my room was such a mess and I left the bathroom sink so dirty that it seemed the only possibility.

My physical needs were met as a child, and I had many friends with whom to socialize. We went on family vacations; I took music lessons and always, *always* looked good. My brother and I were both strong-willed children trying to survive in an emotionally chaotic home, and we did not get along well until adulthood. Today, my parents and I have a close, though still dysfunctional, relationship. I now see how much they did care for me even in their own brokenness, and I have recaptured many of my good memories from childhood. But at the time I felt pain and confusion.

Up until I was thirteen, I experienced inappropriate sexual contact from several males. On one occasion, when I was five, I experienced severe shame from and abandonment by adults who were supposed to be protecting me, but who instead shared in humiliating me with a punishment that had clear sexual overtones. Before I even started kindergarten, I learned to fear men, distrust women, and be ashamed of my body. It wasn't until a life-changing prayer ministry session decades later that I learned where God really was on that horrible night and I came to recognize and find healing from lies I began believing way back then.

To balance the pain of feeling bad and worthless as a child, I began to overachieve in academics and athletics. I started a collection of plaques and trophies that decorated my bedroom walls, yet deep inside I felt unwanted and not special to anyone. I had nightmares and many fears. Many times I packed my suitcase to run away from home. My teachers worried because I never smiled, and I refused to have my picture taken. I hated my face and couldn't look anyone in the eye. I had periodic meltdowns of anger and cried many tears. I did not learn until many years later that this behavior is common after childhood abuse.

Eventually, though, I stopped feeling and just went numb. Life was easier that way. I became fiercely independent, for I couldn't trust anyone to take my side. I began to design a wardrobe of masks that I would wear for the next four decades. Rarely after the age of ten did anyone touch the core of who I was. The world was just not a safe place, and God clearly was not going to protect me. All those church stories about how he loves and takes care of his own weren't true for me, I thought, because I was bad.

Unhealthy boys, and then unhealthy men, seemed to find me. I dated a lot, but I now realize I dated only men with addictive tendencies. I made sure no one ever got to know who I really was—in any way. While still in college, I married a classmate who was an aspiring pastor and the adult child of alcoholics. I felt sorry for him and thought I could help him. It was more of a rescue mission than a marriage. About a year into it, the abuse began.

As a codependent, I thought the spousal abuse was my fault and that I could stop it by being good enough. I wore the mask of a pastor's wife and took care of everyone else's needs, ignoring my own. I worked long hours as a critical care nurse and was the primary source of our household income. I played the piano for every church service, and when I went home I ducked large, flying objects aimed at my head.

Unhealthy men continued to find me. I "danced around the fire" of relational temptation for a while, until finally I wore down. Life seemed hopeless, and I felt trapped. God was far away. I just wanted to be loved for who I was, and my path finally crossed with that of a man who made me feel special. It was one of my most shameful experiences, yet it felt familiar to be bad and hide it.

The verbal and physical abuse at home got worse and worse, until one summer day when it escalated dangerously. I knew in an instant that my life was in serious danger, so I bolted from our apartment and ran across a field to find shelter. I knew that it was time to get out if I wanted to stay alive. My husband and I mutually decided to end our relationship, and strangely enough, after an amends process, we wished each other well and parted on friendly terms. But I had nightmares for years, and I never talked about the abuse to anyone. To my own detriment, I denied and minimized how deeply it had wounded me. I continued to follow the rules I had learned as a child: Don't talk, don't feel, don't trust, and don't rock the boat. I moved to another state and started over.

I soon met another man, and married quickly, but the marriage was in trouble from day one. My new husband was raising three very young children from a previous marriage by himself and needed help. Say no more to a codependent with attachment issues! I was unaware that my new husband was battling a sexual addiction. All I knew was that I constantly felt inadequate and overwhelmed.

In my state of mind, the next best thing to being loved was being needed. I became an instant mom to some very needy babies, and I very much enjoyed parenting. Jimmy, our eldest son, has Down syndrome with medical issues and a huge capacity for love and laughter. Our twin boys were gifted and delightful. The three little guys and I formed a deep bond as their lives and mine began to stabilize. We played tirelessly, tumbling on the floor, climbing trees, reading books, and sleeping under the stars. I recaptured some of my lost childhood and felt safe. We laughed until we were sore, just because it felt good. But some days the laughter never quite reached my eyes and never really covered the pain of what was shaping up to be a second failed marriage—before the age of twenty-seven. But at least this time I wasn't being beaten. I decided to stay for the sake of the kids, confident that if I tried hard enough, my husband would love me the way I wanted to be loved. I soon gave birth to our fourth son.

As if raising four boys was not enough, during this time I completed another academic degree, served on a number of community boards, and took a demanding job on the faculty of a large university. And my husband and I were actively involved in our church. Busyness was my medication for the bad feelings I still carried inside. I told myself I was having fun. I had no idea how insane my life was.

My approach seemed to work for more than two decades. I raised accomplished sons, enjoyed professional successes, and was privileged to serve in ministry. Vacations with friends were a blast. I finally learned to spot unhealthy men early on, and there were no more real-life temptations, only a few leftover fantasies that flared now and then. But I had no insight into how much energy I expended trying to control my husband's addiction, trying to keep him happy enough to stay and not hurt me. While he was addicted to the rush of sexual arousal to medicate his pain, I did not realize that I had become addicted to fixing and controlling him. I depended on our unhealthy relationship to make me feel better about myself.

Life began to unravel quickly after our youngest son left for college. Jimmy was the only one left at home by then, and he required more and more around-the-clock care as his life expectancy grew shorter. Finances were tight with kids in college, so I took a second job, thinking my husband would be happier if we had less financial pressure. I was still fixing him to feel good about myself. But the stress finally took its toll.

On my way to work at the university one morning, I stopped for a routine physical exam by my physician. To my complete shock, the exam detected an aggressive cancer. Worse yet, it had already spread. In a daze, I canceled my classes and went home, too numb to cry. How could God do this to me? How could I not live long enough to see Jimmy through his last days? I began preparations for immediate surgery. Jimmy became my reason to live, as I vowed not to die before he did.

The initial cancer treatment was successful, but life quickly took another ugly twist. I came home early one day from a doctor's appointment and found explicit pornographic websites open on our home computer. I was in disbelief, but there was no denying what I saw and what it meant. With my own body scarred by recent surgery, I felt devastated, then livid. I tried to cover my shame with anger, my most familiar emotion. I had no idea that my husband's sexual addiction had nothing to do with me, that I didn't cause it and my best efforts would not stop it.

Trauma and drama continued to rock my world. The next month, I was a traveling on a plane when one of the engines went out and the pilot announced that we would make an emergency landing. I had heard the joke about what happens when codependents think they are going to die: someone else's life passes before their eyes. Well, it's true. I was so involved in everyone else's stuff that I didn't even know what was mine to review in my ten remaining minutes of life! As we circled the airport until emergency vehicles could line the runway, I promised God I would work harder to be good enough—as if I suddenly had some power over my out-of-control life.

Jimmy was in and out of the hospital a lot by then. It was during those hard, exhausting days that the veil of deception in my marriage was pulled back completely. As I sat by Jimmy's bedside in the hospital one afternoon, the door opened suddenly and a woman walked in and sat down across from me. At first, I couldn't understand why she was there, but I soon realized that she was having an affair with my husband. I could hardly breathe. I clutched Jimmy's hand. The unthinkable had apparently happened. At the lowest point in my life as a mother, I now had to confront my feelings of failure as a wife. I could feel darkness closing in. I fought to stay conscious. I had to block out reality for now. Jimmy needed me. A few days later, he died.

Despite the chaos in my heart and home, Jimmy's funeral was a celebration of his life. But in his absence, I was left very much alone. Crying didn't begin to diminish the pain. I ached to hold him just one more time. I barely remember the next few months. But soon my grief turned to anger and reality came crashing in. I had to pursue the marital deception that could no longer be denied. Drawing on strength that God mercifully gave me, I searched until I found conclusive evidence to confront the addiction that had once again ravaged my marriage and my heart.

My husband and I separated for eighteen months. The losses were more than I could bear. I couldn't grieve Jimmy's death because I was grieving the loss of my core relationship, home, and health. All my efforts to be good enough had failed. All my efforts to be in control had failed. I often describe this as my life "blowing up." I was shattered and had no sense of self. I began to show symptoms of post-traumatic stress disorder, commonly called PTSD, which can occur after a shock, leaving the sufferer powerless and in pain. I could hardly go to work, much less accomplish anything. I was furious with God for not protecting me. He hadn't cared when I was a child or a bruised pastor's wife, and he apparently didn't care now. My long-term habit of using food for comfort took a one hundred eighty-degree swing, and I became anorexic. I developed critically high blood pressure and could spend an entire day crying on the bathroom floor, unable to stand. I hoped I would die. Psalm 6:6-7 reflected where I was at: "I am worn out from sobbing. All night I flood my bed with weeping, drenching it with my tears. My vision is blurred by grief."

During this time, my husband started recovery, and one of his accountability partners led me to a support group for women whose spouses struggle with sexual addiction. Those women accepted my anger and despair and walked me through the chaos. I took the wise advice of my counselor and began to read the Bible with a new eye. Yet I could not fathom that God loved me, because I felt so unlovable and he had allowed such pain in my life.

It took me a while, but I finally began my Step work with a recovery group that had started in my home church. Step Four, on taking a life inventory, was both breathtaking and life changing. As a codependent, I thought everything bad and shameful was my fault. Instead, I learned that I was not to blame for the dysfunction of others. I can only clean up my side of the street and work on my own behaviors. I am powerless to control the choices of others, but I am not alone when I hurt. I learned that I had been programmed to be in addictive relationships since childhood. I learned that I had a self-hatred and core emptiness that had not been filled. Through healthy relationships with my sisters in recovery, I began to do self-care and discovered God's love and acceptance in a new way.

I continued to wrestle, however, with the lie that God didn't care about me and didn't protect me. Through working with my sponsor and pastor, I finally realized that God does not suspend the free will of people just to keep us pain-free and happy. He also does not suspend the consequences of our own sin and poor choices. But the pain that results does not negate God's love for us—or for *me*. God never left me in the hardest of times. He never took his eye off of me. Learning to hold two paradoxical truths—that I suffered, yet was loved by God—was hard, but I am finally getting it and experiencing God's love in amazing new ways.

I cannot say yet that I am glad for all the things that have come into my life. But I can say this: I would not go back to my old life where I was desperately trying to survive under my own power. I would not give up the transformational experience I have had in doing the Step work, especially Steps Six and Seven. Romans 12:2 has become one of my life verses: "Do not conform to the pattern of this world, but be transformed by the renewing of your mind. Then you will be able to test and approve what God's will is—his good, pleasing, and perfect will" (NIV). Am I ever blessed to have my mind renewed and my heart restored!

Eventually, my husband and I decided to reunite to see if our marriage could be resurrected, though wounds were deep and trust destroyed. With perseverance and a willingness to change, things have improved over the past four years. There are still hard days, but they don't stretch into bad weeks anymore. I am beginning to embrace brokenness—his and mine. I am learning to ask for what I need and not feel guilty. I am learning to set boundaries without building walls. My respect continues to grow for my husband as he presses on in his own recovery. As the Serenity Prayer says, I am living one day at a time, one moment at a time, seeking reasonable happiness in this life.

A passage that became dear to me while preparing this testimony is 1 Peter 5:10-11 in *The Message*: "The suffering won't last forever. It won't be long before this generous God who has great plans for us in Christ—eternal and glorious plans they are!—will have you *put together and on your feet for good*. He gets the last word; yes, he does" (emphasis added). If you had seen me just a few years ago, lying on the bathroom floor begging to die, the words "put together for good" would not have popped into your mind. But God gets the last word.

A song that builds on this verse has been an integral part of my healing. It says, "You give and take away. You give and take away. My heart will choose to say, 'Lord, blessed be Your name.'"[11] In closing, let me tell you what I have lost and what I have gained in this sifting season of my life.

I lost my health, my emotional tranquility, my son Jimmy, my innocent and fun-loving relationships with my three surviving sons, many friends who couldn't stand the intensity of my pain, and my entire family of in-laws. Professionally, I lost a number of career opportunities and the income associated with those. But listen to what else I lost, with few regrets: my self-sufficiency, my sense of entitlement, many of my fears, and my need to protect myself from all pain.

Let me also tell you what I've gained: I have gained the truth about who God is and how much he loves me. I have gained trustworthy, authentic friends who love me in the worst of times—and who don't desert me even when my addiction to ice cream flares wildly. I'm gaining tools to break the generational curses of anger, pride, and unforgivingness that have plagued my family for centuries. I've gained hope for a marriage once pronounced dead. And most important, I've gained joy, which doesn't depend on my circumstances or on any other person—a joy that calls out for celebration, a celebration of healing and grace.

God gives and takes away. True. But he has given me *so much more* restoration than I ever dreamed possible. He is a generous God. He has the last word. Blessed be the name of the Lord.

STEP TEN BIBLE STUDIES

Study #1: A Condition of the Heart

This study is based on Matthew 13:1-23 (page 1216 in *The Life Recovery Bible*). Read the verses several times before working on the study.

1. STORY TIME

One of Jesus' favorite teaching methods was using parables. A parable is a simple story used to illustrate a moral or spiritual lesson, often making a comparison or drawing an analogy between something common in life and a spiritual principle. Try to understand this parable, the parable of the farmer scattering seed, from the perspective of the crowd, as if you haven't read Jesus' explanation. How might the crowd on the shore have interpreted what Jesus said?

> *Listen! A farmer went out to plant some seeds. As he scattered them across his field, some seeds fell on a footpath, and the birds came and ate them. Other seeds fell on shallow soil with underlying rock. The seeds sprouted quickly because the soil was shallow. But the plants soon wilted under the hot sun, and since they didn't have deep roots, they died. Other seeds fell among thorns that grew up and choked out the tender plants. Still other seeds fell on fertile soil, and they produced a crop that was thirty, sixty, and even a hundred times as much as had been planted! Anyone with ears to hear should listen and understand.*

MATTHEW 13:3-9

Remembering that a parable is an analogy, what do you think the *seeds* represented to the crowd?

What do you think the *ground* represented to the crowd?

What do you think the *crop* represented to the crowd?

2. A LACK OF UNDERSTANDING

In this parable, Jesus tried to help the disciples understand why not everyone responded positively to the message of God's Kingdom. The crowds were so large that Jesus had to teach from a boat anchored near the shore. But for all his popularity, Jesus met with a lot of resistance and negativity.

The disciples were puzzled. They asked Jesus, "Why do you use parables when you talk to the people?" (Matthew 13:10). Jesus referred to what many of the prophets of Israel were told.

They look, but they don't really see.
They hear, but they don't really listen or understand.
This fulfills the prophecy of Isaiah that says,
"When you hear what I say,
you will not understand.
When you see what I do,
you will not comprehend.
For the hearts of these people are hardened,
and their ears cannot hear,

and they have closed their eyes—
so their eyes cannot see,
and their ears cannot hear,
and their hearts cannot understand,
and they cannot turn to me
and let me heal them."

MATTHEW 13:13-15

In Isaiah 6:9-10, the prophet says the people had hardened hearts and really didn't want to hear or understand. They may have looked, but they really didn't see.

What parallel do you see in today's culture, where someone is popular but not understood?

Why do you think Jesus was not understood?

What do you find hard to understand regarding Jesus and his teachings?

3. GUARDING THE GARDEN

The people loved listening to Jesus, but not even his own disciples always understood the meaning of his parables. They often asked Jesus later to explain what he meant, as they did in this case.

Jesus tells his disciples that if they really want to hear and understand, they would be able to do so. He says that those who seek to understand will have more understanding given to them (Matthew

13:10-12). As part of our ongoing inventory, we seek to understand and we look forward to the increase in understanding that Jesus promises. Now let's look at how Jesus explained the parable to his disciples.

> *Listen to the explanation of the parable about the farmer*
> *planting seeds: The seed that fell on the footpath represents those*
> *who hear the message about the Kingdom and don't understand*
> *it. Then the evil one comes and snatches away the seed that was*
> *planted in their hearts. The seed on the rocky soil represents*
> *those who hear the message and immediately receive it with*
> *joy. But since they don't have deep roots, they don't last long.*
> *They fall away as soon as they have problems or are persecuted*
> *for believing God's word. The seed that fell among the thorns*
> *represents those who hear God's word, but all too quickly the*
> *message is crowded out by the worries of this life and the lure of*
> *wealth, so no fruit is produced. The seed that fell on good soil*
> *represents those who truly hear and understand God's word and*
> *produce a harvest of thirty, sixty, or even a hundred times as*
> *much as had been planted!*
>
> MATTHEW 13:18-23

The crowd on the shore probably tried to understand Jesus' story in a literal way. How did your description of the crowd's interpretation in the previous section compare with what Jesus said he meant?

What kind of ground was your heart before you began your recovery journey?

What kind of ground would you say your heart is today?

What do you think is the "harvest" in your life?

Understanding Jesus' work in our lives is a heart matter. Earlier we saw that, despite his various failings, King David was considered a man after God's own heart because he had a soft, open heart toward God. In the parable of the seed, Jesus suggests that we do the same— that we keep our hearts as "good soil," ready to receive any correction we need along the way.

Study #2: Staying Current

This study is based on Romans 7:18–8:1 (page 1440 in *The Life Recovery Bible*). Read these verses several times before working on the study.

1. ONGOING RECOVERY

To really understand what Paul is grappling with in this passage, we need to go back to Romans 5, where this section begins. In Romans 5:6-11, Paul tells us what condition we were in when Jesus came and died on the cross for us. We were utterly helpless, sinners, and enemies of God (and some translations include *rebellious*). In other words, we were not an impressive lot for whom someone would likely be willing to die.

In Romans 6, Paul speaks against those who said, "Since God loved me when I was a worthless nothing, what difference does it make how I live now?" These people believed that the more they continued to sin, the more they demonstrated God's love. Paul argues to the contrary, that anyone who believes that we should continue to sin doesn't understand the price God paid to provide salvation and a new life.

Then we come to Romans 7. Here Paul addresses the group opposing those he spoke against in Romans 6, people who say that because God loved us in our awful state, we must clean up our lives to prove that we are worth God's love. But Paul finds that this is an impossible task, and by the end of chapter 7, he seems depressed. He expresses the frustration he experienced when trying to clean himself up.

> *And I know that nothing good lives in me, that is, in my sinful nature. I want to do what is right, but I can't. I want to do what is good, but I don't. I don't want to do what is wrong, but I do it anyway. But if I do what I don't want to do, I am not really the one doing wrong; it is sin living in me that does it.*
> ROMANS 7:18-20

In what ways have you struggled as Paul struggled?

How does your current struggle fit with continuing to take personal inventory?

Paul describes a common human struggle. Some have called it our struggle with the "shoulds" of life; whenever we pressure ourselves with something we should or shouldn't do, part of us resists and goes the opposite way. How has this been a part of your struggle?

2. DESPAIR BEFORE RELEASE

Now Paul says that his struggle is something that everyone experiences. He likens it to a war within himself, and thus a common war fought within each of us. The struggle is so great that he ends up in misery. He is depressed by the internal battle. Does that sound like the battle you have had with your addictions, dependencies, or problems? As we discovered in the first three Steps, we end the battle by surrendering, which is what Paul does here.

Paul's original letter did not have chapter breaks, so his thoughts at the end of chapter 7 move right into the beginning of chapter 8, where we discover what happens when we surrender.

> *I have discovered this principle of life—that when I want to do what is right, I inevitably do what is wrong. I love God's law with all my heart. But there is another power within me that is at war with my mind. This power makes me a slave to the sin that is still within me. Oh, what a miserable person I am! Who will free me from this life that is dominated by sin and death? Thank God! The answer is in Jesus Christ our Lord. So you see how it is: In my mind I really want to obey God's law, but because of my sinful nature I am a slave to sin. So now there is no condemnation for those who belong to Christ Jesus.*
> ROMANS 7:21–8:1

"No condemnation!" When we turn our wills and our lives over to God, it's not judgment we encounter—it is no condemnation! Wow, what a loving and faithful God we have who walks with us!

If there is no condemnation for us, why do we continue to take personal inventory?

We see in Romans 6 that just because there is no condemnation doesn't mean we have license to live any way we choose. There is still a goal we work toward in our healing and recovery. How would you describe your goal?

How does Step Ten help you as you pursue your goal?

For many people, the thought that there is no condemnation in Christ is almost too good to be true. But it *is* true. That's what God wants us to understand by his unfailing love for us. When our eyes meet his, we see that his are filled with love for us. In fact, the prophet Zephaniah says, "The LORD your God is living among you. He is a mighty savior. He will take delight in you with gladness. With his love, he will calm all your fears. He will rejoice over you with joyful songs" (Zephaniah 3:17). Not only are God's eyes filled with love for us; he even sings over us!

Study #3: Staying the Course

This study is based on 2 Timothy 2:3-13 (page 1562 in *The Life Recovery Bible*). Read these verses several times before working on the study.

1. THE POWER OF PERSEVERANCE

One of the people the apostle Paul mentored was a young man named Timothy. Timothy had accompanied Paul on a preaching journey, and when they came to Ephesus, Paul suggested that Timothy stay there to lead the local church. He was the pastor to the Ephesians.

This letter is probably the last one Paul wrote that we have. It was written to Timothy while Paul was a prisoner in Rome, around AD 65, just prior to his martyrdom. That's part of why he speaks of suffering. This was also a period of time when Christians were under great persecution throughout the Roman Empire. In addition, false teachers were creating problems for Paul and Timothy and getting Christians in trouble with the government. Paul's advice to Timothy is very relevant to us as we continue our healing and recovery.

> *Endure suffering along with me, as a good soldier of Christ Jesus. Soldiers don't get tied up in the affairs of civilian life, for then they cannot please the officer who enlisted them. And athletes cannot win the prize unless they follow the rules. And hardworking farmers should be the first to enjoy the fruit of their labor.*
>
> 2 TIMOTHY 2:3-6

At times, we grow weary and tired and we may even want to give up on our recovery. When we take our continual inventory, it may seem as though we're not making any progress. As Paul sat in prison, he must have been concerned about what lay ahead, not just for him, but for those he had trained, like Timothy.

How do Paul's words here encourage you?

Paul uses three examples: soldiers, athletes, and farmers. Which is most relevant to you and why?

How would you paraphrase what Paul says about athletes "following the rules"?

What are your "rules of recovery"?

2. FINISH THE TASK

Paul powerfully concludes this part of his letter to Timothy, leaving us with something to ponder. He talks about dying, hardship, denying God, and being unfaithful. We can understand Paul's emphasis on dying and hardship, because he faced both, and the church certainly faced hardships. When the persecution of the church broke out and those who wouldn't deny Jesus were sent to the lions in the Colosseum, many who had professed Christianity apparently denied the Lord. Paul said the Lord would deny them as well. But denying God is not the same as being unfaithful. We may stumble along the way, but we can count on God to be faithful at all times. God cannot be unfaithful—that would be a denial of his character. Regardless of our struggles, God will be faithful to us.

> *Think about what I am saying. The Lord will help you understand all these things. . . . This is a trustworthy saying: If we die with him, we will also live with him. If we endure hardship, we will reign with him. If we deny him, he will deny us. If we are unfaithful, he remains faithful, for he cannot deny who he is.*
>
> 2 TIMOTHY 2:7, 11-13

In what ways have you struggled recently with your recovery?

What has been difficult for you in continuing to take inventory?

Where have you been successful in taking your current inventory?

How does God's faithfulness encourage you?

In several of our studies, we have looked at God's unfailing love for us. Here Paul takes it a step further as he tells us that faithfulness is intrinsic to God's nature. For God to be unfaithful to us would be a denial of who he is at his core. He must always be faithful to us.

Study #4: Growing Forward

This study is based on Hebrews 4:12-16 (page 1582 in *The Life Recovery Bible*). Read these verses several times before working on the study.

1. PREVENTING RELAPSE

Step Ten is our relapse prevention step. If we faithfully continue taking personal inventory and making amends along the way, we will stay centered on our path of recovery and healing. This passage encourages us to continue to be fearless in our ongoing inventories, for we know that nothing is hidden from God. So let's get it on the table, confess it, and make things right.

Notice how the passage begins, talking about the Word of God, the Bible, the *it*. The writer of Hebrews tells us that God's Word is alive and powerful—and so sharp that when we open ourselves up to it, it exposes everything we need to know.

Then suddenly, the passage shifts from the objective "it" of the Bible to God himself—from *it* to *he*. How can this be? What did the writer have in mind in this short but powerful passage? The only way to understand this is to see that the Bible and God are woven tightly together. The Bible is alive and powerful because God is active and alive and powerful within its pages every time we open it. When we read what it says, we are reading what God is saying to us.

> *For the word of God is alive and powerful. It is sharper than the sharpest two-edged sword, cutting between soul and spirit, between joint and marrow. It exposes our innermost thoughts and desires. Nothing in all creation is hidden from God. Everything is naked and exposed before his eyes, and he is the one to whom we are accountable.*
> HEBREWS 4:12-13

What does it mean for you that the Bible and God are at work together?

How has something you've read in the Bible come alive for you?

How has the Bible helped you in continuing to take your personal inventory?

2. HOLD FIRMLY AND BOLDLY

Now the writer shifts the focus from the Word of God and God himself to our great High Priest, Jesus. Everything in our lives—every intimate detail—is exposed to God and to Jesus. Because Jesus sees everything and because he understands our weaknesses—having faced everything we've faced, yet without sin—we can come *boldly* into his presence. We don't have to come to him in shame; we don't have to come to him embarrassed; we don't have to try to hide from him. He understands us and looks at us with unfailing love. He is there to help us!

Though the book of Hebrews was written for Jewish believers in Jesus during the first century, this passage was completely foreign to what the Jewish people had experienced for hundreds of years. After Moses, the only one who could come before the Lord was the high priest, and he could only do so once a year with great care. According to tradition, before the high priest went into what was called the Holy of Holies in the Temple, he would tie a rope around his ankle. That way, if he died while inside the most holy place, the other priests could drag his body out, for no one else was allowed to go in. How freeing it must have been to those Jewish believers who followed Jesus to know that now we can all come boldly into the Holy of Holies—directly into the presence of God.

So then, since we have a great High Priest who has entered heaven, Jesus the Son of God, let us hold firmly to what we believe. This High Priest of ours understands our weaknesses, for he faced all of the same testings we do, yet he did not sin. So let us come boldly to the throne of our gracious God. There we will receive his mercy, and we will find grace to help us when we need it most.

HEBREWS 4:14-16

Regular Bible reading was central to those who developed the Twelve Steps and is important to anyone serious about recovery. As you put these two passages together, how would you explain the importance of reading the Bible regularly?

Prior to beginning your recovery, you may have come into God's presence with anger over his failure to do what you asked. How has this now changed for you?

When you come before the Lord, you can find mercy and help. What does this mean to you?

In these five verses, the writer of Hebrews weaves together the reality of God, the accessibility of God, the reality of Jesus, and the living power of the Bible. He makes no distinction between them. He moves easily from the "it" of the Bible to the "him" of God and Jesus. The point is that the living God is ready to meet us in the pages of the Bible. Meeting Jesus through the Bible shows us what we need to work on as we take our personal inventories and admit our wrongdoing.

STEP ELEVEN

We sought through prayer and meditation to improve our conscious contact with God, praying only for knowledge of his will for us and the power to carry it out.

Devote yourselves to prayer with an alert mind and a thankful heart.

COLOSSIANS 4:2

Sarah's Story of Recovery: What It Means to Be a Child of God

Ever since I gave my heart to Jesus fifteen years ago, I have desired to get to know God in a more intimate way. In my personal quest, I have learned what works and what doesn't work for me. If any of my experiences are helpful to even one other person, I will be grateful. I'm happy to share how God has changed me and the tools he used to get me to where I am today. I should add that where I am today is far from perfect, but it's far better than where I came from. I may not be as far along as I would like, but thank God I am not where I used to be!

Though I had a brief encounter with Catholicism in elementary school, I did not grow up in church. My parents drank heavily, fought often, and showed very little love or gave very little structure to our lives at home. I am happy to say that they are both sober today, have found their own Christian church, and have been transformed by knowing Jesus Christ as their Lord, but none of that happened until I was an adult and living outside their home.

I am the youngest of three children and the only girl. Both of my brothers made choices similar to mine growing up, but both are now sober as well and walking toward a new way of living.

My story is not much different from that of other alcoholics or addicts, but it is my story. Before I finished sixth grade, I had experimented with beer, wine, marijuana, and a few other drugs. In fact, by the time I was five, I had a wineglass that my folks would fill for me on special occasions. I learned quickly that if I offered to refill my mom's glass for her, I could take a few gulps and top it back off before handing it to her.

After getting sober, I looked back and realized this was an early sign of my addictive nature and a stronghold that would easily take hold in my life. My family has a very long and complex history of addiction on both sides—with suicides, abuse, and loss of life all directly related to alcoholism.

I am also the child of a now-retired military officer, so we moved often while I was growing up, staying in each new place for only a short time. That, coupled with my low self-esteem, made it hard for me to feel as if I fit in anywhere, and I often gravitated toward others with similar backgrounds. My lack of healthy relationships and my distorted view of who I was wove their way into every aspect of my life.

The most glaring manifestation of this was my choice in men. It should come as no surprise that I became aggressively sexually active before my thirteenth birthday—initially with a twenty-two-year-old man. From that point forward, I would sleep with just about anyone. I had no moral fiber to speak of and tended to attract much older men who were as unhealthy as I was. For years, I joked that I was a "garbage magnet," which meant that when I walked into a room, the sickest, most dysfunctional and abusive man would make a beeline for me. But I wasn't willing to do anything about it. Today I believe that "like attracts like," and we tend to gravitate toward people who share our beliefs and values—no matter how good or bad. The good news, however, is that the moment we receive Christ, he gives us "the right to become children of God" (John 1:12). Now that I'm a follower of Jesus, I'm no longer a garbage magnet and have not been for a long, long time.

I can clearly remember my first Alcoholics Anonymous sponsor telling me that eventually the spirit of God would be so strong in me that I would "turn off the people of my past" in a way that they would not even understand. In the midst of my drinking, sex was such a big part of my life that I took jobs in strip clubs to immerse myself in the lifestyle to which I had grown accustomed. I dressed the part all the time, leaving little room for imagination. I showed every part of my flesh possible, short of getting arrested. I learned that dressing provocatively got me things—drugs, money, attention (good and bad—any kind would do), and what I thought was love. Clearly, I had no idea what real love was, and it took me a lot of work to discover godly love—unconditional and without limit. Until I truly became willing to change, I never understood why men thought it was okay to make overt sexual comments to me. I used to blame men for their bad behavior, without looking at my own actions.

The first time I became aware that my behavior affected how men perceived me was while chatting with some people before an AA meeting. We were celebrating the anniversary of a man with many years of sobriety, and some of the men thought a sex toy would be an appropriate gift. One guy asked me if I would like to borrow it before the meeting started. My first reaction was to make a lewd comment in an effort to play along, but thankfully the Holy Spirit convicted me and put a bridle on my tongue. I politely declined and walked away. I left that group soon after, because it did not represent AA or recovery well. But that moment was eye-opening for me and helped me realize that God could only do so much to change me if I wasn't willing to conform to his will. I could pray for change, but I also had to be willing to take steps to honor God and facilitate change.

Over the next few months, I experienced many more revelations just like that one; within eighteen months, I can honestly say that many of my old habits, attitudes, and behaviors had fallen away, never to return. During that time, as a single woman, I decided to recommit my body to Christ, which meant complete abstinence until marriage, no matter how long it took. I figured that God still needed to do a work in me—boy, was I right!—but I underestimated the freedom that came with those changes. I surrounded myself with people who lived for God, walked in the Spirit, and showed love to all. Friends that I'd had for years did not understand my decisions. Some came along for the ride, and others just faded away. But I had a lot to learn about living a new life; I still had a lot of old ideas floating around in my head, with many lies and strongholds from years of abuse and addiction.

Some change was immediate and radical, but most took time and commitment, along with a willingness on my part to seek and do God's will. When I saw the pure joy and satisfaction that some believers had, I decided I wanted what they had; I wanted *all* God had to offer and nothing less. I quit listening to the music I had grown up on and instead filled my spirit with worship tunes and teaching tapes. I gave up TV, with the exception of a few teaching series and videos that were good for my soul. To this day, I guard my heart closely and choose very carefully how I spend my time. I have invested a lot of time in reading God's Word and prayer—often flat on my face.

Eventually, I asked God for a life mate, a husband that *he* would choose for me, not someone that only I thought would be good. I remember asking a friend about my desire for a husband, and she told me to make a list of everything I wanted in a husband and share it with her. When I came back with what I thought was a reasonable and acceptable list, she agreed, but then said, "Now, Sarah, you can't expect a man to be all of these things to you, unless you first are all of these things yourself." *What?!* Some of the characteristics on my list were *patient, tolerant, even-tempered, reliable, punctual, kind, affectionate, truthful, loving, accepting,* and *non-judging*—well, you get the picture.

True to my friend's suggestion, God did not bring Tom into my life until we both had made major changes in our lives. Just so you know, that took about six or seven years! But I thank God every day because our marriage today is *solid*, and by the time we began dating, we had known each other for years—there were no surprises and no secrets. We stood before the Lord on our wedding day like two virgins, completely restored, new creatures in Christ.

What I haven't told you is much about my drinking years, but there was a lot of trauma during that time. It all started with my parents telling me what a screwup I was, how I would never amount to anything, and that I was an embarrassment to them. Because I believed those lies, it was only natural for me to find that type of attention from men. Strongholds developed, and patterns repeated themselves over and over. For years, I was abused by men, raped, viciously beaten within an inch of my life several times, and belittled in just about every form possible. I got pregnant four times and terminated each pregnancy—all before my twenty-first birthday.

When I finally got sick and tired of my life, I was living with a man, smoking crack and drinking daily, and using whatever means available to get my drugs, including my body. But one night, after smoking crack for three days straight, I reached the ultimate bottom and found myself crying in a corner. I vividly recall saying these words out loud: "God, if you are there, and if you care at all about me, please help me stop living like this. Please help!"

I was so filled with shame that I did not believe anything would happen—but it did. For the very first time in my life, I totally lost the desire to use drugs or drink, and I found myself in an AA meeting the very next day. I am overjoyed to report that I picked up a chip at that meeting to show that I desired a new way of life, and I have been clean and sober ever since.

Over the course of the next few months, I learned that prayer would help, and I used it the only way I knew how—just talking honestly to God. I eventually asked him to send someone into my life who could teach me about him, and of course he did. He sent an on-fire follower of Jesus into my life, and she rocked my world. Through Pam, I learned how to depend on God. I learned that to be rid of my old self, I had to renew my mind and let go of the things of this world so that I could be transformed. I could not act on my feelings and expect to experience true freedom in my life. Things I never considered harmful, such as gossip, certain TV shows, or music, could squelch the Spirit that now dwelled inside of me. By God's grace, I stopped smoking and changed the way I talked and dressed—because, for me, these things hindered my relationship with God.

No matter our past, we have all sinned, and in order to change and grow into Christ's image, we need renewal through immersion in God's Word and accountability with other believers. Even seasoned Christians get stuck, discouraged, and unwilling to look in the mirror. (I can share evidence of that in my own walk.) The good news is that God gives us a way to restore our broken relationships with him and with others.

I've learned to stop describing myself by what I *do*—I am a mother, a wife, a business manager, a bus driver, or a programmer—and instead think of myself according to *who I am*. As believers in Jesus Christ, we are children of God. Before I met Pam, I had no frame of reference for living as a Christian, nor did I understand who I had become when I submitted to Christ. Only by studying God's Word and other recovery materials have I begun to grasp God's truths about what it means to be a child of God.

For me, the change began when I started to develop relationships with godly women who held me accountable for my actions. They called me out on my bad behavior and reminded me to focus on God. I worked through the Steps of AA, personal Bible studies, and other recovery materials. These tools have given me another method to face Satan and understand his lies and attempts to draw me away from God. What is great is the depth of knowledge I have gained from this profound but simple-to-use material. I am better equipped as a believer, but also in my roles as a friend, mother, wife, and daughter, among other things.

It is my desire that everyone would know his or her *true* identity in Jesus Christ—what we are and what we are not—to stop the enemy in his tracks and prevent him from influencing God's children. God desires us to be free, full of joy, and at peace, not living in the past, which was full of doubts and fears.

"Therefore from now on we recognize no one according to the flesh; even though we have known Christ according to the flesh, yet now we know Him in this way no longer. Therefore if anyone is in Christ, he is a new creature; the old things passed away; behold, new things have come" (2 Corinthians 5:16-17, NASB).

I am accepted. I am secure. I am significant.

STEP ELEVEN INSIGHT

If we look back at our prayers, we often discover they consist mainly of asking God to deliver something we want. "Give me, forgive me, bless me, fix me, show me, protect me"—that about sums up the content of most of our prayers. We contact God to *get* things from him. We are consumers, wanting to consume more of what the world, or God, has to offer. In the process, we miss having a genuine relationship with God. We forget about the source and become fixated on the results that he gives. That's why we need Step Eleven to cause us to pause and reflect and reconsider the composition of our spiritual lives. Step Eleven invites us to move beyond our self-centered motivations into a godly desire to know God better and know better what he wants us to do with our lives.

As in every Step, some key words in Step Eleven make a huge difference. The first significant word is *sought*: "We sought . . . to improve our conscious contact with God." A relationship with God doesn't just happen. We must desire it, seek it, pursue it. The idea of *seeking* leads us away from waiting for God to do what he wants *us* to do. This Step points to the priority of seeking after God rather than waiting for him to intervene.

When we actively seek contact with God, we're not just calling on him for help. We want to be with him, dwell with him, and experience as much of him as we possibly can. David expresses this well in Psalm 27:4: "The one thing I ask of the LORD—the thing I seek most—is to live in the house of the LORD all the days of my life, delighting in the LORD's perfections and meditating in his Temple."

David truly was a man after God's own heart. Though he was an imperfect man, capable of some extreme acts of immorality, he wanted to live his life in God's presence. He wanted to live with God every day he was alive. This was a man seeking to improve his conscious contact with God.

Experiencing God in a deeper and richer way requires time. You can't get there by rushing through your day and thinking about God only when it's convenient. If you want to improve your conscious contact with him, you need to carve out some time. Perhaps you think you can't fit another thirty-minute block of time into your schedule. Most likely you could, but if not, ten minutes is better than no minutes—even five minutes is better than nothing. We must decide that improving our contact with God is enough of a priority that we are willing to make it a daily reality.

Prayer and meditation are two processes we can use to make this happen. If we want our prayer time to be valuable, we can follow the instructions given by Jesus in Matthew 6:5-6.

> *When you pray, don't be like the hypocrites who love to pray publicly on street corners and in the synagogues where everyone can see them. I tell you the truth, that is all the reward they will ever get. But when you pray, go away by yourself, shut the door behind you, and pray to your Father in private. Then your Father, who sees everything, will reward you.*

Contact with God occurs best when we step away from the hustle and bustle of our daily lives and commune with him privately in prayer. Yes, we can ask for things. But we also want to be sure to thank him, praise him, and wait for him to light up our hearts, minds, and spirits. If we find it difficult to pray, we can use God's Word as a source for our prayers. We can pray the Psalms as if they were coming from our own hearts. We can meditate on them and consider their deeper meaning. In the process, we can hide God's Word in our hearts, as it says in Psalm 119:11: "I have hidden your word in my heart, that I might not sin against you."

If we are having a tough time feeling the presence of God, we can use this check to be sure we are ready for what God has for us.

> God's light came into the world, but people loved the darkness more than the light, for their actions were evil.
>
> JOHN 3:19

That sounds pretty serious—and it is. Perhaps at one time we were very committed to doing evil things. Now that we have been saved from that life, we must be certain there is no residue that infects our time with God. We need to be sure we really want God's light in our lives and are willing to live with it. When we are ready, God's light shines within us, and we come to understand ourselves, others, and God in a whole new way.

The second part of this Step is good instruction for everyone. It directs us to pray for only two things. First, we are to pray for the knowledge of God's will for us, rather than asking God to fulfill our requests and submit to our will for ourselves. Praying to understand God's will is a way of relinquishing control to him. It makes God the focus, the purpose, the direction, and the reason for our recovered lives. We come to a wonderful place of peace and serenity when our greatest desire and motive is to know what God wants us to do.

Second, we are to pray for the power to carry out God's will.

> But those who trust in the LORD will find new strength.
> They will soar high on wings like eagles.
> They will run and not grow weary.
> They will walk and not faint.
>
> ISAIAH 40:31

It is pretty clear that faith in God will give us the power we need to carry out his will. But we must not misunderstand the nature of the trust and faith we need to have. Faith does not mean *feeling* more trust; it means *taking action* as a result of our trust in God, rather than doing nothing because we're letting God take over our lives. When God takes over our lives, we don't retire; rather, we are called to action.

While trusting God means connecting with him privately, it also involves connecting with healthy and supportive people who can build us up and provide us with renewed hope. We need to work our recovery program so that we clear up the past and its residue. As we get rid of this baggage, we become energized by the lighter load we carry. We use up less energy on anxiety because we are more comfortable in the presence of others, as well as more at ease in our own skin. Life is lighter, better, and more meaningful. We experience God's renewing strength as we seek to carry out his will, grow closer to him, and experience his presence in a more meaningful way.

"The LORD is good to those who depend on him, to those who search for him" (Lamentations 3:25). God favors us; he is good to us and blesses us when we depend on him and when we search for him, which is an ongoing process. We can never get too much of God. We must never stop searching for all of his dimensions. Our challenge is to continue in prayer and meditation so we grow closer to God and know more about what he wants us to do with our lives of recovery.

Keith's Story of Recovery: Pick Up the Phone and Call Somebody

In Step One, "we admitted that we were powerless over our problems and that our lives had become unmanageable." Many years ago, I was taught that I need to work the first Step 100 percent every day because if I lose track of Step One, I'm going to be stepping out and I'm going to be drinking.

The first word of that Step is *we*. That means we can help each other. The most important thing for Alcoholics Anonymous and any other Twelve Step program is that we need to be there for one another.

I had sixteen years of sobriety, and things were going well. I had a connection to a higher Power. I had a sponsor. I was going to meetings. And then it started to fade. I stopped going to meetings. I stopped calling my sponsor. And I drank. After sixteen years of active participation in AA, I took that first drink.

I don't know if you have ever been told that there will come a time in your life as an addict when God will be the only thing between you and a drink. Well, I had a "god of my understanding," and it wasn't God. At first, my god was a rock star from a rock band. Just the image, you know. I wanted a rockin' God. The point is, I drank. And I drank for a while.

I'm one alcoholic who didn't *lose* anything. No, I *gave it away*. I gave away my family, my job—everything I had achieved in sixteen years—for the right to drink alcohol.

I ended up getting divorced, but a couple years later, we got back together. The reason we got back together is because my wife had a healing heart, and she wanted to heal the family and give it another shot. She got that healing heart from God.

Today, I'm a Christian. I'm a follower of Jesus Christ. I firmly believe that God works miracles. The healing of my family was such a miracle that I'm still amazed.

One thing about alcoholism—and this is what I faced when I took that drink—I *knew* I was going to drink. There was no, "Gee, I wonder . . ." There was no concern about the consequences of a relapse. There was none of that. I was going to drink.

What I found from talking to other addicts during my sixteen years of sobriety, and from talking to people since, is that a day will come when the pain of alcoholism will get so bad that you'll be left with three options:

1. Take a drink. (That's the option I chose.)

2. Harm yourself. (That's the option I'm glad I didn't choose.)

3. Pick up the phone and call somebody. (That's the option
   I should have chosen.)

I hope you remember number three—*pick up the phone and call
somebody.* I don't care how many meetings you've attended or how
good your sponsor is—if you work the Steps, there's going to come a
time in your recovery when the pain will get so bad that you're going
to have to pick up the phone. I hope you do. I pray to God you do.
Or I hope you go to a meeting. You don't have to waste your sobriety
like I did. When the time comes, make the call.

Here's what's going on in my life right now: I have liver cancer,
and it looks like it's terminal. It's a by-product of sharing needles
in the seventies. I had hepatitis C, and now it's turned into cancer.
I've got a tumor fifteen centimeters long on my liver, and I'm going
through chemo. I'm going through it with faith. What will be will
be. But what I've learned from this new challenge, first of all, is that
my wife, Anita, and my son, Troy, have my back twenty-four hours
a day, seven days a week.

Through the miracle of Alcoholics Anonymous and the coming
together of people at my church, brothers and sisters come to see me
and hold me up on a daily basis. We started a men's group, and when
I got pretty sick, the men from the church came to my house for a
Bible study. I never had that in AA. It's my church that has really
shown me unconditional love. And every time I walk around, people
come up to me and thank me for inspiring them to show compassion. What I want to do is thank *them*, because without them, I'd
probably already be dead.

STEP ELEVEN BIBLE STUDIES

Study #1: Knowing Our Creator

This study is based on Psalm 8 (page 684 in *The Life Recovery Bible*). Read the psalm several times before working on the study.

1. THE MAJESTIC GOD

Two of our goals as we work on Step Eleven are to improve our understanding of the nature and character of God and to improve our relationship with him. The Step suggests we do this through prayer and meditation. As we meditate on this psalm, we will first bask in an awareness of God's majesty and power. As we consider this image of God, we will feel small and insignificant in comparison.

Then the psalmist shows us our place in God's creation—crowned with glory and honor and above everything else in creation. As we work through the issues of our recovery, we may feel like failures, like we don't really matter in the big picture. But the psalmist tells us that when we have a right understanding of God in all his majesty and power, we are not to think less of ourselves. We are the crown jewels of God's creation. That means we are each to see ourselves as crown jewels in God's creation. We begin, though, with the image of God.

> O LORD, our Lord, your majestic name fills the earth!
>   Your glory is higher than the heavens.
> You have taught children and infants
>   to tell of your strength,
> silencing your enemies
>   and all who oppose you.

PSALM 8:1-2

What do you think the psalmist means when he says that God's "majestic name fills the earth"?

The words *majestic* or *mighty* are used in Psalms to describe kings (Psalm 136:18, NASB), heroes (Psalm 16:3, NASB), mountains (Psalm 76:4), and waves hitting the seashore (Psalm 93:4). When you consider the words *majestic* and *mighty* in those contexts, what other similar words come to mind?

We also see that the psalmist uses two other words to describe God. One relates to his "strength." In what ways has God been a *strength* for you in your recovery?

The other word is really a phrase—"silencing your enemies." How is this an extension of *majestic* and *strength*? How has God used your recovery to silence those who opposed you?

2. KNOWING GOD

What goes through your mind when you watch a beautiful sunset or look at the sky on a clear night? Have you ever driven in the mountains and seen the sun shimmering on a far-off ridge? Have you ever stopped and just enjoyed the view? This is what the psalmist does in Psalm 8. But he is also doing more than meets the eye. The false religions of his day worshiped the sun, moon, and stars. The idol worshipers believed the heavenly bodies had power and were worthy of worship. But to David, the author of this psalm, they are nothing to be worshiped in themselves, for they are merely the handiwork of the true God. Next time you see a beautiful sunset or an awesome array of stars, think of the God who created them. Think of God's power and majesty, and remember that he is also the God of your recovery.

When I look at the night sky and see the work of your fingers—
  the moon and the stars you set in place—
what are mere mortals that you should think about them,
  human beings that you should care for them?
Yet you made them only a little lower than God
  and crowned them with glory and honor.
You gave them charge of everything you made,
  putting all things under their authority—
the flocks and the herds
  and all the wild animals,
the birds in the sky, the fish in the sea,
  and everything that swims the ocean currents.
O LORD, our Lord, your majestic name fills the earth!

PSALM 8:3-9

When we compare ourselves to the sun, moon, and stars, we truly are insignificant. But what does it mean to you when the psalmist says we are "crowned . . . with glory and honor"?

In Genesis 2, God tells Adam to tend to the garden and name the animals. By having Adam name the animals, God gave him authority over them. The psalmist asserts the same thing—that we are above the rest of creation and that we have authority over it. What does this mean to you about how God views you?

God has, by design, given you dignity and honor. Addictions, dependencies, and problems seek to rob us of our dignity and honor. In what way does this make God the God of your recovery?

In our healing, we need to recover an image of ourselves based on how God sees us. Our addictions, dependencies, and problems have filled us with guilt and shame. But God seeks to fill us with *honor* and *glory* and restore our sense of *dignity*. When we see ourselves as God intended us to see ourselves—as just a little lower than the angels— we begin to restore the image of God in ourselves. The psalmist makes this very clear.

Study #2: The God Who Blesses

This study is based on Psalm 84 (page 739 in *The Life Recovery Bible*). Read the psalm several times before working on the study.

1. MORE OF GOD

In this psalm, the writer expresses his deep longing for God. It's as if he's saying, as Step Eleven says, "I long to improve my conscious contact with God!" When he talks about the Temple, or the courts of the Temple, he is really talking about God's presence. He not only longs to be in God's presence, but he "faint[s] with longing to enter the courts of the LORD."

Again, we are building a more accurate picture of the God to whom we have surrendered our wills and our lives. The psalmist finds that he is not judged or condemned when he comes into the presence of God. Instead, he experiences great joy! That same promise applies to us: As we continue to heal and recover, we will experience an increase in *joy*.

> *How lovely is your dwelling place,*
> *O LORD of Heaven's Armies.*

I long, yes, I faint with longing
to enter the courts of the LORD.
With my whole being, body and soul,
I will shout joyfully to the living God.
Even the sparrow finds a home,
and the swallow builds her nest and raises her young
at a place near your altar,
O LORD of Heaven's Armies, my King and my God!
What joy for those who can live in your house,
always singing your praises.

PSALM 84:1-4

On a scale from 1 to 10, to what degree do you experience joy at the thought of being in God's presence?

When the psalmist wrote this psalm, he was far from the actual Temple of God, where the people believed God's presence dwelt. What helps you anticipate joy in getting to know God better?

What are still some roadblocks for you? What keeps you from experiencing the joy of God's presence?

2. STRONG IN THE LORD

Now the psalmist begins the journey, or pilgrimage, to Jerusalem. He makes it clear that the journey will not be easy, but for those who stay the course, their weeping will lead to a place of blessing. Even when they become exhausted and feel like giving up, they keep moving toward their destination—Jerusalem.

Recovery is hard work, and in many ways it goes against what seems like an easier path. But we've already discovered that the easy way takes us away from our goal of healing and recovery. When we grow weak and face temptation, we need to meditate on these verses and their promise: As we seek the presence of God, he will give us strength for the journey.

> *What joy for those whose strength comes from the LORD,*
>> *who have set their minds on a pilgrimage to Jerusalem.*
> *When they walk through the Valley of Weeping,*
>> *it will become a place of refreshing springs.*
>> *The autumn rains will clothe it with blessings.*
> *They will continue to grow stronger,*
>> *and each of them will appear before God in Jerusalem.*
> *O LORD God of Heaven's Armies, hear my prayer.*
>> *Listen, O God of Jacob.*

PSALM 84:5-8

If we were to rewrite the opening words of this section to read, "What joy for those whose strength comes from the LORD, who have set their minds on healing and recovery," it might help us see that our strength for the recovery journey comes from the same God we are growing closer to each day. How has God given you strength so far?

Where do you most need added strength today?

God is the source of our strength, and Step Eleven tells us to "improve our conscious contact with God." How can we accomplish this through prayer? How has your prayer life been lately?

What does this passage say that helps you better understand how to meditate on God?

3. GOD, THE AUTHOR OF JOY

People often say, "All I want is to be happy," or they ask, "Where's the joy?" The problem with happiness and joy is that they can't be the object of our quest. They are by-products of our journey. We all know people who are miserable. Misery is the same as happiness or joy—we think it depends on our circumstances, but it is actually the result of how we perceive what's going on in our lives. It's a matter of *attitude.* That's what the psalmist means when he says he would rather be a gatekeeper in the house of God than live the good life anywhere else. It's a description of his attitude. He knows that if he has the right attitude and remains in the presence of God, God will bless him and the result will be joy.

> *O God, look with favor upon the king, our shield!*
> *Show favor to the one you have anointed.*
> *A single day in your courts*
> *is better than a thousand anywhere else!*
> *I would rather be a gatekeeper in the house of my God*
> *than live the good life in the homes of the wicked.*

For the LORD God is our sun and our shield.
  He gives us grace and glory.
The LORD will withhold no good thing
  from those who do what is right.
O LORD of Heaven's Armies,
  what joy for those who trust in you.

PSALM 84:9-12

In what way can you see that happiness, joy, and misery are consequences of our perceptions and attitudes?

In the next study we'll see the importance of our thoughts in shaping
our attitudes. What are some thoughts and attitudes that keep you
from experiencing the joy the psalmist talks about?

What, if anything, keeps you from fully enjoying the presence of God
in your life?

We may not be able to choose our circumstances at all times, but we
can choose how we respond to those circumstances. But our response
is not just something we *will* to make happen. This psalm tells us
that joy, happiness, and good things all come to us when we desire
to be in God's presence. That's what this Step is all about—and this
Step gives us the means to do so, through prayer and meditation on
the goodness of God.

Study #3: New Ways of Thinking

This study is based on Proverbs 4:1-13 (page 790 in *The Life Recovery Bible*). Read the entire chapter several times before working on the study.

1. GOD'S WISE ADVICE

One of our problems before we started our journey of healing and recovery was that we thought we could do it on our own or do it our own way. We've learned that we need to walk the journey of recovery in the company of other people, many of whom are working toward the same goal. Here, Solomon, the writer of Proverbs, tells us to think back and listen to the wisdom we've heard from our parents. For some, that seems impossible; their parents were more lost than they have ever been. If that's the case, we might think back and listen to the wisdom some wise adults tried to give us when we were getting off track. Somewhere in our past, wisdom was offered to us and we didn't listen. But we can listen today.

> *My children, listen when your father corrects you.*
> *Pay attention and learn good judgment,*
> *for I am giving you good guidance.*
> *Don't turn away from my instructions.*
> *For I, too, was once my father's son,*
> *tenderly loved as my mother's only child.*
>
> PROVERBS 4:1-3

In the past, who tried to speak wisdom into your life?

What made it hard to listen?

What makes it hard to listen to the wisdom of others today?

Were there people in your past who fed you what sounded like wisdom, but later turned out to be terrible guidance? If so, when did you realize it was bad advice?

2. LOVE WISDOM

When we read the word *commands* in this passage, we need to see that Solomon is talking about God's principles for life. He says that we are to listen to our fathers when what they say is in line with God's Word. Wisdom here is godly wisdom, not just any old idea our fathers may have said.

Wisdom is not related to intelligence. (In Proverbs 30, even ants show wisdom.) Wisdom has to do with how we live our lives—how we speak and act in various situations. In the first two chapters of 1 Corinthians, Paul contrasts two kinds of wisdom. One is the wisdom Solomon talks about, God's wisdom; the other is the wisdom of the world. These are the bases of two ways of life. We've already spent a lot of time living out the wisdom of the world; our healing and recovery are based on *godly* wisdom.

> My father taught me,
> "Take my words to heart.
>   Follow my commands, and you will live.
> Get wisdom; develop good judgment.
>   Don't forget my words or turn away from them.
> Don't turn your back on wisdom, for she will protect you.
>   Love her, and she will guard you.
> Getting wisdom is the wisest thing you can do!

And whatever else you do, develop good judgment.
If you prize wisdom, she will make you great.
    Embrace her, and she will honor you.
She will place a lovely wreath on your head;
    she will present you with a beautiful crown."
PROVERBS 4:4-9

Who has been a source of wisdom in your life?

What has he or she taught you so far?

What are the benefits described here for those who "prize" God's wisdom?

3. COMMON SENSE

Now we come to the promise—the prize. When we pursue godly wisdom, we experience benefits. According to Solomon, we will have a long, good life; our paths will be straight, or clear; and we will be secure as we move forward, for there is nothing in God's wisdom that will trip us up or deceive us.

My child, listen to me and do as I say,
    and you will have a long, good life.
I will teach you wisdom's ways
    and lead you in straight paths.
When you walk, you won't be held back;
    when you run, you won't stumble.

Take hold of my instructions; don't let them go.
　　Guard them, for they are the key to life.

PROVERBS 4:10-13

Later in the chapter, Solomon describes the path of the world—or, as he calls it, the path of the evildoers. It is crooked, filled with things to stumble over, and those who walk on it thrive in darkness. How does that describe your life before recovery?

How does the straight path of God's way help you in your healing and recovery?

If we really understand the difference between the two paths set before us, the choice seems obvious. But there is something in human nature that wants to learn every truth by experience. The good news is that if we've been living our lives according to worldly wisdom, we can switch over to the right path. When we are tempted to go back to our old ways, we can quickly get back on the path of godly wisdom. The more we understand that God loves us, that he cares about the intimate details of our lives, and that his ways lead to fulfillment, not punishment, the more we will love his wisdom.

Study #4: Trapped by Perfectionism

This study is based on Matthew 25:14-27 (page 1236 in *The Life Recovery Bible*). Read the parable several times before working on the study.

1. THE CHALLENGE

One of the biggest challenges almost everyone faces in recovery is a struggle with perfectionism. When things don't go perfectly, some people use it as an excuse to use. For others, it's a constant battle with making certain that everything is perfect for others. Some use perfectionism to procrastinate, while others have "pockets" of perfectionism, meaning they strive for perfection only in certain areas of their lives.

If you have struggled with perfectionism, you know it can lead to paralysis. We become so afraid that something won't be perfect that we do nothing. At the root of perfectionism is fear, mostly a fear of being criticized. What's ironic is that when we give in to perfectionism, we are often criticized anyway. In this parable, Jesus doesn't discuss perfectionism directly, but one of the servants acts out his perfectionism. He is the loser when all is said and done.

> *Again, the Kingdom of Heaven can be illustrated by the story of a man going on a long trip. He called together his servants and entrusted his money to them while he was gone. He gave five bags of silver to one, two bags of silver to another, and one bag of silver to the last—dividing it in proportion to their abilities. He then left on his trip.*

MATTHEW 25:14-15

Why do you think the three servants got different amounts at the beginning?

In some translations, the bag of silver is referred to as a "talent." If we think of literal talents, how does that add to the meaning of the parable?

2. THE RESULTS

If we understand that *talents* are a measure of currency, we see that there is a lot of money on the table here. A talent of silver was about 75 pounds, so the first servant got 375 pounds of silver to invest!

> *The servant who received the five bags of silver began to invest the money and earned five more. The servant with two bags of silver also went to work and earned two more. But the servant who received the one bag of silver dug a hole in the ground and hid the master's money. After a long time their master returned from his trip and called them to give an account of how they had used his money.*
> MATTHEW 25:16-19

The master trusted his servants, for he was gone "a long time." What do you think the servants must have thought as they waited for his long-delayed return?

What must the third servant have thought as he hid the money?

3. THE PARALYSIS OF PERFECTIONISM

Now comes the time of accounting. The master has returned, and it's time to give a report. The first two servants were faithful in doing what the master wanted. They must have had a positive picture of the master in their minds, one that motivated their work. But the third servant failed at the task. Jesus says the master calls the servant "wicked and lazy" and gives him a harsh consequence for his inaction. The problem with this servant is that he focused so much on the harshness of his master that he lost sight of what he was supposed to do. If he knew the master was harsh in his judgments and demanded results, why didn't he respond as the other two servants did? That's a good point to wrestle with as you finish this study.

> *The servant to whom he had entrusted the five bags of silver came forward with five more and said, "Master, you gave me five bags of silver to invest, and I have earned five more."*
>
> *The master was full of praise. "Well done, my good and faithful servant. You have been faithful in handling this small amount, so now I will give you many more responsibilities. Let's celebrate together!"*
>
> *The servant who had received the two bags of silver came forward and said, "Master, you gave me two bags of silver to invest, and I have earned two more."*
>
> *The master said, "Well done, my good and faithful servant. You have been faithful in handling this small amount, so now I will give you many more responsibilities. Let's celebrate together!"*
>
> *Then the servant with the one bag of silver came and said, "Master, I knew you were a harsh man, harvesting crops you didn't plant and gathering crops you didn't cultivate. I was afraid I would lose your money, so I hid it in the earth. Look, here is your money back."*
>
> *But the master replied, "You wicked and lazy servant! If you knew I harvested crops I didn't plant and gathered crops I didn't cultivate, why didn't you deposit my money in the bank? At least I could have gotten some interest on it."*
>
> MATTHEW 25:20-27

Why do you think the third servant lost sight of the master's expectations?

The key to understanding perfectionism is to understand fear. How would you describe this servant's fears?

When have you held back and felt paralyzed by fear?

Have you done this in your recovery and healing journey? When and how?

Remember, this is a parable, so Jesus is making a point here. We didn't include the paragraph where Jesus tells what the master did, but you can read it in Matthew 25:28-30. Jesus says that if we aren't faithful in using what we have, we may end up losing what we are trying to keep. On a more positive note, Jesus also says that when we faithfully use the gifts, talents, and opportunities we've been given, the master (God) will give us more. He will enrich our efforts. In other words, the more we work on our problem of healing and recovery, the more God will add his grace to our efforts.

STEP TWELVE

Having had a spiritual awakening as the result of
these Steps, we tried to carry this message to others
and to practice these principles in all our affairs.

Dear brothers and sisters, if another believer is overcome by some
sin, you who are godly should gently and humbly help that person
back onto the right path. And be careful not to fall into the same
temptation yourself.

GALATIANS 6:1

Tyrell's Story of Recovery: Sharing the Message with Other People

I'm a recovering crackhead and a recovering alcoholic.

In Step Twelve, "having had a spiritual awakening as the result of these Steps, we tried to carry this message to others [alcoholics, addicts, codependents] and to practice these principles in all our affairs." I've had quite a few opportunities over the past eight years to share my experience, strength, and hope with other people. When I share my experiences, I always try to let people know where I came from and some of the things I've done.

After spending two weeks in jail one time, I was released into a residential recovery program, where I gained about ten pounds in one week. Praise the Lord. I had one tooth, and the rest of them were broken off in the gums. My pride and joy was a long ponytail, but they made me cut it when I came into the drug program. Regardless of how bad I looked on the outside, on the inside it was a million times worse. I had no spirit, no spirit at all. The god of my understanding was Mr. Crack Cocaine and the pipe I walked around with, and I served that god diligently all day, every day. And I did a lot of things in order to get Mr. Crack Cocaine—a lot of things.

When I came into the program, I wasn't afraid of going back to jail, because I had been in jail many times. I wasn't scared; I was just tired of that empty feeling on the inside—the one where your heart seems like it's in your belly and you're just feeling bad all the time. And then you use Mr. Crack or Mr. Meth or Mr. Alcohol to get over that feeling, but it always comes back. I was tired of feeling like that. So I started going to the mandatory meetings, and they said, "You know, you need to get a sponsor."

Now, let me tell you, some of the first AA meetings I went to were in Sacramento, California, and I could not relate to the other folks who were there. Let me put it this way, without being racist, but there were these old white guys walking around, and their "bottom" just tripped me out.

"Well, at my bottom, I was in my million-dollar condo with a bottle of Chardonnay."

I'm like, *Get outta here. You've gotta be kidding.* Right off the bat I'm thinking, *This ain't gonna work, because they do not understand.* I grew up on the streets of South Central LA. I spent a lot of time downtown, on skid row. These guys don't know what that's like. They don't know what it's like to be over at the rescue mission. They don't know what it's like to sleep in a doorway. I thought there was absolutely nothing I had in common with these people.

A few weeks later, my friend Robert, this brother named Demetrius, and I were down in Stockton, and by the grace of God we went to a recovery meeting there. It was a mixed meeting, and there was this brother up there sharing his experience, strength, and hope to everybody. And when he started talking about the things he had done, I thought, *I don't believe he's saying that. I don't believe he's admitting that.* But the thing was, I could relate to every bit of it.

When he got to the tail end and started sharing his hope, he started saying the same things those white guys in Sacramento had said. The exact same things. Go to meetings. Get a sponsor. Work the Steps. Be of service. Except he said it in a way I understood, that was familiar to me. And I was thinking, *I've got to talk to this dude.*

After the meeting, people were swarming all around him, and I said, "Dude, Dude. I need to talk to you."

"Can you relate?" he said.

"Yeah. Yeah. Yeah. I can relate a little bit." Then I asked him, "Dude, how were you able to stand up there and tell all of that in front of all these people? And more important, how did you get past it?"

He gave me the commercial pitch again: Go to meetings. Get a sponsor. Work the Steps. Be of service.

I had heard that line the whole time I was in recovery. I was getting tired of hearing that stuff. They always made it sound like a commercial: *You can get well if you just go to meetings.* But laying all jokes aside, it works. It works. So when this particular dude said it, I knew it had to be right.

Back in Sacramento, I jumped into the program. I went to that little old white guy who had hit bottom with a bottle of Chardonnay and asked him to be my sponsor. I started working the Steps. And the Steps helped me to find God.

See, I had a thing about God. I felt he had abandoned me quite a few years back. But when I started working the Steps, it helped me to feel God inside of me. It helped me to see God right in front of me. God was tangible. God was telling me he loved me. He said, "No matter what you've done, I love you and I forgive you." When I turned to God in prayer, he started showing himself to me in a major way.

After about a month of not doing crack cocaine, all the crud in my life, everything I had done for nineteen years—the kind of stuff I had started smoking crack to try to forget—came back to my mind with a vengeance. Stuff like "street hustling." Let me give you an example. Street hustling is taking someone's money to go get a big package of rock, and then breaking off some for yourself before you deliver. Street hustling is offering some girls a piece of dope and telling them you've got some more waiting for them if they'll go out and turn a couple of tricks. That's street hustling. But here's the bite: Street hustling eventually turned on me. Mr. Crack told me, "You can't get anybody to hustle for you, so you go out there yourself." So guess what? I became a male prostitute, and I hustled my own tricks to supply my own addiction. Yeah. Years and years of that.

When I started working the program, I had to ask God to help me through all this, because I would wake up at night crying, hurting, remembering all that dirt, feeling that dirt. And God answered my prayers. He helped me to forgive myself. God helped me to step past that man I was, and he started to make a new man out of me.

If you are new to the program, or if you're an old hand, and you're at a point where you're just hurting and you don't think you can get past that hurt, or if you think you need the drugs or alcohol or whatever to get past it, there is a better solution, and there is hope.

That's what Step Twelve has been for me: *hope*. See, if I had never heard that brother speak and share the dirt he had done, I never would have felt comfortable enough to do the same thing. He showed me there was hope. He showed me there was a better life.

God started to change me. As I worked the Steps, my sponsor told me it was imperative that I share the message with other people—that I pass it on. If you are two days sober and know someone who is one day sober, you can share the message. You can let that person know what you did to stay sober one day longer than he or she has.

I've had opportunities across the country to share my experience, strength, and hope. Once or twice a year, I speak at a local high school. I get chances to go to juvenile hall and share my experience, strength, and hope about how the program and God delivered me from my past. The first time I spoke in front of those kids, I was scared as the dickens. I was thinking, *Lord, I don't wanna mess them up*. But the woman who has run that prison ministry for a long time quieted my fears by saying, "Just share your experience, your strength, your hope. Just tell them what God has done for you." And I felt good about that.

Then God took me another big step. My church had a recovery ministry, and a vision to help the people of Uganda. I was asked to be a part of taking AA to Uganda, a place where alcoholism and drug addiction rules, a place where they have nothing like this, no program at all.

I remember that first AA meeting in Uganda. God took me a little bit further. He took a drugged-out crackhead, a shopping-cart-pushing, womanizing, blankety-blank like me, and he used me to carry the message of strength and hope clear across the world. So you see, this story is ultimately not about me. It's about how powerful God is— the God we serve. It's about a program of recovery that can take you at your weakest point and start you on a path to where you can change the world. It's about carrying that message. It's about showing that love.

I was blessed to accept Jesus as my Savior. I don't push religion, but I definitely talk about relationship. Relationship with the God of my understanding got me to the point where I am now. I still have a lot of growing to do, you know. I have a long way to go. But hey, God has already brought me a long way.

So, if you have two days sober and you see a person with one day sober, help him or her along the way. Spread the love and share the hope.

STEP TWELVE INSIGHT

People often vacillate between good and bad, right and wrong, religious and rebellious. They go from having a good day where they do not relapse to a bad day where they do. One day they treat people with respect, and the next day they tear them down. One day they faithfully seek to know God's will, and the next day they seek their own way. They struggle alone and wonder where God is and whether the promise of abundant life that so many Christians talk about really exists. Where is the upside of not using or abusing? they ask.

Along the way, they may discover that they have not fully surrendered or agreed to comply long enough to experience what sobriety or serenity really feels like. When they finally surrender *totally*, life starts to get better, many things work well, and healing takes place. But something still seems to be missing. There has to be more than just feeling better and doing better and communing with God.

Well, there *is* something better and more meaningful. There is a *cause* to get behind. There is a reason to get up in the morning, a purpose greater than the all-important "I." It is called *the missional life*. In this life, we go from being focused on ourselves and our recovery to being focused on others and contributing to their lives. Step Twelve is all about the missional life as a recovering person.

But first things first. This Step has three major elements to consider: having a spiritual awakening, carrying the message, and practicing the principles.

The first component of the Step, "having had a spiritual awakening," is a great place to start. As soon as we find recovery, it is natural to want to share it with others. It is normal to want others to experience what we are experiencing. But we must temper that zeal just a bit. It is tempting to want to carry the message to others before we have lived the message ourselves. We can fall into the trap of becoming "instant authorities" on recovery, even though we hardly know anything about it. Thus, Step Twelve starts with an assumption that we have worked *all* of the Steps, and that, as a result, we have experienced a spiritual awakening. If you haven't worked all the Steps, you need to stop working on this Step and go back to where you left off. That way you'll be able to go beyond telling people what you've stopped doing and start telling people how you're now living.

Spiritual awakening is quite a mystery and a miracle at the same time. For some, it is an instant grand finale to their obsession or compulsion, with a supernatural remission of the urge to use or abuse. Sometimes—and we emphasize *sometimes*—the desire instantly goes away as the person is delivered into a new state. But that is never enough. Being delivered *out* of something or *from* something is a gift, but it is just a beginning. It does not complete or accomplish the process of recovery. No one is delivered from the desire to do something harmful into instant character and maturity. No one instantly becomes the most godly human being on the planet, doling out wisdom from a totally transformed heart. No one grows in recovery unless he or she gets into the process of working the Steps. Working the Steps is a necessary process that will provide opportunity for more spiritual awakening and growth.

For many, the craving for the object of their addiction or dependency continues, and every day is a challenge to live free. Connecting, praying, working the Steps through the pain, and accepting the struggle as part of recovery often draws a person closer to God and provides for spiritual awakening. But there's a danger in thinking about spiritual awakening as an *event* rather than a process. We may become discouraged if we do not experience a major or sudden shift in our desires or thinking. But if we are open to the spiritual things of God, looking for God's hand in all that happens to us, and moving *toward* God and not away from him, then we can be confident that we have begun a spiritual awakening.

When we are spiritually awake, we realize that others are not. We are aware that others continue to struggle in darkness and blindness, and we are motivated to help them, which brings us to the second component of this Step—carrying the message to others.

Here is a story to illustrate: Once a man fell into a hole and began screaming for help to get out. A physician passing by yelled down into the hole that if the man could find a way out he should come by the clinic and have his injuries treated. A lawyer came by and informed the man that he had a good case for a lawsuit, and if he ever got out to be sure to come by his office. A third man heard the cries and realized they came from his best friend, so he jumped down in the hole with him.

The man who had fallen in could not believe it. He told his friend he needed help getting out, not someone to jump into the hole with him. The friend replied, "Don't worry, I jumped down on purpose. I've fallen in this same hole myself, and I know how to get out." He told the man to follow him and he led him out of the dark hole.

That is both what we need and what we need to do for others. We need help from those who have been in the dark hole where we find ourselves. And once we get out, we need to be willing to jump back in the hole so we can help others find a way out. When we've been healed, it is our turn to carry the message of hope to others.

> *If another believer is overcome by some sin, you who are godly should gently and humbly help that person back onto the right path.*
>
> GALATIANS 6:1

We are instructed to carry the message, and we are to carry it with *gentleness* and *humility*. It is easy to become arrogant when we try to help someone who doesn't have things together like we do, but we must be careful. The remainder of Galatians 6:1 says, "And be careful not to fall into the same temptation yourself."

Humility and gentleness help us keep our motives in check and prevent us from being so arrogant that we find ourselves in the same shape as the person we are trying to help. We need to help—we need to carry the message of hope and strength—but we need to do it carefully.

The last part of this Step is a very difficult one, but it sums up a life of recovery. To practice the principles found in the Steps in all our affairs produces a life of serenity, purpose, and meaning. It creates a manageable lifestyle in which we find ourselves connected to God in a new and intimate way, and we are drawn to others like never before. We experience all of this because we adhere to the principles found throughout the Twelve Steps—the principles that are the foundation of our new lives.

In reviewing these life-changing principles, we find that *love* is at the top of the list and also a part of every principle on the list. We accept and experience God's love for us. We feel loved and then share that love with others. We learn to love first. We accept rather than reject. We try to understand rather than judge. We reach out to others rather than cocoon ourselves in a flawed attempt at self-protection.

Love spills from us because we are loved and are so full of love. It is tangible and contagious. Love becomes our priority because no matter what we do or how much we do it, if we do not love others through it, our actions are worthless. We become missional and share the love as we share what recovery has done in our lives.

The love of God in us and through us results in a generous freedom that few are fortunate enough to experience. What joy we experience when we are free to be generous with our time, our efforts, and our money! When we are full of love, we maintain healthy boundaries, but we do not hold back what we have discovered, because we find joy in giving. We experience the fulfillment of getting out of ourselves and into other people.

Practicing the principles of the Steps in all our affairs truly makes a remarkable difference in our lives. Our lives now contrast greatly with our old way of living, surviving, and coping. Look how marked the difference is:

From		To
Control	$\longrightarrow$	Surrender
Earning favor	$\longrightarrow$	Grace
Wishing	$\longrightarrow$	Hope
Deception	$\longrightarrow$	Truth
Fear	$\longrightarrow$	Courage
Bondage	$\longrightarrow$	Freedom
Secrecy	$\longrightarrow$	Confession
Emptiness	$\longrightarrow$	Fullness
Excuses	$\longrightarrow$	Responsibility
Compulsions	$\longrightarrow$	Self-control
Pain	$\longrightarrow$	Relief
Intentions	$\longrightarrow$	Actions
Resentment	$\longrightarrow$	Forgiveness
Idolatry	$\longrightarrow$	Worship
Negativity	$\longrightarrow$	Optimism
Stress	$\longrightarrow$	Serenity
Isolation	$\longrightarrow$	Community

The contrast is amazing. It is worth working for. It is worth the price. It is worth pursuing for the rest of our lives.

To go from a self-obsessed life of defeat and agony to a missional life of joy and fulfillment is a miracle, something we should never take for granted. This miracle gives us a chance to avoid the downside of life. But it is so much more. It is our chance to live and experience life in all of its joy and wonder and purpose. It is the beginning of a blessed life where we are free—free to become the people God has created us to be and to introduce others to this wonderful way of life: the life of recovery.

Scott's Story of Recovery: I Am More Present for My Life

The oldest of four children, I was born into an alcoholic family, though I was not aware of that. My father was a veteran of World War II, where he had been a scrub nurse in the South Pacific and seen a lot of bloodshed. I now believe that he drank to quell the memories, regrets, and missed opportunities of his life. He drilled into me responsibility and hard work and gave very little nurturing and relationship to the family. His perfectionism left wounds of shame and the sense that I would never measure up. In high school, I began drinking to medicate the pain, although I would have told you it was to party and have fun.

After discovering pornography, I began to act out sexually. My high school girlfriend was pregnant when we graduated, and we were married just after graduation. Less than two years later, we had our second child. I worked many retail jobs just to make ends meet. Truthfully, alcohol was becoming more important than my family. I was not any better at relationships than my father had been.

When I was twenty-five, after working with the youth group at our church and being influenced by the pastor, I heard God call me into vocational Christian ministry. At that time, I believed it was not "spiritual" to drink, and I was able to go two years dry. My anger and irritability soared, and food and pornography became my "drugs" of choice. Eventually, of course, I went back to drinking—although secretly, late at night. This pattern continued even after I enrolled in seminary and became an ordained pastor. The years in ministry were difficult, due to my anger and control issues, which were displayed with parishioners. They had no idea that I drank to relieve the stress and be able to sleep.

In 1988, my wife was diagnosed with breast cancer, a tragedy that initiated my search for another way of life. The cancer was a virulent form that attacks younger women, very resistant to treatment. During the three years of her illness, I came face-to-face with a sense of helplessness and inadequacy that I had never experienced. Drinking was a constant, everyday occurrence by now, and it escalated even more after my wife's death. I was overwhelmed with grief and the responsibility of rearing our third child, a preteen at that time. My nightly drinking helped me cope, I told myself. But I began having blackouts more regularly.

During that dark time, I became reacquainted with a friend from the past who had been transformed physically and emotionally by working a recovery program. She had no idea that I was a closet alcoholic, but she invited me to some open Alcoholics Anonymous meetings. I went to be supportive of her, but I was shocked to hear people tell *my story*—talking openly about the secrets I was living with. But they had hope. They were facing the challenges of life, but without drinking. I could see and sense the difference.

I heard about the Twelve Step program and was amazed to hear the spiritually sound faith that the members reported and how God had worked in their lives to stop their drinking. I began to attend meetings regularly, and I began a new life without alcohol.

The first year was one of challenges and changes. I had to learn to deal with my anger in a constructive way and to maintain relationships. I had to face fears of moving on in my life rather than avoiding and hiding. Most of my extended family still drank, and when I stopped drinking, they had no reference point to deal with me. Although it grieves me to say it, I must still keep some distance from them to protect my recovery.

Now, twenty-three years later, I am so grateful that I stepped out in faith for this life of recovery. I was able to marry again and have two more children, who have never known me under the influence of alcohol. That is truly a miracle! Relationships are much better because I am more present for my life. God also allowed me to have another vocation, counseling and assisting people in recovery to find God's path to wholeness. When I think about it, I can see that my life is divided by alcohol. In my adult life, I have now had as many years sober as I spent drinking, and each year from now on will tip the scales in a positive direction. I was not really living until God removed the compulsion, filled me with the Holy Spirit, and set me on the path of life and service. Thanks be to God!

STEP TWELVE BIBLE STUDIES

Study #1: Speak Out!

This study is based on Psalm 107:1-22, 32 (page 756 in *The Life Recovery Bible*). Read the entire psalm several times before working on the study.

1. SPEAK OUT!

This psalm is the beginning of a section in the book of Psalms that relates to Israel's return from exile. For years, they had been in Babylon, prisoners of a foreign king. Years earlier, the Babylonian king and his army had destroyed the cities of Israel and had taken the people from their homes. They lived a strange life in a strange culture, learning a strange new language and way of life. Finally, they were allowed to return to their homeland, and this psalm celebrates the recovery of their lives. It begins with an exhortation to speak out about what God is doing for his people. Similarly, Step Twelve tells us to speak out. We are to take what we have learned and share it with others as we continue to apply these principles to our lives. We don't wait until we have "made it"—no, speaking out is part of our journey and our healing. Sharing what we have learned contributes to our recovery; it makes what we have accomplished more concrete and holds us accountable to continue *doing* what we are sharing.

> *Give thanks to the LORD, for he is good!*
>   *His faithful love endures forever.*
> *Has the LORD redeemed you? Then speak out!*
>   *Tell others he has redeemed you from your enemies.*
> *For he has gathered the exiles from many lands,*
>   *from east and west,*
>   *from north and south.*
>
> PSALM 107:1-3

How was your previous way of living like being in exile?

How would you describe to someone else what the psalmist means by being redeemed?

Who have you told about your healing and recovery? Who *could* you tell about what God is doing in your healing and recovery?

2. SATISFIED BY GOD

The wilderness the psalmist refers to can be a number of things, most obviously a place of dryness and emptiness, where a person can literally die of hunger and thirst. But when the person cries out, "LORD, help!" and surrenders to God, he or she is rescued. Notice, all the person does is cry out—there are no instructions or demands given to the Lord. It is clearly a cry of surrender.

> Some wandered in the wilderness,
>   lost and homeless.
> Hungry and thirsty,
>   they nearly died.
> "LORD, help!" they cried in their trouble,
>   and he rescued them from their distress.
> He led them straight to safety,
>   to a city where they could live.
> Let them praise the LORD for his great love
>   and for the wonderful things he has done for them.
> For he satisfies the thirsty
>   and fills the hungry with good things.
> PSALM 107:4-9

Describe your wilderness experience.

What have been some of the surprises as the Lord has led you to safety and recovery?

In what ways are you experiencing the feeling of being satisfied?

3. FREED BY GOD

Now the psalmist focuses on those who have been in exile because of a rebellious spirit. He is speaking to those of us who have left the path of godly wisdom and gone our own way. When we rebel against God's path of wise living, he makes life harder for us. He tries to get our attention in the midst of our rebellion. So when our rebellion takes us to dark places, God makes things worse in some way in an attempt to get our attention. When he eventually gets our attention, the chains that have bound us are broken and we are set free.

> Some sat in darkness and deepest gloom,
>   imprisoned in iron chains of misery.
> They rebelled against the words of God,
>   scorning the counsel of the Most High.
> That is why he broke them with hard labor;
>   they fell, and no one was there to help them.
> "LORD, help!" they cried in their trouble,
>   and he saved them from their distress.
> He led them from the darkness and deepest gloom;
>   he snapped their chains.
> Let them praise the LORD for his great love
>   and for the wonderful things he has done for them.
> For he broke down their prison gates of bronze;
>   he cut apart their bars of iron.

PSALM 107:10-16

Here is an accurate picture of the power an addiction can have over us: we are "imprisoned in iron chains of misery." In what ways was your experience like being in chains?

Even the patterns of dependencies and the oppression of unresolved problems can feel like a prison. How has this been your experience?

In what ways did your life go from bad to worse before you surrendered your will and your life to God?

4. EXALTING GOD PUBLICLY

Here the psalmist talks about fools—the ones who, in many ways, created their own misery. But once again, when they surrender and cry out to God, they are rescued and healed. Now the psalmist tells them to exalt the Lord publicly—to carry the message of hope to others in need.

> Some were fools; they rebelled
>   and suffered for their sins.
> They couldn't stand the thought of food,
>   and they were knocking on death's door.
> "LORD, help!" they cried in their trouble,
>   and he saved them from their distress.
> He sent out his word and healed them,
>   snatching them from the door of death.
> Let them praise the LORD for his great love
>   and for the wonderful things he has done for them.
> Let them offer sacrifices of thanksgiving
>   and sing joyfully about his glorious acts. . . .
> Let them exalt him publicly before the congregation
>   and before the leaders of the nation.

PSALM 107:17-22, 32

How have you expressed your gratitude to God for helping you in your recovery and healing program?

How have you expressed your gratitude publicly?

Identify at least two people whom you could share your gratitude with, and then make it a point to do so.

Sharing our stories is not punishment, though for some it may feel that way. It is not only a key principle of recovery, as expressed in Step Twelve; it is also a principle of growth. We don't grow toward greater health by living in isolation. We grow as we interact with other people. So when we are encouraged to "carry this message to others," we are growing stronger and healthier. Exalt the Lord publicly!

Study #2: A Slow Miracle

This study is based on Mark 8:22-26 (page 1264 in *The Life Recovery Bible*). Read these verses several times before working on the study. Also read Mark 8:14-21 and 8:27-30 for the context of the story.

1. A STRANGE HEALING

At some point in our healing and recovery, we become impatient. We want to see results, and they don't come quickly enough. In this brief event, which is only recorded in the Gospel of Mark, Jesus seems to take his time in healing the blind man. We don't know exactly why it took two attempts for the man to see clearly, but that's what happened. If we read what Mark records just before this event, we see that Jesus challenged his disciples because they were worrying about not having enough bread. He reminded them that he had fed five thousand people with five loaves of bread and four thousand with seven loaves of bread. Then he asked, "Don't you know or understand even yet?" (Mark 8:17). He was asking if they understood who he was and what he could do and he implied that apparently they didn't yet understand, but someday would. When they arrived in Bethsaida and a blind man was brought to Jesus, the people begged Jesus to heal him. It's almost as if Mark is saying that these people understand Jesus' power better than the disciples.

> *When they arrived at Bethsaida, some people brought a blind man to Jesus, and they begged him to touch the man and heal him. Jesus took the blind man by the hand and led him out of the village. Then, spitting on the man's eyes, he laid his hands on him and asked, "Can you see anything now?"*
> MARK 8:22-23

In what ways has your healing and recovery been a gradual miracle?

Which parts of your healing and recovery have been instantaneous?

2. THE HEALING COMPLETED

The context implies that Jesus' healing of the blind man was for the benefit of his disciples. As Jesus and the disciples were leaving Bethsaida, he asked them, "Who do people say I am?" After the disciples give several options, Jesus asks the real question: "But who do you say I am?" Peter gives a quick and clear response: "You are the Messiah." It is possible that Jesus slowed down the miracle of healing so that the disciples would better understand who he is. If that is true, then we can look at the slower parts of our recovery as an opportunity to better understand who Jesus really is and how he wants to be a part of our lives.

> *The man looked around. "Yes," he said. "I see people, but I can't see them very clearly. They look like trees walking around."*
>
> *Then Jesus placed his hands on the man's eyes again, and his eyes were opened. His sight was completely restored, and he could see everything clearly. Jesus sent him away, saying, "Don't go back into the village on your way home."*
>
> MARK 8:24-26

This is a "slow-motion" display of Jesus' healing power. What have you learned about yourself in the "slow-motion" parts of your healing and recovery?

What have you learned about God, and about Jesus, in the "slow-motion" parts of your healing and recovery?

Sometimes, when our healing is sudden and complete, we can overlook the incredible nature of what has happened. As we experience "slow-motion" healing, we learn things that will serve us well in the future—things we didn't learn when we should have and that were a part of our addiction, dependencies, and problems. So pay close attention to what you have learned along the way.

Study #3: A Debt of Love

This study is based on Luke 10:30-37 (page 1308 in *The Life Recovery Bible*). Read verses 25-29 for the context of the story. Then read the parable several times before working on the study.

1. WHO IS MY NEIGHBOR?

Jesus makes several points in this discussion that are relevant to our ongoing recovery and healing. When Step Twelve directs us to share our journey with others, our old patterns of shame and rejection get stirred up and we think, *Who am I that I think I can help anyone?* But that's just the point. Who better to help someone get on the path of healing than someone who is a little farther along that path? In this parable, the "professionals" didn't know what to do or were certainly unwilling to do what was needed. For us, the professionals haven't been where we've been and don't really know by experience the path out of addictions, dependencies, and ongoing problems. Those with experience are best capable of giving help to someone uncertain about how to move forward on the path of healing.

> *The man . . . asked Jesus, "And who is my neighbor?"*
>
> *Jesus replied with a story: "A Jewish man was traveling from Jerusalem down to Jericho, and he was attacked by bandits. They stripped him of his clothes, beat him up, and left him half dead beside the road.*
>
> *"By chance a priest came along. But when he saw the man lying there, he crossed to the other side of the road and passed him by. A Temple assistant walked over and looked at him lying there, but he also passed by on the other side."*
>
> LUKE 10:29-32

Why do you think the two religious leaders passed the man by?

Some might think they passed the injured man because of pride, fear, or busyness. Regardless of the reason, how does their passing prepare the way to answer the question, "Who is my neighbor?"

2. THE DESPISED SAMARITAN

When the pagan Assyrians conquered Israel, they left large numbers of Assyrians in the land to keep things peaceful. Many of these Assyrians intermarried with the Israelites who were left behind. Their offspring were called Samaritans. When the Israelites returned from exile, conflicts arose between them and the Samaritans, partly over the question of where they were to worship. The Samaritans wanted to worship on Mount Gerizim, and the Israelites wanted to worship in Jerusalem. Their hatred came to a head when the Jewish king destroyed the Samaritan temple on Mount Gerizim in 126 BC. (You can get another picture of the break between the Jews and the Samaritans in John 4:1-42.)

To Jesus' listeners, Samaritans were the scum of the earth. A practicing Jew would have nothing to do with a Samaritan. They hated each other. Jesus' audience must have gasped when they heard that the hero of the story was a Samaritan.

> *Then a despised Samaritan came along, and when he saw the man, he felt compassion for him. Going over to him, the Samaritan soothed his wounds with olive oil and wine and bandaged them. Then he put the man on his own donkey and took him to an inn, where he took care of him. The next day he handed the innkeeper two silver coins, telling him, "Take care of this man. If his bill runs higher than this, I'll pay you the next time I'm here."*
>
> LUKE 10:33-35

Who have been the "Samaritans" in your recovery and healing? In other words, who were you surprised to see caring about you and your recovery?

Two silver coins equaled four days' pay for the average person at that time and represented a sacrifice on the part of the Samaritan. Who has sacrificed to help you in your healing and recovery?

The parable implies that the injured man never knew or even met his rescuer. He had no way to show gratitude. How have you shown gratitude to those who have been your support during this time of growth and healing?

3. THE QUESTION AGAIN

No one listening to Jesus was prepared to hear that a despised Samaritan would help a Jew, so they were in shock as they listened. But the answer to Jesus' question was clear. Only the Samaritan was acting in love. The man to whom Jesus asked the question couldn't even say the word *Samaritan*. All he could say was, "The one who showed him mercy." But he got the point. And the point is this: The law of God—the "straight path" or the "path of wisdom"—is summed up in the simple phrase, "Love your neighbor as yourself." Love is more than an emotion or a sentiment; it involves our actions.

"Now which of these three would you say was a neighbor to the man who was attacked by bandits?" Jesus asked.

The man replied, "The one who showed him mercy."
Then Jesus said, "Yes, now go and do the same."

LUKE 10:36-37

Describe how this parable illustrates the law that says we are to love our neighbors as we love ourselves.

Who in your life has shown you that kind of love?

Can you think of ways you have shown that kind of love?

One might read this story and say that the Samaritan was just being a good codependent. It may seem hard to differentiate between codependency and acting in love. But this is not a picture of codependency because the Samaritan did for the man what the man was incapable of doing for himself. That's what Jesus calls loving behavior. But when we do things for others that they can and should do for themselves, that's codependency.

Study #4: We Will Make It!

This study is based on Philippians 1:3-11 (page 1520 in *The Life Recovery Bible*). Read these verses several times before working on the study.

1. GOD CONTINUES TO WORK

Two important parts of Step Twelve are that we carry the message of recovery and healing to others, and that we continue "to practice these principles in all our affairs." This means that no matter how many times we go through the Twelve Steps, we are still in the process. It becomes a way of living. God promises us that the results lie in his hands—we are only called to faithfully follow through. God took the initiative, and he can be trusted to continue what he started.

Recovery is a task that is never finished. We can never sit back and say we've arrived. The biblical word for recovery is *sanctification*, which is also an ongoing, lifelong process. As long as we breathe, we are either moving forward or moving backward. God's desire is to keep us moving forward.

Every time I think of you, I give thanks to my God. Whenever I pray, I make my requests for all of you with joy, for you have been my partners in spreading the Good News about Christ from the time you first heard it until now. And I am certain that God, who began the good work within you, will continue his work until it is finally finished on the day when Christ Jesus returns.

PHILIPPIANS 1:3-6

The apostle Paul prayed this prayer for the Philippians, but because it is God's Word, Paul was also praying this prayer for you and me, with joy. Once again, we come face-to-face with God, and despite our past, God looks at each of us with grace and unfailing love. How has that become more of a reality for you as you've worked through these studies?

The promise in this passage is that the same God who started the work of our healing and recovery will continue his work in us "until it is finally finished on the day when Christ Jesus returns." How does that promise encourage you in your healing and recovery at this point?

2. CONFIRMING THE TRUTH

Paul wrote this letter from a Roman prison while facing the possibility of execution—which later became a reality. By writing to the Philippians, he reconnected with people who had been very important in his life and work. He knew he could not face what lay ahead of him without the support of the people who were important in his life. He had no intention of facing it alone.

> *So it is right that I should feel as I do about all of you, for you have a special place in my heart. You share with me the special favor of God, both in my imprisonment and in defending and confirming the truth of the Good News. God knows how much I love you and long for you with the tender compassion of Christ Jesus.*
>
> PHILIPPIANS 1:7-8

Who have been the people in your life to whom these words would ring true?

Have you shared your gratitude with any of them?

3. A PRAYER FOR OUR FUTURE

As we continue to seek the deepening of our spiritual awakening, Paul gives us a model prayer that we can pray daily for ourselves. All we need to do is change the wording so that we are praying for ourselves. For example, "I pray that my love will overflow more and more, and that I will keep on growing in knowledge and understanding. For I want to understand what really matters, so that I may live a pure and blameless life until the day of Christ's return." You can finish it or add to it to make it personal and then make it part of what you pray each day.

> *I pray that your love will overflow more and more, and that you will keep on growing in knowledge and understanding. For I want you to understand what really matters, so that you may live pure and blameless lives until the day of Christ's return. May you always be filled with the fruit of your salvation—the righteous character produced in your life by Jesus Christ—for this will bring much glory and praise to God.*
> PHILIPPIANS 1:9-11

Write your version of the prayer here:

Afterword

If you've completed these studies, you have worked your way through both the Old and New Testaments and are more familiar with themes that run through the entire Bible. These are the kinds of studies you can repeat on your own or in a small group. Prayer and meditation on the Bible are two crucial practices you need as you journey toward a healthier future and greater peace and serenity in your life.

Please stay in touch with us. Let us hear of your recovery and learn from your story. You can contact us through drstoop@cox.net and sarterburn@newlife.com.

Notes

1. *Merriam-Webster's Collegiate Dictionary*, 11th Edition, copyright © 2008 by Merriam-Webster, Incorporated, s.v. "surrender."

2. Rembrandt's "Return of the Prodigal Son" is on display in the Hermitage Museum in St. Petersburg, Russia. It may be viewed online at http://www.hermitagemuseum.org /html_En/03/hm3_3_1_4d.html.

3. André Gide, *The Return of the Prodigal Son*, Aldyth Thain, trans. (Logan: Utah State University Press, 1960), np; authors' paraphrase.

4. Francois Fénélon, *Let Go* (Anderson, PA: Scroll, 2007), 9.

5. *The Confessions of St. Augustine*, Albert C. Outler, trans. (Philadelphia: Westminster, 1955), 1.

6. *Merriam-Webster's Collegiate Dictionary*, s.v. "inventory."

7. Council of Trent (1551): DS 1680 (ND 1626); cf. St. Jerome, In Eccl. 10, 11: PL 23:1096. For more on the Council of Trent see http://www.catholicculture.org /culture/library/catechism/index.cfm?recnum=4677.

8. Frank Buchman, quoted in *Foundations for Faith*, Harry J. Almond, ed. (London: Grosvenor, 1980), 21.

9. *Alcoholics Anonymous: The Story of How Many Thousands of Men and Women Have Recovered from Alcoholism*, 3rd ed. (New York: AA World Service, 1976), 13.

10. Ibid., 76.

11. Matt Redman and Beth Redman, "Blessed Be Your Name," Thankyou Music, 2002.

About the Authors

STEPHEN ARTERBURN IS the founder and chairman of New Life Ministries—the nation's largest faith-based broadcast, counseling, and treatment ministry—and is the host of the nationally syndicated *New Life Live!* daily radio program on over 180 radio stations nationwide, Sirius XM radio, and on television. Steve is also the founder of the Women of Faith conferences, attended by over 4 million women, and of HisMatchforMe.com.

Steve is a nationally known public speaker and has been featured in national media venues such as *Oprah*, *Inside Edition*, *Good Morning America*, *CNN Live*, the *New York Times*, *USA Today*, and *US News & World Report*. In August 2000, Steve was inducted into the National Speakers Association's Hall of Fame. A bestselling author, Steve has written more than one hundred books, including the popular Every Man's series and his most recent book, *Healing Is a Choice*. He is a Gold Medallion–winning author and has been nominated for numerous other writing awards.

Steve has degrees from Baylor University and the University of North Texas as well as two honorary doctorate degrees. Steve resides with his family in Indiana.

DAVID STOOP, PHD, is a licensed clinical psychologist who received a master's degree in theology from Fuller Theological Seminary and a doctorate from the University of Southern California. He is a co-host on the *New Life Live!* radio and TV program. David is the founder and director of the Center for Family Therapy in Newport Beach, California. He is also an adjunct professor at Fuller Seminary and serves on the executive board of the American Association of Christian Counselors. David is a Gold Medallion–winning author and has written more than thirty books, including *Forgiving the Unforgivable* and *You Are What You Think*. He resides with his wife, Jan, in Newport Beach, California.

FIND HEALING IN GOD'S WORD EVERY DAY.

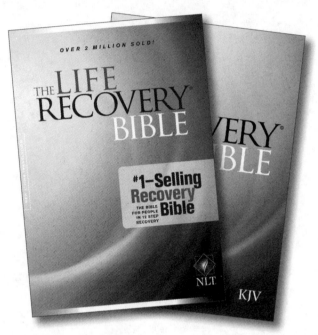

Celebrating over 2 million copies sold!

The Life Recovery Bible is today's bestselling Bible for people in recovery. In the accurate and easy-to-understand New Living Translation, *The Life Recovery Bible* leads people to the true source of healing—God himself. Special features created by two of today's leading recovery experts—David Stoop, Ph.D., and Stephen Arterburn, M.Ed.—include the following:

Recovery Study Notes: Thousands of Recovery-themed notes interspersed throughout the Bible pinpoint passages and thoughts important to recovery.

Twelve Step Devotionals: A reading chain of 84 Bible-based devotionals tied to the Twelve Steps of recovery.

Serenity Prayer Devotionals: Based on the Serenity Prayer, these 29 devotionals are placed next to the verses from which they are drawn.

Recovery Principle Devotionals: Bible-based devotionals, arranged topically, are a guide to key recovery principles.

Find *The Life Recovery Bible* at your local Christian bookstore or wherever books are sold. Learn more at www.LifeRecoveryBible.com.

Available editions:
NLT Hardcover 978-1-4143-0962-0
NLT Softcover 978-1-4143-0961-3
Personal Size Softcover 978-1-4143-1626-0
Large Print Hardcover 978-1-4143-9856-3

Large Print Softcover 978-1-4143-9857-0
KJV Hardcover 978-1-4143-8150-3
KJV Softcover 978-1-4143-8506-8

CP0107

Check out these great resources to help you on your path to recovery:

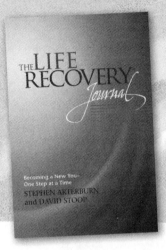

The Life Recovery Journal has been carefully created to guide you through the recovery process. The questions and quotes will help you to write honest reflections, reinforce what you're learning, and give insight into your recovery as a whole person.

The Life Recovery Workbook is about transformation: from death to life, from addiction to recovery. As you work through each of the Twelve Steps, the challenging spiritual lessons will strengthen you to live free from addiction.

The easy-to-read, down-to-earth meditations in *The Life Recovery Devotional* are designed to help you find the recovery, rest, and peace that Jesus promises. They will help you understand the struggles we all face— in recovery, in overcoming temptation, and in getting back on track after a relapse.

BLESSINGS AND WISDOM
FOR YOUR LIFE RECOVERY JOURNEY

978-1-4964-0269-1

978-1-4964-0270-7

From the creators of the bestselling Life Recovery series, *The Twelve Gifts of Life Recovery* and *The Twelve Laws of Life Recovery* illuminate the wisdom and gifts that God imparts as you travel through the Twelve Steps of Life Recovery.

With expert insight and biblical truth, recovery pioneers Stephen Arterburn and David Stoop explore the life recovery "laws" that God honors, as well as the blessings for those who seek him. These powerful books reveal God's faithfulness in your everyday walk, enriching your life in ways you've never imagined as you invite him to work within you.

Find out more at **LifeRecoveryBible.com.**